THE TWO-PARENT FAMILY IS NOT THE BEST

June Stephenson, Ph.D.

Diemer, Smith Publlishing Company, Inc.
3377 Solano Avenue, Napa, California 94558

Copyright © 1991 by June Stephenson
ISBN 0-941138-10-0

All rights reserved. No part of this book may be reproduced in any form or by any electronic or mechanical means including information storage and retrieval systems without permission in writing from the publisher, except by a reviewer who may quote brief passages in a review.

Other Books by June Stephenson

The Administrator
It's All Right to Get Old
Women's Roots
A Lie is a Debt
Womankind
Innocent Weapons
Humanity's Search For The Meaning of Life
Men Are Not Cost-Effective

*Photography front and back covers by Marissa.
Napa, California*

Diemer, Smith Publishing Company, Inc.
3377 Solano Avenue, Napa, California, 94558

Dedicated to the women who participated in this research and gave us insight into family structures which are seldom seen from the inside.

Acknowledgments

I most gratefully thank the 368 women who participated in this research. The writings of their deepest feelings in growing up formed the basis for the implications in this book. Their great contribution should change the way we look at family structure and at methods of child-raising in the future.

My great thanks to my two research assistants, Rochelle Abend, Ph.D., and Katherine Smith, Ph.D., who helped me develop the Research Questionnaire and code the answers. Sadly, Rochelle Abend died unexpectedly before the research was completed, but her expertise in research techique is present in this study. Katherine Smith was, as always, a steadying hand. She ensured that the results were understandable and not so heavy with statistics as to turn readers away from this important work. Her humane approach to understanding personal interactions within families was basic to this research.

Thanks, too, to Kirk Richter who set the design for incorporating the massive number of coded answers from the questionnaires into the computer. Thanks to Nancy Brennan for spending interminable hours loading information into the computer program, and to Garry Carter who set up the design for further analysis of the results.

I thank the people at The Consulting Psychologists Press in Palo Alto, California, for the use of their Adjective Check List and permission to print their Descriptions of the Scales in Appendix C.

Thanks to Evelyn Smith for her proofreading, interest and enthusiasm for this project. And I thank Joanne Macy for her final proofreading and important suggestions. Thanks, too, to my daughters and my friends, who, for the past several years have been interested in this study and have been supportive. Thanks to my husband who urged me on to completion when it seemed I was becoming over-burnened by the volume of work involved. I thank him for his continual encouragement and faith in me.

June Stephenson

Table of Contents

INTRODUCTION i

PART I - GROWING UP 23
Fathers "There For You?" 25
Mother "There For You?" 31
Parental Help In Child's Bereavement 37
Close Knit Family? 47
Unburdening Unto Children 60
Financial Security In Childhood 66
Gender Equity In The Home 78
Childhood Responsibilities 86
Older Than One's Years 97
Lost Childhood? 101
Singled Out As Different? 105
What People Said 111
Others Permitted To Play In Your Home? 118
On Your Own More Than Others? 123
Allowed To Take More Risks Than Others? 128
Encouraged In Things Others Were Not? 136
Role Models 144
Fantasy Mother 148
Fantasy Father 151
Who Told You The Facts Of Life? 158
Parental Dating 160
Parental Remarriage 161
Parental Alcoholism 172
Physical Abuse 176
Sexual Abuse 182
Parental Pride In Daughters 188
What Admire/Dislike About Father 197
Fathers Who Don't Communicate 210
What Admire/Dislike About Mother 215
What Was Missed Not Having Mother 226

What Was Missed Not Having Father 232
With Mother How Life Would Have Been Different 238
With Father How Life Would Have Been Different 243
Father/Mother Have Two Parents? 248
Evaluating Fathers 249
Evauating Mothers 255
Childhood Happy Or Unhappy? 260
Miscellaneous Letters 262

PART II - THE PRESENT 285

Level Of Education Achieved 287
Occupation 289
Marital Status 291
Physical Condition 292
Organizations 294
Political Party 295
Relationships With Men 297
Relationships With Women 300
Sexual Preference 303
Are You Different? 306
Personality Traits 317
Parents Embodied In Their Children 320
Desired Qualities In Mate 323
Opinions On Equality 326
If Not Married, Why Not? 332
If Have No Children, Would you Like To? 333
Most Important Thing About Mothering 334
Most Important Thing About Fathering 335
Things A Mother Can Do Which A Father Can't 337
Things A Father Can Do White A Mother Can't 338
Know Anyone Else Raised By Father/Mother Only? 340
Can Father Be A Good Substitute For A Mother? 342
Can Mother Be A Good Substitute For A Father? 343
How Do You Evauate Yourself As A Mother? 344
How Your Children Evaluate You 346
How Has Upbringing Affected Your Parenting? 347

PART III SUMMARY AND ANALYSIS 348

What Has Been Learned? 348
Two-Parent Family Is Not The Best 349
Single Father Daughters, Feminine Traits 355

Single Mother Daughters, Masculine Traits 358
Single Parent Families Have Advantages 363
Most Children With Step Mothers Were Absued 372
What Is A Mother? 377
What Is A Father? 383
What Is A Family? 390
Implications For The Future 398
Rewriting The Myth Of The Two-Parent Family 398
Rewriting The Dogma Of Motherhood/Fatherhood 400
Daughters Of Single Parents 402
Conclusion 405

APPENDIX A: Research Questionnaire 409

APPENDIX B: Gough Adjective Check List 416

APPENDIX C: Description Of Check List Scales 432

BIBLIOGRAPHY 445

THE TWO-PARENT FAMILY IS NOT THE BEST

INTRODUCTION

This is a book about parenting and the human relationships involved in the process of raising children. It evaluates how well parents did in raising their children by what the children, now grown, say about their childhood. It will indicate some do's and don'ts for today's parents.

Children often hide their hurts, either fearful of telling their parents how they feel, or not knowing how injured they are until they're grown. If we listen to the adults in this book, we hear of the joys and the anguish lingering from childhood, either praising or condemning the way their parents treated them.

How do we really know what children feel? What could be a hidden anguish may burgeon to a full blown breakdown in adulthood. What better way to learn the effects of family composition and customs than to listen to yesterday's children?

The children in this book, now grown to adulthood, speak out from four different family groups. These groups are composed of 368 women who were raised by single fathers, or by single mothers, or by both biological parents, or by a step parent. Their answers to a lengthy questionnaire asking a multitude of questions were compared from group to group. The results indicated that where there is one

THE TWO-PARENT FAMILY IS NOT THE BEST

strong and loving parent, the children were often better off than where there were two parents. Fathers, in the two parent families, barely participated in child raising. There were fathers in three of the groups studied, but the only group as a whole, where fathers did a credible job of parenting was where they were the *only* parent.

This book is about young girls, how they were raised and how they are now as adults. The initial quest was to learn about girls raised by single fathers, but the study was then expanded for comparison purposes. The next book will be about boys growing up in different family situations.

Other things were learned in this research. One is that there is no family composition, that by its structure, is better than another family structure. All family groups had good family relationships and all family groups had disastrous family relationships. What matters in families is not whether there is a father or a mother, two biological parents, or a step parent, or even if any of the people are related. What matters is how the people treat each other. This study should dampen the assumption that the two biological parent family is the best for all children, because that did not prove to be true.

Among the other things that were learned were that single parent families have advantages over two-parent families, that girls growing up in single father homes have strong feminine characteristics, and girls growing up in single mother homes have strong masculine characteristics, and most girls growing up in step mother families are emotionally and physically abused.

INTRODUCTION

My hope, as I conclude this research, is that parents in the two-biological parent families will reevaluate their interactions with each other and with their children, and not assume they are intrinsically better than the single parent families primarily because they have provided two parents for their children. They may actually be doing a very good job, but so many two-parent families in this research were not, that, I suggest, it behooves parents in all two-parent families to take a closer look. Is father "there" for his children or does he leave almost everything up to his wife?. What kind of a pattern is father setting for his sons if all of the housework is left to the mother?

I hope, also, that single parents, male or female, will take heart and gain confidence from what is learned in this study. They need not feel "*second rate.*" In fact, the advantages to children in single parenthood may actually be greater than the perceived advantages of dual parenthood, if other elements are compensatory. That is, for instance, if the children in the single mother family do not suffer from financial hardship, or if a girl, she is not deprived of healthy male companionship.

I hope also that parents in step parent families will be at least as concerned with their children's emotional yearnings as they are with their own. I hope when married people with children are widowed or divorced, they will thoroughly consider the consequences of remarriage on their children. In many cases in this research, step children, especially in step *mother* families, would have been better off if their biological parents had not remarried. It

THE TWO-PARENT FAMILY IS NOT THE BEST

seemed the death of a parent, which was terrible in itself, was not as damaging to the children as the intrusion of a denigrating step parent. Unlike step children whose original parents had divorced, the step children in this study had nowhere else to go because one of their parents had died.

This is not to say that considerations for children should always come first. Parents have physical and emotional needs too. But if the child is considered a subordinate appendage whose needs are frequently submerged, she has a slim chance of developing a healthy personality. The child is a child for only a short time, and in that time she needs to believe wholly that she is as important in the family function as any other member so she can grow up and be on her way as an adult with pride and self-confidenc.

On a personal note, I am a daughter raised by a single father. I had one brother two years older. As a girl raised in this very different family situation, I had always felt somehow different from other girls. Of course I was different in that I had great responsibiities for a child, but there were feeings I could not identify. I remember my father telling me that my aunts descended on him after I lost my mother. The two of them came to California from Denver to decide how my brother and I should be divided up. Since Aunt Edna had a son, maybe she should have my brother, or would it be nice for her little boy to have a sister? I wasn't aware of this at the time because I was only six months old. My father relayed this to me many years later.

4

INTRODUCTION

Aunt Edna told my dad she decided I would be the one she would take, and Aunt Edith would take my brother. Aunt Edna said she could give me a college education, and that must have stung my father. He worked in a factory, and in 1920, college was unheard of for children of factory workers.

Aunt Edna's husband worked in a bank and wore a starched collar everyday. The only time my father wore one of those collars was on special occasions, like at Christmas or funerals.

Well, from what I was told, my father listened to his sisters-in-law, considered what they had to say, made them as comfortable as he could in our two bedroom home, and had coffee ready for them when he left for work each day. Even though he had just lost my mother, and I know he loved her very much, he apparently went about his life as he usually did, going to work, and cultivating his garden on weekends.

When he came home from work one day, my aunts were packing and finalizing their plans for their departure, which also meant the departure of my brother and me. My father simply told them that we were staying with him.

"But you can't raise these children by yourself."

"I've hired help."

That must have surprised them, but I learned through the years that my father got things done without much fuss.

"I hired a woman who will be moving in when you leave."

"But these children need a mother!"

THE TWO-PARENT FAMILY IS NOT THE BEST

He told them he knew that, but he would do the best he could.

"I went and talked to Sven last Sunday," he explained. Sven was his best friend, a man who had gone to law school at night and was then a lawyer. My father loved him because they had shared so much in their youth. And my father respected his opinions.

"Sven advised me to keep my children. He said if I give them up I will have nothing left."

My aunts couldn't argue with that, but still Aunt Edna tried, no doubt with sincere good intentions. "But a man can't raise a girl! And she's just a baby! I'll take her. You'll still have the boy."

"We all stay together."

And that was the way it was.

We stayed together for over twenty years, and after that my brother went to work for an oil company five hundred miles away and I married and traveled with my husband who had been inducted into the army at the beginning of World War Two.

But what of those growing up years?

Back in those days it was most unusual for a father to raise his children by himself. If a man lost his wife, it was almost automatic that any children would live with relatives. Or they might be placed in orphan asylums, or the father might remarry soon in order to provide a mother for his children. If a father were separated from his children, he would probably visit with them now and then, possibly see them in their new home, adjusting to a new set of parents. If

INTRODUCTION

the father were physically separated from his children he would undoubtedly become more remote from them.

Historically, even fathers who had not lost their wives, have been distant family participants. Actually in prehistoric times a family consisted of a mother and her childen. There was no father in the family. Men lived in the men's house and were merely visitors to the women and children.

This was the time about 15,000 B.C. when a father's role in procreation was unknown. It was assumed that a woman became pregnant for any number of reasons, maybe because she swam in a lagoon when the moon was at a certain height, or she walked by a specific tree in the jungle, or she was visited by the Child Spirit in one of her dreams.

As fatherhood was unknown until about the time of the domestication of animals, women, before that time, were considered supernatural because they could create human life. Even today in some tribes, in the Trobriand Islands, for instance, there is no word for father.

But when fatherhood was realized, fathers began to take possession of their children because they were valuable assets as workers. And girls could be traded as wives to neighboring tribes in exchange for cattle or pigs or other valuables So the knowledge of paternity changed the family structure from women and their children, to what has been termed the "*natural* or *nuclear* family," -- a father, mother, and children, though the "*natural*" family did not initially include a father.

THE TWO-PARENT FAMILY IS NOT THE BEST

While fathers claimed ownership of their children, and in later years took financial responsibility for their upbringing, it was always the mothers who had primary responsibility for raising children. In more modern times, when fathers interacted with their children, it was more with their sons than with their daughters, and then, not until the sons had matured considerably. The earliest years in child raising were left to the mothers, or in upper economic classes, to nannies and nursemaids, but almost always to women.

It was not until the late 1970's that an increasing number of fathers began to take an active role in caring for their young children. In fact, as recently as 1977, a father's taking custody of his child in a divorce case, was extraordinary enough to be highlighted in a movie, "*Kramer Vs. Kramer.*" Generally, for a father to have custody of his children in a divorce case the mother would have to be declared an unfit mother.

Single motherhood, which began with the advent of human beings on earth, has been taken for granted throughout history. But single fatherhood, on an increasing scale, is a new phenomenon in social history. This may have been activated by the generation of the 1960's which encouraged both men and women to get in touch with their inner feelings, or prompted by the encounter group movement of the 1970's which urged men to permit their softer, nurturing side.

Single fatherhood is breaking new ground in the history of paternity, and as a consequence there have been only a few studies made about this sub-

INTRODUCTION

ject. As for any study specifically on father-raised daughters, a computer check at the University of California at Berkeley revealed only one study written into a book in 1972, *Motherless Families*, which discusses the problems facing single parent fathers from the social welfare roles in England. Emphasis is on situations the fathers face, not on the development of the children. Little is known regarding the effect upon daughters of having a father, but no mother, with whom to identify.

Yet there are many questions. How, for instance, do women who were raised by their fathers fare in their adult lives? Without having been *"mothered,"* how do they do as mothers? How do these women compare with women who were raised in other situations?

I wondered if it would be possible to find other women who had been raised by their fathers to see what could be learned from our experiences. It would be interesting to compare our unusual growing up years. And, further, what we might learn could be helpful for single fathers today who are raising their daughters.

Just *"to test the waters,"* I put an advertisement in the Berkeley, California weekly newspaper, *The Bay Area Guardian*, asking women who had been raised by fathers to volunteer for a research study. I was surprised to get several responses from women enthusiastic to participate. All of the women said they had never known anyone else raised by a single father, and were eager to communicate. Encouraged, and now wanting to expand my initial curiosity into a reliable research study, I needed to find research participants from different geographical, economic, ethnic and educational backgrounds. I also needed to find women willing to participate who were not raised by their fathers so I would have one or more control groups for comparison. Maybe my feeling "different" because of the way I was raised, is not significant. Maybe women raised in other situations also feel different. To secure a more balanced sample, I then put advertisements in *Ms. Magazine, Graduate Woman, 50 Plus, National Enquirer, True Romance, Modern Romance, Psychology Today, Mother Jones, Globe, The Sun,* and *The Examiner,* and *True Story.*

The ads asked for volunteers in four categories: women raised by fathers only, women raised by mothers only, women raised by both biological parents, and women raised by one biological parent and one step parent, where the biological parent had died at about the time the woman had been five years old. This latter category was set up so that there would not be respondents with two sets of parents. The ads asked simply for women to volunteer to answer a questionnaire for a research project, and to indicate their category.

After I had received numerous letters of interest from women responding to the magazine advertisements, I elicited the assistance of two research associates. One, Katherine Smith, had been a student with me when we both received our Ph.D.'s in psychology. She has considerable experience in psychotherapy. The other associate, Rochelle Abend, has an M.A. in statistics and a Ph.D. in psychology and also a great deal of experience as a

INTRODUCTION

social psychologist, instructor, researcher and counselor. Sadly, the second associate died unexpectedly after two years of working on this study. As for me, I have been a high school teacher of English and history, a Dean of Students, and am currently a writer and research psychologist. I have written, among other books, *Women's Roots*, a history of women from prehistoric times to the present, and *Humanity's Search for the Meaning of Life, a Brief Survey of History, Philosophy, Religion, Art, Music, and Architecture*.

The three of us developed a sample questionnaire which was sent to ten respondents on a trial-run basis, asking them to complete the questionnaire and to criticize it freely. Good suggestions came from the trial-run group. The questionnaire was revised and eventually sent to all women in all four groups. In order to assure the respondents anonymity, the questionaires were coded and I am the only one who has the key to the code.

Interesting comments accompanied the initial letters sent when the women volunteered. Father-raised women said, "*Its' about time someone studied motherless children.*" Some women raised by both biological parents commented how pleased they were to be included since they were not generally considered to be "*unusual*" enough to warrant a study. One letter came from a man in New York who said he had seen my advertisement in *True Story* magazine. He wrote, "*I read your ad in the True Story magazine I found at the laundromat. It said you had a questionnaire called, 'How are we different.' I got custody of my eight year old daughter after a very dirty*

THE TWO-PARENT FAMILY IS NOT THE BEST

divorce case. I had to move home with mom to let her watch my daughter when I was at work. I want to raise my daughter right since I'll be around her more than her mother who hasn't seen her in two years even though she lives only one mile away.

If you have any advise or think your questionnaire can help me raise my daughter better I could use all the help I can get as I don't plan on getting married yet."

As for the questionnaire, approximately seventy percent of all women who volunteered returned the nine page questionnaire. There are over 120 questions, and with a few exceptions, all respondents answered the same questions. The question, for instance, "*How did you lose your parent?*" was not asked of respondents with two biological parents. Respondents were also encouraged to write personal narratives about their growing up. These are heartfelt explorations which illuminated the individual lives of women in all groups.

By the time we were ready to number-code the answers so they could be computerized, we had a good medium-sized sample. There are 119 respondents from the "*Single Fathers*" group, 106 from the "*Single Mothers*" group, 92 from the "*Biological Parents*" group, and 51 from the "*Step parents*" group, with a diversity of ethnic, religious, educational, economic, and geographical backgrounds, ages 18-83.

Many of the questions had "*yes,*" or "*no,*" answers, but as many had open-ended questions. These latter answers were coded into categories by

INTRODUCTION

the three of us, after compiling all the answers to a specific question and then determining applicable categories. Not all open-ended answers fit into the determined categories, but most did. Those that did not, were classified under miscellaneous. Two college students were hired to enter the coded answers into the computer on a dBase III Plus computer program which then derived percentages.

In addition to the questionnaire which we developed, included as Appendix A, we also used The Gough Adjective Check List, included as Appendix B. This is a standardized test of 300 adjectives. The respondent is asked to check which adjectives describe herself. We believe that the use of this check list, in conjunction with our own questionnaire, helps to validate our findings. When applicable, the results of the questionnaire on certain questions, and the results of the Adjective Check List are correlated. For instance, one question on the questionnaire asks if the respondent was permitted risks which other girls were not permitted. The results from this question were then compared with the results on the Adjective Check List, specifically the Creative Personality Scale. Are girls who are permitted more risks, more apt to develop creative personalities compared to girls who are not permitted risks? The Adjective Check List indicated that the answer to that question was "*Yes*."

It was not known what the results of this study would be until all the answers to the questionnaires were compared from group to group. When these were analyzed there were five major surprises: 1. The biological parents group offered no clear ad-

THE TWO-PARENT FAMILY IS NOT THE BEST

vantage to children; 2. Single parent families have advantages over two-parent families; 3. In the step parent group, most children who had step *mothers* suffered distinct childhood trauma; 4. Single father daughters develop strong feminine traits; 5. Single mother daughters develop strong masculine traits.

These first three will be discussed here briefly, and all five in more detail later.

Two Parents - No Clear Advantage

My initial intent was to learn how women raised by single fathers had fared in their adult lives. I had always heard that one learns to "*mother*" from one's mother. How did we, who had no mothers, get along as mothers ourselves. To learn this, I needed to compare women who had been raised by their fathers, with women raised under different parental circumstances. But as the answers to the questionnaires were returned I could see there was much more to explore than I had originally intended.

I had expected to learn that women raised by both biological parents had a happier childhood, more parental support from both parents, less family trauma, and would consider themselves better mothers than women in the other three groups. That is not what the results indicate. Women raised by both biological parents, as a group, seem to be no better off than women in the other three groups, and may not be as well off in such areas as independence, financial capabilities, creativeness and resourcefulness as women from single parent homes.

INTRODUCTION

First there was the surprise that the two parent family, *as a group*, did not stand out as the family providing the best situation for raising children in terms of parental alcoholism, martial arguments, physical and sexual abuse of children, and lack of important ingredients such as father presence, family closeness, gender fairness among brothers and sisters, and freedom to explore on their own.

It is generally assumed that the best family situation for children is for them to have two parents -- one of each sex. This is an assumption I had always made. I *knew* when I was growing up that I should have had two parents, that was the *normal* and the best way, and that my brother and father and I were only doing the best we could under the circumstances.

When I had observed my many childhood friends in their two-parent families, I don't recall that I ever envied them, though I thought it would be wonderful to be called home to an already cooked dinner, as my friends were, rather than having to go home to cook. But aside from that, and the fact that my girl friends had nicely ironed dresses, and mine were wrinkled in the days before permanent press fabrics, and before I learned to iron, I did not feel that I was missing anything. Since I had never had a mother, I did not miss her.

But many father-raised daughters in this study had lost their mothers late enough in their childhood so that they had clear memories of mother-love, and nostalgic memories of the things their mothers did for them and their families. But,

TWO-PARENT FAMILY IS NOT THE BEST

whether we had memories of a mother or not, without one, and I know I speak for most of the father-raised daughters in this study, we knew our families with only a father-parent were different enough to almost be wrong. I believe this speaks for the women raised by single mothers also. Several women in the single mother group said she felt "*ashamed*" that she had no father.

The assumption that it is best for children to have two parents is so prevalent that it is almost a foregone conclusion. Yet, once again, that assumption ignores the evidence that families existed, as women and their children, for thousands of years in prehistory, not only without a father, but without the knowledge of the father's role in procreation. Will Durant in his book, *The Story of Civilization*, writes:

Since it was the mother who fulfilled most of the parental functions, the family was first (so far as we can pierce the mists of history) organized on the assumption that the position of the man in the family was superficial and incidental while that of the woman was fundamental and supreme. In some existing tribes, and probably in the earliest human groups the physiological role of the male in reproduction appears to have escaped notice....

Single Parent Families Have Advantages

In this research there was also the surprise that rather than being handicapped by having had only one parent, most respondents from the single father and single mother groups stressed that this ex-

INTRODUCTION

perience prepared them for coping as adults. Having had great childhood responsibilities, most said they were self-reliant and confident. Almost all had an especial closeness with their one parent, said they were free of parental fighting, had close knit families, more gender fairness among brothers and sisters, and were free of parental "*snoopervision.*"

Mention has been made that single fatherhood is a growing phenomenon. So also is single motherhood. We have always had single motherhood, but never before in the United States have there been so *many* single-mother families. Today an astonishing statistic informs us that there are eleven million single mothers. This provokes the question: "*What is a family?*" When we hear politicians speak of maintaining "*family values,*" which families are they speaking of?

Step Mother Group - Distinct Childhood

Trauma

In this research the step parent group was at times further separated into two groups, that is, one group with step mothers and biological fathers, and another group with step fathers and biological mothers. In almost all cases where children had step *mothers*, the children were at a distinct disadvantage. Not only was there, in many cases, a lack of love, but there were various forms of cruelty. There were exceptions. Several women reported very loving step mothers, but these percentages were low.

Not only were the children at a disadvantage because of their particular step mother, but their biological father who was also in the home, did not seem to be as attentive to his daughter as did fathers in the other groups. All of this is discussed in more detail later.

As there are more and more children growing up in step parent homes today, this small study might indicate the need for further study of the relationship between step mothers and their step daughters. This particular study included only women whose biological mother or father had died, so she did not have the "other" family to go to as do many step children today whose divorced parents have remarried. However, much of what is learned in this study could apply to most step families and particularly to families with a step mother and a biological father. The step mothers need to know of the craving for love their step children feel, and the biological fathers need to know about the dynamics between their spouse and their children. The biological father who has remarried should continue to play an important part in his children's upbringing, rather than ignoring his children's emotional needs when he acquires a new wife as was often noticed in this research.

RESPONDENTS' COMMENTS

Because we are moving into a changing family pattern of an increasing number of single father

INTRODUCTION

and single mother families, and also of step parent families, anything we learn about these family groups should be helpful. This research is based on information which comes from the women who have lived their childhood in these family groups, who looked back and evaluated that childhood, and then looked at themselves now as the results of their upbringing.

Nothing is ever an absolute comparison. There are too many variables that affect all situations. All we can really speak of are *"indications."* What we learned about yesterday's parenting may not *exactly* apply to today's parenting because so much has changed since the women in this study were raised. Many attitudes are different now, including attitudes about divorce, welfare, and single parenthood. But the dynamics of family living are fairly constant. The way human beings treat each other, especailly the way adults treat children, is what this book is about. Human nature seems relatively consistent through the ages. We love, hate, take advantage of, help, protect and abuse others. Children's needs have also been relatively consistent through the ages. The needs for all children to grow up with financial and emotional security has not changed.

With the assurance of anonymity, many women in this research freely wrote of their memories. It was not initially intended that the open-ended answers to the questions would do more than provide the statistics. But so much written commentary accompanied the the answers on the questionnaire that to simply present the computerized results

THE TWO-PARENT FAMILY IS NOT THE BEST

would be to write a sterile analysis. As a consequence, the personal, heartfelt commentaries are a vital part of this study.

No woman in this research was indifferent. All people are inextricably connected to their childhood. Whatever happened to us in our childhood, can either be a springboard to a fulfilling adult life, or it can be something which we deny, or try to overcome throughout our lives. We are born with trust in the people who bring us to life. Will they ignore us, abuse us, or nurture us?

In the writing that follows, Part 1 focuses on the growing up period of the respondents, Part 2 on the present situation of the respondents, and Part 3 is a summary and an analysis of the results of the questionnaire and the Gough Adjective Check List. In Parts 1 and 2, the questions are followed by the text which includes the percentages from each of the four groups as they answered the particular question. Charts of these percentages are also included. These charts simply present another way of looking at the percentages.. Then written comments from the participants follow.

In some instances there may be more written comments included from the single father group than from the other three groups. It was decided not to try to achieve a balance in this respect for two reasons: One, the women from the single father group were motiviated to write lengthy anecdotes about their growing up, mostly because no one had ever asked them before about their particular family situation; Two, of the four groups, the single father family was, and still is, the most unusual. As this is a

INTRODUCTION

growing phenomenon, it is good to learn more about this group without in anyway diminishing the vital contribution from the women in the other three groups.

It is a compliment to the three research associates that the 368 respondents, who were unknown to any of us, would write about their innermost feelings of their childhood. The comments come from women now grown. Though society is different now and is ever-changing, the needs of children do not change. Though many respondents wrote that we could use their names, that has not been done except for one poem where credit should be given. Otherwise the trust of anonymity holds fast.

Written comments included in this book may be recognized by respondents and may evoke remembered emotions, some painful and some happy. The purpose in using these comments is to elucidate the family interactions in a way that cannot be done otherwise. These comments bring forth images and permit society to look through a window into the childhood of many children growing up in different family situations. They serve the great purpose of educating us all.

The charts will make a case. They will numerically indicate which parental situations appear to be more generally satisfactory and which are detrimental, in answer to specific questions. But the numbers and charts are sterile information. This study is brought to life by the eloquent voices of the women who write of their experiences with such fullness that we are either hurt by the cruelty they ex-

THE TWO-PARENT FAMILY IS NOT THE BEST

perienced, or warmed by the loving kindness. Many voices are filled with devotion and appreciation for their parents; many voices reflect the suffering of childhood trauma; many vent long-simmering anger.

The reader will hear the richness of voices from women speaking from childhood reflections. On their voices we are transported back into their childhood. From their voices we are helped to understand which family dynamics undermine self-worth and optimism, and which family dynamics provide the best opportunity for nourishing and encouraging the healthy development of children.

PART I

GROWING UP

Of the women who participated in this research some are saying in effect, "*These attitudes and actions of my parents helped me become a fully functioning person,*" and some are saying, "*These attitudes and actions of my parents nearly destroyed me and left me emotionally crippled.*" The question is, what attitudes and what actions help children and what attitudes and actions harm them? First there is the parents' availability for his or her child. What chance does a small child have to get help from a single working father? Or a single working mother? What chance from either or both of her own biological parents, or a step parent?

For many years the child is completely dependent on parents. While parents have a wide range of personal relationships -- usually a spouse, other children, their own parents, siblings and friends --

THE TWO-PARENT FAMILY IS NOT THE BEST

the infant or young child is focused primarily on one or two parents. The child looks to the parent, but the parent looks everywhere.

The power which parents have in developing the character of their children is second only to that of a supernatural being or a despot. Parents may emotionally ruin their children with neglect, humiliation or abuse, or they may, through encouragement, attention and love forge fully functioning human beings.

We think of childhood as a carefree, joyful experience, but childhood is a serious business. Though it lasts only a short time in a life span, it is with us forever. One has only to scratch the surface of recollections to remember childhood joy or disappointment. Childhood unhappiness may be submerged, but it is not forgotten.

It takes so little to make children happy, and if there are minor hurts along the way, children forgive and forgive again, as long as they know parents care about them. Even when there is major damage, such as parental sexual abuse, the child forgives however unhealthily, for many reasons, one of them being because she needs the love of her parents, even as they are destroying her.

Did the parents of the women in this research care about their children? How was this caring or lack of caring perceived by each group? Were the parents present when needed?

FATHERS 'BEING THERE' FOR DAUGHTERS

"My father was distant and withdrawn from the family and was extremely critical of any one who was different."

A question was asked *"Was your father there for you?"* This was asked only of women in the groups where there were fathers, that is, it was not asked of women in the single mother group.

Single Father Group

By a wide margin, the group having the highest percentage of women saying their fathers were *"there for them,"* was the single father group. Most of these women grew up in a household where they could easily go to their only parent for advice, comfort, or help in difficult situations.

It is very likely that fathers who raised their families by themselves decided to do that. They probably *chose* to raise their children rather than to pass them on to a relative. This choice would be in contrast to the situation for single mothers who most likely *had* no choice. Though several women had mothers who left their children in the custody of the father, this was because either their mothers had no job skills, or if they did, these mothers could not

THE TWO-PARENT FAMILY IS NOT THE BEST

make enough money to support themselves and their children, whereas their father could.

Even though the children were left with their father, he had more of a choice to pass children to relatives than did *women* left alone with children. It was not then, and still is not now, socially acceptable for a mother, single or otherwise, to turn her children over to someone else. But a man can give his children to others and heads would nod in understanding. The mother would be criticized, the father would not.

Most of these men who chose to keep their children were possibly nurturing type men to begin with, and therefore men whose children could go to them with hurts and bruises, both real and imagined, and these nurturing type men would be there for their children.

Some fathers, when asked for help from their daughters, put the responsibility for solving problems onto their child. "*If I had a problem and went to him for help,*" one woman wrote, "*he would say, 'You're bright. You'll figure it out.' And I learned to do that.*" Another who had asthma remembers how her father used to sit up with her at nights when she had an attack.

And in another case, one woman who was only two and a half years old when her mother died, wrote, "*My father was both father and mother to me and my younger sister...His life was devoted to rearing us and to his work as a rancher. Because of his type of work he was able to take us with him as he did his chores -- checking the cattle, mowing and hauling the hay, etc. He took us to movies, occasionally, and in those pre-T.V. days we visited friends after going to weekly Sunday Mass...Even though we had a parade of housekeepers, my Dad always did the 'mothering.' Whenever he hired a housekeeper he'd take my sister and me along to make sure we approved...My wish when I married and started having our family was that I'd be half as good a parent as he was to me.*" Another woman wrote, "*My dad did the cooking and laundry and he made every attempt to be there for us when a parent was required. Even the Mother-Daughter dinner with the Girl Scouts. He must have been the only man there.*"

But not all women raised by fathers were as fortunate. Of those who said their fathers were *not* there for them, several women responded that their fathers, when they were not drunk, were there for them, but alcohol got in the way. There are a few women raised by fathers who later had stepmothers. Several, but not all of these, indicated that their fathers were there for them until their stepmother moved into the house. One woman said she seldom went to her father for help because she knew her father would overreact to anything. Another mentioned that her father didn't know how to give her a hug or any praise and "*I couldn't express any opinion of my own without an argument.*"

A strong comprehensive negative statement came from a woman who said, "*My father was incapable of being one. He didn't have the necessary tools for interaction with people, therefore, how could he possibly relate to a child left in his care by a woman who had been totally responsible for the child's wellbeing.*" Some fathers were described as being too uncomfortable with closeness to be helpful.

THE TWO-PARENT FAMILY IS NOT THE BEST

In spite of the negative responses, it was clear that single fathers *as a group* did a better job of interacting with their daughters than did fathers in the other groups.

Two Biological Parents

Fewer fathers in this group were *"there"* for their daughters than were fathers in the single father group. Several of the positive answers were hedged. For instance, "*I only turned to him in dire emergency,*" or "*I very rarely confided or never confided in him. He did not seem to be aware of my problems.*" One wrote that she went to her father, "*but on his terms, not mine.*" And another, "*My parents didn't like 'messy' emotional problems.*"

Of the women in this group who said their fathers were *not* there for them, one wrote, "*I feared my father -- he was a volatile man and he criticized his children and his wife.*" Other comments included, "*My problems were just kid stuff to both of them.*" "*I never tested him because I was too frightened of him,*" and "*He was an authority figure who was there for me when I was 'good'.*" And "*My father was not really a part of my life.*" Another wrote, "*There was no honesty in my family, no communication, no discussion. We were the children. We did as we were told and if we didn't, we were punished usually with a razor strap. My father demanded respect and he got it. Actually, we were terrified of him.*" Another wrote, "*I feared my father -- he was a volatile man and he criticized his children and his wife as if he expected and demonstrated perfection.*"

One wrote of the neglect of both of her parents. "*I now know that my parents' unhappy marriage, and our difficult family life, along with their neglect and emotional abuse of their three kids, provided me with no confidence or self-esteem or ability to have healthy relationships. I really can't imagine why having biological parents or not would matter. What's important in my estimation is whether the environment is generally healthy or not. I don't remember ever feeling afraid my dad would leave. Maybe I knew he wasn't really there anyway.*"

Step-Parent Families

While fewer women growing up with two biological parents were able to go to their fathers for help than were women in the single father group, they apparently were freer to discuss things with their fathers than were women raised with a step parent. In this study there are approximately the same number of step mothers as step fathers.

It is in the step parent family that a distressing picture emerges. More *step* fathers were helpful than were the daughters' *biological* fathers. One woman with a step father wrote, "*He was always calm and ready to hear my side of the story when there was trouble.*" Another with a step father wrote, "*The father I learned to love was my step father who did not reject me.*"

One woman with a biological father and a step mother said her father was there but always seemed to be preoccupied. Another says, "Y*es he was*

THE TWO-PARENT FAMILY IS NOT THE BEST

there for me. He bailed me out of difficult spots a lot. Encourages and compliments me when I need it." Another said, *"He was busy running a business. If I asked for help he never refused, but he did not sense my need."* Another who said her father was there for her, added, *"But he was usually too tired to do anything and has a hard time communicating."* Another with a biological father writes, *"I don't remember my Dad paying much attention to me."*

WAS YOUR FATHER THERE FOR YOU WHEN YOU WERE GROWING UP?	
	Yes
Bio. F.*	55%
Sing. F.	75%
Step F.	36%
Bio. F. St	32%

* Bio. F. stands for Biological Father; Sing. F. stands for Single Father; Step F. stands for Step father; Bio. F. St. stands for Biological father in the step parent group.

MOTHERS 'BEING THERE' FOR DAUGHTERS

"Yes, but I couldn't tell her my true feelings."

Two Biological Parents

How emotionally available were mothers to their daughters? One would think that mothers are more apt to *"be there"* than fathers because they are assumed to be more nurturing, and because they may be in the home more. *But in no group were mothers more available to their daughters than were the fathers available in the single father group.*

Where there are two biological parents, more mothers are available to their daughters than are mothers in the other groups. Almost no woman in the biological parents group wrote comments after she had checked that her mother or her father *had* been there for her. A few positive responses included, *"My mother was not there for me when I was a child, but, yes, when I was an adult." "Yes, she was there for me, very much so." "When I was a child I could call her at work."*

Of the negative responses, women in this group wrote: *"I never really used her. Too judgmental." "Due to her critical nature as I matured, I didn't go to her." "My Mom avoided conflict so she did not often support me." "She was there for me but I couldn't*

THE TWO-PARENT FAMILY IS NOT THE BEST

confide in her because she'd throw it up at me or tell Dad." "I never felt I needed her." "Physically, yes, emotionally, no." "I never got along with my mother. We couldn't hold a single conversation without her saying some little thing that convinced me she thought I was still a baby." "My parents belonged to the 'school' that did not believe in praising a child. It might make one conceited or 'spoiled.' They did not hesitate to criticize. I grew up feeing homely and fat."

Single Mother Families

Not as many women in the single mother group as in the biological parents group said that their mothers were there for them. One gets the picture in reading about these single mothers who were helpful that they were out of the home working each day, raising a family with little money, yet listening to their children and helping where they could. These women wrote about their mothers, "*Yes she was there for me! Always!!! and still is!!*" "*Sometimes we acted as friends rather than mother and children.*" "*We were always more like sisters than mother and daughter.*"

One woman who indicated that her mother was *not* there for her, wrote, "*The greatest sadness of my life comes in not having had a close and loving relationship with my mother. I can never once remember being held, kissed, patted, or being told that I was loved by my mother.*" Women who had lost their fathers either through death or divorce or desertion, had mothers who had to go to work, who had previously been home with their children. So, unlike the women who had lost their mothers, whose father had daily gone to work before this loss, the child who had lost her father felt a double loss, because now her *mother* had to be away from home a lot. When these women were asked if their mother was *"there for them,"* many said that she had to work and was too tired or too immersed in her own problems to be very helpful. *"I think,"* said one, *"she felt guilty about not being there for us all of the time." "Seems like my mother worked all the time -- didn't have time for us." "My mother never had the time nor interest in fun things, nor listening to me or my side of things. I had no voice in the house." "She wouldn't know what to do anyway."* But most of the daughters of single mothers gave their mothers great credit for doing a difficult job.

Step Parent Families

The child in the step parent family who was left with her own mother had a better chance of having her *"there"* than did the child who had a step mother.

But of those in the step parent group who said their *step* mother was there for them, some wrote, *"She was always at home. She never did anything. However we didn't really have any communication then, as we don't now." "Yes, but it wasn't any good." "Yes! She still is!" "Twice. Once when I wanted to date a guy and once when I wanted to move out of the house." "I am forever grateful for my stepmom. She loves us more than any mom I know. She is kind, gentle, warm, loving, approachable, accepting and has a great sense of humor. She saved me from many beatings. She played no favorites between us and her two biological kids when raising us and continues to be fair today. We may have lost a biological mother but the one we gained was a whale of a replacement."* This woman's biological father was described as, *"rigid, angry, and not emotionally approachable."* Another with a step mother writes *"My step mother has always been very warm and loving."*

One in the step mother group wrote, *"We have always struggled with our relationship and I often wonder if the antagonism between us is related to her youth at the time when she married (20 years old) and inherited me, and to the fact that I, as a child of a violent, alcoholic home, was left to take care of myself because neither of my parents were in a position to do so."*

MOTHER THERE FOR YOU	
	Yes
Bio. M.	70%
Sing. M.	54%
Step M.	32%
Bio. M. St.*	60%

*Bio. M. St. stands for biological mother in step parent group.

Another wrote of her step mother, "*She never said a kind word to me in my life. All I heard was, 'You're not a nice girl; nobody likes you.'*"

Conclusion

What does this say about a young girl's growing up and being able to go to her parents when she needs them? In single *father* families more girls had caring fathers than in any other group. In the two biological parent families, more girls had caring *mothers* than in any other group. It might be that where there are two biological parents, the father assumes his wife will take care of his daughters' emotional needs, whereas in the single father family, that father *knows* he is the only one to listen to his daughter, and so he does. But most daughters in step parent families were listened to primarily only if the mother in that family was the girls' biological mother. Otherwise most daughters in the step parent group had neither their step mother nor their biological father available to them.

Fortunately children whose parents or step parents are not available to them to listen to their problems, often have other people who do help them, such as grandparents, neighbors, or friends' parents.

When a child knows that the person responsible for providing food and housing, also cares about such things as whether or not they have friends, or whether they should take a certain class in school, or if they are maturing satisfactorily, then that child is likely to be living in a physically and mentally healthy family. This is a security that all children should expect but many do not have. If all that is provided for a child is food, shelter and clothing, an important part of that child is starved.

It has been said that if emotional needs are not met at specific stages in a child's development, they can never later be met. The best that can happen is that one may learn to *compensate* for the need. There are projects where disturbed adults have been brought back to their infancy, have been required to crawl on the floor, and to sort of "start over," so that therapists can try to learn what was missing and can attempt to provide the nurturing that was not provided in early childhood.

This is not to suggest that women whose fathers or mothers were *not* "there for them," should resort to such extremes to capture what they had missed. Since most are now fully functioning adults, they have no doubt long ago learned to compensate for the deprivation of their parents' total support.

But the child who can go to her own parents when she needs them, grows up with a sense of being important to the people who are important to her. This gives her a sense of her own value and will affect the choices she makes in life and the choices she makes will determine the quality of her life.

Lucky are the children, boys and girls, who can, without fear of ridicule or reprisal, open their hearts to those who mean the most to them. It is the beginning of learning to trust. How desolate the child who cannot turn to a protector for help, or just to listen.

PARENTAL HELP IN CHILD'S
BEREAVEMENT

"I think the cruelest thing one could ever do is ignore a grieving child."

In the most traumatic time in a child's life -- the loss of a parent -- the child's emotional trauma can be overwhelming. Is the remaining parent, at this sensitive time, helpful? Or is the remaining parent so traumatized or angry that he or she is unable to help the children? Also, is there a difference in help for children if the parent is lost through death, or if the parent is lost through divorce or desertion? Is the way a parent relates to children in such extreme disruption, in turn, related to her or his own grief and/or anger? And what effect does the parent's reaction have on the children?

The question was asked, "*Was your father/mother helpful at this time?*" The question was not asked of women with two biological parents.

Single Father Families

In the single father group, more women lost their mothers because of death than because of divorce or desertion. And about the same number of women answered that their fathers were helpful as those who said their fathers were not helpful. Several

THE TWO-PARENT FAMILY IS NOT THE BEST

said they couldn't remember because they were too young at the time.

Some women said their fathers were very grief stricken, yet were helpful. Some said they were too grief stricken to help. One woman whose father fought for her custody when she was seven years old, says she was very angry. She blamed him for her not having a mother.

Another woman whose father took her away from her mother because her mother was physically and mentally abusive to her, said her father was helpful at times and at times not. She was afraid of her mother because her mother blamed her for the divorce. One wrote that her mother left home many times before her daughter was seven years old. That last time," *she stayed gone."* Others wrote that their fathers were too busy trying to support the children to be helpful, and one said her father had to work especially hard, *"to pay off all the bills left by my mother."* One wrote that her father wasn't aware of her grief. *"I didn't cry at her open casket funeral. I didn't cry until a lot later."* Another wrote she didn't remember if her father was helpful or not. *"I only remember the day my mother was buried. I didn't know then what was happening...."*

Another wrote of the value of seeing her father cry. *"My father, I remember, cried and was quite obviously grief stricken. That I had never seen before. It served to add to the fear but was also reassuring since there seems to be a need to know others are also crushed with sorrow."* When parents hide their tears after a death, to protect children from the trauma of seeing them cry, the children are apt to wonder if the parents feel grief. The question occurs to them, *"Would my father cry if I died?"*

Of those whose mothers left the house and never returned, there was a different kind of grief accompanied by the ever-present hope that she would return. *"She said she was going to the movies and never returned. I lived my life not knowing if she were dead or alive. I used to fantasize that she was always watching me in the streets -- from afar-- assuring herself I was a happy, healthy child. This, of course, was a mere fantasy, not connected to anything but my deep yearning to be loved and valued as a child."*

Another woman wrote, *"I knew when she told me she would be gone for awhile that something was wrong and I organized my siblings into a spy team to try and find where she went. When my father came home from work, I told him what I knew. He made phone calls and various relatives came and he questioned me. Annoyed and frustrated he said to me, 'I wish you'd watch things more around here!' It was a very humiliating moment. I felt like I'd not done enough, but I didn't know what more I could have done. I was ten years old."*

One whose mother went away with another man wrote, *"I longed for her intensely. Whenever an airplane went by, my brother and I waved hoping she was coming to surprise us. I used to cry a lot for her and that continued through adolescence, but only at night so no one ever knew. Dad never bad-mouthed her, so that was nice."*

THE TWO-PARENT FAMILY IS NOT THE BEST

Single Mother Families

More women raised by their mothers lost their fathers because of divorce than because of their father's death. In the single mother family, fewer mothers were helpful to their children at the time of the loss of the father, than was true for single fathers. Many women indicated that their mother was so angry at the time their father left that they failed to recognize, or were unable to deal with the terrible sense of loss the children were experiencing. Several women said they waited endlessly for their father to return. Some are reminded often of the trauma of their father's leaving. "*I've never lost sight of the pain I felt the day my father left. I remember it as clear as if it were yesterday. I felt as though it weren't happening. It was like watching a movie, only the pair wasn't fantasy.*" The scene holds another woman's memory. "*I still remember the scene when my father said good-bye. For a time I expected him to come back and remember asking the adults in the house when Daddy was coming back. I don't remember anyone explaining it to me, or maybe I just didn't understand.*" She was six years old then.

One woman whose mother was helpful, is still perplexed at her father's action. "*The fact that he was able to walk away from his family has puzzled me over the years. He never contacted us or supported us in any way.*"

Many also wrote that throughout their childhood they feared they would also lose their mother, and then where would they be? No women raised by fathers referred to that kind of anxiety.

Some who indicated their mothers were helpful were also glad that their fathers had left. Comments included, "*I was glad my father left because now my parents would stop fighting.*" "*If my parents had not divorced, say 'for the sake of the children,' my life would be changed for the negative. They'd argue for sure and I can't see letting much feminism in.*"

A victim of incest was understandably relieved when her mother got her "*father out of the house to protect me.*" One who says her mother was not helpful laments "*My mother denied my father his privileges to see me.*"

In answer to the question of helpfulness, one woman whose mother was deserted by her father writes, "*Actually, I guess she did what she thought was 'correct' -- she told me nothing!*"

While some mothers were angry at their husbands over a desertion or divorce, others were angry at their husbands for dying and could offer little help to their daughters. As one wrote, "*As an adult I can see clearly now that she resented Dad dying. After all, he had no cash, no life insurance, no possessions and he was on alcoholic, who abused her often, then left her with nothing but six very young children. She had a mess to clean up. She hurt, but she survived the impossible. Someone should write about these type of women. They need recognition.*"

Another said, "*Losing my father was of course one of the most painful experiences of my life. One of the worst things about it was that I was told of his death, then rushed off to Bible school. The Bible School teacher, who had been told, didn't say a word of comfort to me. I was not allowed to attend his funeral, al-*

though I begged to go. I carried my grief for years. It took a long time to work through. I think the cruelest thing one could ever do is ignore a grieving child." One whose father died when she was two years old answers the question of whether or not her mother was helpful with "*NO!!!*"

Step Parent Families

The step parent group was recruited almost exclusively from a pool of women who, at the age of around five years old, had lost a biological parent through death. It was evenly divided as to whether or not the remaining parent was helpful. Also some did not remember, and for some, their parent's death was not discussed with them. For instance, "*My mother's death was kept secret from me until I said something at age eleven. It remained a subject to be avoided until a few years ago.*" "*Exclusion from the grieving process seems to facilitate denial.*" One whose mother was killed in a car accident was told, "*She'll be along later.*" The little girl kept waiting until she realized six months later her mother was never coming home.

The parent's helpfulness was significantly determined by whether or not the remaining parent was the girl's biological father or her biological mother. Biological mothers were, for the most part, helpful; biological fathers were not.

Asked if her remaining parent was helpful, a woman writes, "*As much as she could be, but she was devastated.*" Another who had lost her mother wrote that her father couldn't be helpful "*because he was so lost himself.*" One with a biological father who was planning his remarriage writes that her father had "*offered to place us in an orphans' home when they married.*" This didn't happen but the relationship with her stepmother was not good. Were other people helpful to this girl in her bereavement? She writes, "*I can remember sitting in a sunny spot on the carpet in my grandmother's living room during mother's funeral wondering why I was not allowed to attend. Several months later an older cousin, possibly jealous of the attention we had received from other's family members, informed my sister and me that the only reason people were being nice to us was because our mother had died -- as though that made us different from the rest of the family, not loved but pitied.*"

Another who couldn't attend her mother's funeral said, "*I was not allowed to grieve over my mother's death and the anger I expressed in temper tantrums during the year after her death was to be controlled. No one in the family ever connected these tantrums with her death.* " She also writes of the attitude which was assumed after her father remarried. "*...the overwhelming family belief required of us all was that we were a 'normal' family in which no adoptions, remarriages, etc. had happened. It was supposed to be 'as if' our parents had always been our parents.*" What confusion that must have caused for this girl!

THE TWO-PARENT FAMILY IS NOT THE BEST

	REMAINING PARENT HELPFUL IN BEREAVEMENT		
	Yes	No	Too Young
Sing. F.	43%	42%	15%
Sing. M.	27%	41%	31%
Bio. M. Stp.*	73%	19%	8%
Bio. F. Stp.*	20%	62%	18%

Bio. M. Stp. stands for biological mother in step parent group; Bio. F. Stp. stands for biological father in step parent group.

CONCLUSION

Generally, children who lived with a single *father* have experienced the death of their mother, whereas children who lived with a single *mother* have experienced a divorce. In single father families, whether the loss was from death or divorce or separation, the father's helpfulness was approximately the same.

In single mother families, where divorce was twice as apt to be the cause of the child's loss of her father, the single mother was not very helpful.

In the step parent family, a girl could expect consolation and help if the remaining parent was her biological mother. Biological *fathers* were generally not helpful to their daughters.

The absence of a spouse because of *death* often leaves the remaining parent so distraught they are unable to help their children in their sorrow and loss. The absence of a spouse because of a *divorce* or desertion often leaves the remaining parent so angry they cannot show compassion to their children who are suffering from the loss of a parent. This anger which is often translated by fathers to a hatred or fear of women in general, does not seem to be generational. Daughters of these men who are angry at women do not themselves seem also to be angry at women.

On the other hand, *women* who have been divorced or have been deserted by men and who often translate this anger to a hatred of men in general, *do* seem to pass this on to their daughters. One might say that this dislike of the opposite sex is transmitted from male to male and female to female.. The daughters of single mothers write of their being uncomfortable with men, of not being accepting, and of being fearful. This may also be because children in single mother homes may not have many good relationships with men as they are growing up.

But where there had been a death and it had not been communicated to the children, even kept from them for a long time, or they had been prevented from attending the funeral, or where there was no discussion about the absence of the parent or what had caused the parent to die, the children suffered greatly. Children in these circumstances, now grown women some with children and grandchildren are even today resentful about having been excluded from vital information about the person most important to them. Women who had

THE TWO-PARENT FAMILY IS NOT THE BEST

been excluded from the grieving process are still suffering greatly from the loss which occurred so many years ago. As some women have said, they are afraid to get close to other people because they are afraid of losing them and they are terribly afraid of loss.

The adjustment a child makes after a death of a parent depends on whether or not she is included in the grieving process. After a divorce, the child's adjustment depends on how much she is included in the reforming of the family situation, how much discussion there is about the loss of the parent and what needs to be done for smooth continuity. If the child is "*protected*" from grief or "*protected*" from understanding at least the basic cause of the divorce, desertion or separation, she is left feeling even more alone. If the child is not somewhat included she is left free to wildly assume anything. "*Daddy/Mommy left because she/he didn't love me. I wasn't good enough. I'm not a good girl.*"

Many children in these circumstances suffer lowered self-esteem, lowered performance in school and poor personal relationships. However painful it might be for adults to include their children in their own grief or trauma, to let the children see the weeping or the angry frustration, in the long run including them is more apt to help than to hurt the children. Including children in family grief includes them in the humanity of the family. It shows them that each family member's absence will be grieved, including their own, should that happen.

CLOSE KNIT FAMILY

"My father's love and guidance in serving both roles seemed more bonding than other families I saw."

The question asks, "W*as your family closer knit than other families?*" A few women in each group answered that they couldn't compare their families because they had no inside knowledge of other families. But most women had strong feelings about whether or not their families were close knit.

One is apt to think of close knit families as always being a positive quality. But there are situations where being close knit may be for negative reasons, as for instance when family members keep silent because of evil secrets such as incest, alcoholism, or drug dealing. However, this question was answered in the sense that it was asked and it is assumed here that being in a close knit family is a healthy, positive situation.

In addition to answering if their families were close knit, women in all groups were asked to explain *why* they believed they were close knit or not. All of the positive answers were listed and then categorized, as, for instance, "*closed rank,*" "*dependent on one another,*" "*fun and recreational,*" or "*other.*" which included, "*good communication,*" "*lots of love.*" The negative categories were: "*poor situational,*" "*fighting and tension,*" "*no affection,*" "*expectations too high.*"

THE TWO-PARENT FAMILY IS NOT THE BEST

Single Father Families

Half of the women from single father families said theirs was a close knit unit and half said they were not. A few of the explanations from women who felt their families were close knit were, "*A la Helen Reddy, it was 'Dad and Me Against the World.'*" "*It seemed at times to be 'us against them.' The struggle to survive pulled us together.*" "*My father and I seem to get along better than other families and we tend to do more together.*" "*My father seemed to spend more 'playtime' with us than other fathers did.*" "*We learned to rely on each other.*" "*Especially close father-daughter relationship. Most women don't experience the friendship we had.*" "*My father and I always went everywhere together and I always had his undivided attention.*" "*We became very protective of other people hurting us, but we fought among ourselves.*" "*We felt we had to stick together, versus his in-laws who often tried to influence his child-rearing.*" "*We were very close before and after my mother died. This aspect of family life didn't change so I'd say we were like other families that had mothers.*" "*We all shared the hurt, and talked all the time about how we felt.*" "*We felt we were different and 'stuck together.'*" "*We fought among ourselves, but outsiders were not allowed to put any of us down.*"

When fathers are appreciated for having kept their family together, women write, "*I've always been so grateful to my father for not giving us up for adoption or to relatives who offered when my mom died. My father was a far from perfect dual parent, but I give him a hell of a lot of credit for his efforts.*" Another said,

"*When our paternal grandparents offered to take me and my younger sister my father refused to even consider it, and never turned away from his raising his children. We were close.*" And, "*Until our stepmother appeared, we were all close and at our best.*"

Of those women from single father families who said their families were *not* close knit, many wrote that their father was uncommunicative. Some talked about the friction among siblings because of the tension of not having a mother in their home. One said their mother had been the "*life*" of the family and without her, things were not good, or as one said, "*After mother died our family became very cold.*" Several said their father worked so much that they didn't have a chance to be close, and one said "*There was more tension and hostility toward us that previously had been targeted for my mother.*" And another viewpoint, "*We were expected to be perfect little children who were held up to the town as children of Mr. So. and So. who were polite and helpful to everyone.*" One of the reasons given which was often repeated, was "*There was jealousy and competition between the children -- little intimacy with father.*"

Nevertheless half of the women in the single father group regarded their family as close knit, with the principal reason being that they were dependent on one another. Forty-four percent said their families were not close knit.

THE TWO-PARENT FAMILY IS NOT THE BEST

Single Mother Families

With the highest percentage of women in the four groups who recalled their families as close knit, many women in the single mother group explained their reasons much as the single father group did, such as. "*I think our troubles brought us together.*" One of the differences between the single mother group and the single father group is apparent in that in the mother group, as one wrote, "*We are all females, my mother, sister and I . . .*" In this respect one woman points out the relative position of her brother in the family. "*My mother, sister and I are quite close; my brother is a sort of appendage, though, almost an outsider.*"

Of the women in the single mother families who said their families were *not* close knit, that is, 40%, several remarks are similar to those of the negative responses from the single father family, that is, that there was a lot of quarreling. Some women mention feelings of isolation, even within their own family, such as, "*Although we physically moved as a group, emotionally we did not discuss anything.*" "*We were four lost souls, no parenting, no routine, very survival-minded.*" "*It was very difficult. I had three bosses, mother, grandfather and grandmother.*"

But generally, comments from women who felt that their families were close knit were voiced quite like the following: "*I do believe that my family was very tight-knit, partly because of my father's absence. We had some very good times together -- talking, staying up real late. Sometimes we acted like friends rather than mother and children!*"

Two Biological Parents

A few more women in the biological parents group reported that their families were *not* close knit than were close knit.

It could have been expected that women from the biological group would have had the highest percentage answering "*Yes*," to this question. Children growing up with two biological parents generally have access to two parents rather than just one parent, and with this access it could be assumed that children have the warmth, security, and comfort that two parents can provide. Theoretically, also, there is a female/male balance in discussions and decisions which concern the children and a sense, therefore, that the biological parent group is more intact, more "*whole*" than other family groups. Why, then, does there seem to be less family closeness in the biological parent group than in the single parent groups?

One reason is that in a family where there are two parents, these two adults have each other to communicate with and may not communicate as much with their children as single parents. Also, the two parents together may make the decisions which concern the family, treating the children as children, rather than as more equal participants, not bringing them into the decision-making, a process which helps to create a sense of unity. Also, the family may not feel threatened from the outside as single parent groups may have felt. In the two biological parent group there may have been no urgency to "*pull together*" as there often is with single parent families.

THE TWO-PARENT FAMILY IS NOT THE BEST

Then, too, the parents may be so close that they, unknowingly or otherwise, exclude their children from the warmth of their own love. As one woman wrote, "*I did not feel wanted and I did not feel loved. I hungered for love. Having a single mother, single father, or two parents living together is not as important as being wanted, loved, and cared for.*" Another woman whose parents married when they were 18 and 19, felt rejected and wrote, "*I believe my parents were concentrated on their own growing up and unusually close love. I must have been a nuisance to them and I believe my mother was jealous when she saw a closeness beginning to develop between my dad and me. I look back from age 60 and am still profoundly convinced I was a rejected child, quite isolated within my small family.*"

Another woman wrote that her parents, who were estranged, stayed together "*for the children.*" This, she said, "*puts too much responsibility on the children.*" She adds, if she were in a marriage with a no-win situation she "*would have the strength to leave and if I did not, to place the responsibility for my staying with myself, not on my children.*"

Most in the biological group who reported a close knit family situation said it was because they "*did fun things together.*"

"*We spent a lot of time together. We were too poor to 'go out' or even own a T.V.*" "*Family outings, summer vacations, evenings reading, playing games, watching T.V. together, family suppers.*" "*Family outings took precedence over everything else.*" "*Blood is thicker than water.*" "*We always ate dinner together, went to the movies every week.*" Many women in the

GROWING UP

biological parents group mention *going to the movies together a lot* in response to the question. Others talk about supporting each other or always being able to count on each other. One woman was extremely grateful for the closeness she felt with her family. "*I always felt loved and that I belonged. I count myself one of the very fortunate to have known, lived with and loved both parents.*"

Another believes that all two-parent families are as happy as hers was. "*I feel our family was closer knit because we learned to share and work together to achieve harmony. The roles we each learned and performed were quite common in all two-parent families, I feel. The emotions, whether up or down, good or bad, were observed on a more equal basis as opposed to observing only a male or female-oriented behavior.*" One woman wrote of her father's teaching her how to fly an airplane, and how they both took glider lessons together. She adds, "*Our family was very close.*" Another wrote of her parents, "*All my life I heard them say to each other, 'I love you.'* I think hearing that and the fact that they talked openly about bills, kids, shared responsibilities, didn't turn me off to marriage.*"

But most women in the biological parent group did *not* feel a family closeness. Several women wrote comments similar to this: "*My parents were so close I felt like an outsider.*" "*My parents were lovers. I felt outside their circle of warmth.*" And then there were the remarks that were the opposite of those saying how much the family did together. In the negative remarks, women wrote that they never did anything together as a family. Or, "*Closed against the world, but not warm inside.*" And "*We were at war with*

THE TWO-PARENT FAMILY IS NOT THE BEST

ourselves, each other, and most of the world around us." "The four of us acted independently." "Father was preoccupied and involved with his patients." "Mom and Dad played head games with each other and us." "Lots of marital fights, mostly about alcohol." "We were there but not close." "The 'Father Knows Best' family wasn't a reality for anyone I knew." "My friends' homes and family seemed warmer than mine." "We were close as far as duty and obligations, but for activities and love, 'No.'" "We never had any fun or enjoyed anything." "Little emotional attachment or feelings expressed." "My mother believed her children should be seen and not heard. She was incapable of giving even the slightest sign of caring or affection and I have always felt that I was cheated out of having a mother." "I often wished I was an orphan who was 'found' by a long-lost aunt who was affectionate, educated, supportive, nonjudgmental and fun as well as firm and helpful. I never enjoyed helping my mother since she always 're-did' my work, claiming it wasn't done correctly or completely." "I was often certain I did not belong to this family." "For some reason during all my growing up, despite my having both biological parents, I still continue to be estranged by them." "My tendency has been to look upon closest friends as 'family,' whereas my biological family lived in one house almost as roommates. My strongest memories of my childhood center around my friends and not the 'family unit.'" Another with an alcoholic mother wrote, "I really feel cheated that I wasn't brought up in a supportive loving atmosphere. I feel really angry and I'll never forgive my mother for putting me through that life and I'll never forgive my father for not doing anything about it."

Step Parent Families

Three quarters of the step parent families said their families were *not* close knit. In answers to almost all questions there was the ever-present dislike voiced about the step parent. A few women spoke of their step parent with kindness, love and admiration. But most mentioned their step parent with hostility and lasting anger. Not in any sense did these women as a group feel that they were in close knit family units.

Because of the particular circumstances of step parent families where a powerful person moves into the home to replace the child's missing parent, there is in many cases tension and resentment and fear of the unknown. There is an *"instant Dad,"* or *"instant Mom."* Mother or father can't *"be there,"* as she/he was before. One women said, *"It felt like we were a 'put-together' family."* Another wrote, *"Two sets of children just caused rivalry and friction."* *"My step mother packed up and left many times. We were not close except maybe my father and me."* *"We were just a group of people living together."* *"I was reminded constantly that my step dad adopted me because he loved me and that he didn't have to take me in."* *"Too much tension and I got a lot of pressure from my grandmother."* *"My step mother had three children, my father had two. We were always fighting."* *"I was never a part of the family."* *"I envied kids with two real parents."* *"My mother married a man who admitted he never should have married. He didn't have love to give to children -- only to his wife."* *"There were two sets of children. That was a problem."* *"Our image to the

THE TWO-PARENT FAMILY IS NOT THE BEST

public was totally dishonest. We were forced to play the role, but there was nothing but hatred."

"*We had a lot of fights - my step sister and Mom.*" "*With two families we just lived together. We never became one family.*" "*My step father was too stern and had problems with drinking.*" "*My stepmother had two children of her own. She pitted them against us. They were allowed to live normally. We had to stay in our bedrooms.*" "*The situation may not have been so bad if my step mother had not had a child of her own, but with her doing that, I was able to see the difference of how she treated my step brother and saw that there was a difference -- a big difference. My father through all this time was basically unaware of the actual dynamics of the situation, either that, or knew what was happening but just not what to do about it. In all, I don't blame him because I think he tried to do the best he knew how to. My only regret is that my childhood had to end at age 6.*"

Another in the step mother group wrote, "*I was never a part of the family and felt no closeness.*" And another, "*I feel that my step mother, my father and their children tried to be a family...I was odd-man out.*"

Those women in the step parent group who wrote favorably about their family unit said, "*My stepfather played no favorites. My parents showed it was not necessary to be pleasant all the time to be a family. Love was never diminished.*" "*My stepfather was like a natural father as far as I knew.*" "*My parents never ever fought, but my friends' parents did.*" "*As a teenager most of my friends hated their parents but I never did.*" "*I was so young when my mother remarried that I never thought of my father as a 'step' father." "We were close because we were never treated differently from one another. Care was always shown." "We all attempted to understand one another." "We all counted on each other very much." "There were eight children and my parents made it very clear that this new family unit was to be successful; otherwise too many people would be let down."*

Men and women who have lost a spouse often remarry with the intention of providing their children with the mother or father who is missing. In many cases this appears to be a successful arrangement with possibly two families blending together, step children becoming friends, and step parents loving and winning the love of their step children. But in many more cases, at least in this research, step children suffer by the tension which is created, by the fighting between step children, by the lack of love from the step parent and often by the withdrawal of love or attention from the biological parent.

It is possible that the biological parent in the step parent family may sense what is going on in the treatment of his or her children, but may be fearful of earning spousal displeasure and that biological parent lets the situation persist. Or the biological parent who had been a single parent may be so grateful for the assistance with the children that he or she turns them over to the step parent who then takes on the role of principal disciplinarian. Being a disciplinarian can give that person a strong sense of power and maybe, indirectly, a sense of overpowering the missing biological parent by over-disciplining the step children. Where children had accepted

THE TWO-PARENT FAMILY IS NOT THE BEST

discipline from their biological parent, they often resent it from a step parent.

When women and men are considering remarriage it should be for many more reasons than *"for the sake of the children,"* It appears from this research, that most children in single parent families feel more closeness to their family unit than do children with two biological parents or step parents.

	Close Knit Family
	Yes
Bio.	48%
Sing. F.	50%
Sing. M.	55%
Step	27%

	Explain Why Close Knit			
	1	2	3	4
Bio.	10%	15%	43%	16%
Sing. F.	15%	31%	25%	28%
Sing. M.	38%	32%	11%	19%
Step	3%	29%	47%	21%

1. Closed ranks
2. Dependent on each other
3. Fun and educational
4. Other

Conclusion

As the family is the first social unit children know, they need to feel its cohesiveness. Maybe the family is only the mother and child, but if the child feels the two are a unit, sharing the problems of doing small chores, or sharing the joys of, for example, watching a new puppy and cleaning up after it, then he or she can feel a part of this first social unit. A cohesive family is a place *from* which children can safely step and *to* which they can safely return. Even if children and their single parent, or two parents, should move to many different towns in the growing-up years, wherever their parents are, that is their home, their safe place, if they are included as participating members and not as tag-a-long appendages.

Children who grow up in families splintered by angry and unresolved arguments, alcoholism, lengthy silences, feel they do not belong. They constantly await the day when things will get better and the family can feel good again. At time things do get better, but the good times don't hold. Father gets drunk on Christmas Day, the very day the children have been waiting for all year. Or mother spends too much money when the family had agreed to get out of debt. The family feels doomed again and children learn to distrust their own hopes. Skepticism and negativism become part of their personalities.

Children have an especially strong start in life when they can grow up in families where family members are concerned for the good of other members and live that concern.

UNBURDENING ONTO CHILDREN

"Dad didn't discuss his problems. He just left the house."

In single parent households, with no other adult in the home, do parents "*unload*" their problems onto their children? And if so, is this a burden for the children? Without another adult available for communication, do single fathers and single mothers discuss with their young children aspects of adult life which the children may not be ready to assimilate and which then become burdensome. The questions asked, "*Did your father/mother talk about his/her personal problems?*" and, "*If so, was this a problem for you?*" These questions were asked of all groups, not just single parent group.

Fathers Unburdening

More single fathers talked about their personal lives than did fathers in the other groups, but of those who did, most did not present a problem for their daughters. .

Comments from this group included, "*To our knowledge, our father had no personal problems, except for fishing. He complained about money a lot.*"

Another, "*He didn't share with us.*" One woman who said her father spent most of his free time with his children, said, "*He did not have a personal life.*" In answer to whether or not her father talked about his personal life, one woman wrote plaintively, "*I wish he would have.*" And another whose father *did* discuss his personal life, and on whom this was a burden, said, "B*ut I was also proud of hearing confidences.*"

True to the stereotypical male, most single fathers did not discuss their problems with their daughters. But then, neither did fathers in the other groups. However, in the biological group, most of the daughters of fathers who discussed their problems reported that these discussions were a problem for the daughters.

One in the biological parents group said both her mother and father discussed their personal problems with her and this caused her to worry about money, which was what her parents worried about. Another said her father discussed, "*Only family problems.*" One complained, "*He lashed out constantly at what was going on around him, whining and chastising.*"

Few fathers in the step parent group discussed their problems, and of those who did, only one caused a problem for his daughter.

FATHERS UNBURDENING ONTO CHILDREN	
	Yes
Bio. F.	*9%*
Sing. F.	*27%*
St. Grp.	*8%*

OF THOSE BURDENED, WAS THIS A PROBLEM?	
	Yes
Bio. F.	81%
Sing. F.	29%
St. Grp.	0%

Mothers Unburdening

As could be expected, since women do seem to talk more freely about their problems than men, mothers in all three "*Mother*" groups talked freely with their daughters about their personal problems. the single mothers were more apt to discuss their problems, but it was the mothers in the biological parents group who were more prone to burden their daughters by these discussions. One woman in this biological parents group said her mother did not "talk *with*" so much as "talk *at*," "*constantly muttering and bitching.*" One said her mother would not *admit* to any personal problems.

In the single mother group, one women, in writing about her mother discussing problems, said, "*She had none. She learned to drive at age 32, even though she had no car.*" Another said, "*She always treated me as an adult.*" One who said her mother's conversations were a problem to her, wrote, "*Only to tell us how we were a constant burden to her, how much her life could have been improved without us.*" Another wrote about the burden,"*She talked about money and how hard everything was for a woman alone." One woman said, "*Not until I was an adult did she talk to me about her romances.*" Was this a burden? "*No. I loved the stories.*" One was very emphatic about whether or not her mother discussed her personal problems. "*NO!!!!!! She still doesn't.!!!*"

Very few women in the step parent group added comments to their answers of whether or not their mothers, or their fathers, talked about their personal problems, though one did say her mother talked freely, "*But she only spoke to complain.*"

MOTHERS UNBURDENING ONTO CHILDREN	
	Yes
Bio. M.	37%
Sing. M.	46%
St. Grp.	33%

OF THOSE BURDENED, WAS THIS A PROBLEM?	
	Yes
Bio. M.	74%
Sing. M.	42%
St. Grp.	37%

Conclusion

Single fathers and single mothers discuss their personal problems more freely with their children than do other parents and this is generally

THE TWO-PARENT FAMILY IS NOT THE BEST

not a burden to children of single parents. However, while fewer fathers and mothers in the biological parents group discussed their problems, those that did, created a burden for their children.

The burden which children feel when either their mother or their father, in a two biological parent family, discusses personal problems may be related to a sense of disloyalty to the non-present parent. Maybe the mother complaining about the child's father never fixing things around the house. Maybe the father is complaining to his daughter that her mother is more interested in her job outside the home than in taking care of her family. What is the child to do? Side with one against the other?

That personal-problem discussions are a burden in the two biological parent family could also be because children in these families are not as often taken into discussions which involve problems. Possibly they are more often maintained as children longer, protected by their parents from learning about disturbing possibilities such as a parent's impending unemployment, or protected from the knowledge that one of the parents is really quite ill.

In a single parent family it would be difficult to conceal many personal problems. Children who depend entirely on one parent may be more keenly sensitive to that parent's moods. Also the single parent usually has no other adult at home to help him or her cushion the effects of a bad day at work, for instance. The child in the single parent home, who usually already has many family responsibilities, also

GROWING UP

often assumes and expects to assume the role of listener and at times of advisor.

FINANCIAL SECURITY IN CHILDHOOD

"My [single] mother worked in a factory alongside men who made more money because 'they were supporting a family.'"

Children pick up on the worries of adults and accept them as their own. One of the age-old worries of adults, is the worry about money. What were the relative financial situations of the women in the four groups in this research study when they were growing up? Did their financial situation affect their happiness/unhappiness and their attitude in general?

Because men, on average, make more money than women, children growing up with fathers usually have more financial security than children growing up with single mothers. The 1991 figures on the gender differences in wages are that women earn on average $18,000. a year whereas men earn on average $27,000. a year. In two-parent families, especially where both parents work outside the home, children see more money being spent on non-essentials than they do if they life in single mother families. How much does the lack of financial security affect children? Apparently quite a lot.

Children never forget growing up in poverty. If every family in their sphere were poor, the lack of money would make no difference to their attitude. But as children make comparisons, and acquisition seems to be part of human nature, they wonder why the children in their neighborhood have a tricycle and they do not. Of course there's a limit to how much is enough to give a child even in wealthy families. But the child in this country who has no good clothes, no toys other than cardboard boxes, and is seldom taken to entertainments which cost money, begins to wonder about her worth compared to her friends. Peers, especially during teenage years, can be very cruel about children who are not dressed in current fashion.

It takes a tremendous amount of parental attentive love and creative play to help a poor child maintain a sense of equilibrium with his playmates in this period of extreme materialism. Today many children are given computers by the age of seven and electronic keyboards the following year. T.V. cartoons are interspersed with bombardments of commercials for millions of toys with movable parts, or with human voices, all enticing the youngster to beg her parents of for these things or she'll be the only kid on the block without. This is difficult enough for parents and children with money, but what does it do for the children who know their parents have no money?. And this is not only about toys. It's about clothes, cars, housing, and food.

In the days the respondents in this study were growing up, several were too young when T.V. began to be a part of the furniture in most homes. The median age of the women in this research is 36. T.V. began to be a household item about forty years ago. So most of these women grew up with T.V.

But watching T.V., with its barrage of advertised toys, is not the only way children learn what they might like to have, which their parents can't afford.

THE TWO-PARENT FAMILY IS NOT THE BEST

They may also notice the other children in school with their fashionable clothes, stylish haircuts, newest lunch pails and good school equipment which may even include computers, to realize a sense of deprivation.

For the women in this research who grew up financially insecure, it was a painful part of their childhood. Many are left with a great fear of being poor. Some received welfare and that created a shame. One whose parent had been on welfare, wrote, if she had to go on welfare again, "*death would even seem preferable.*"

It is the women from the single mother group who were most affected by the lack of money. Because many had been deserted by their fathers who paid no child support, many of these women are angry at men. Being poor and the reason they were poor has affected their relationships with men. Many are fearful of putting their trust in men. A positive outcome of their childhood poverty is that they have put their trust in themselves, ensuring their own financial security by getting themselves educated and qualified for employment which pays enough to support them.

Not all women in this study who grew up poor are from the single mother group, but most are. Many, in all groups who experienced poverty, wrote of how, though they had little, their childhood was happy because they "*pulled together*," or they "*made do*" with what they had. This was especially true of women who were children before there was T.V. And also very true of women who grew up on farms, or who lived on farms far away from neighbors.

It isn't that children who are poor need to be emotionally injured. If the parents are themselves depressed about their situation, as well they might be, they may continually complain about their plight and be unable to focus attention on their children's needs. The parents may develop in the children a feeling of guilt that they are costing their parents too much money. This is a situation where parents who not only cannot help, can actually damage children and cause psychological problems in their future. But if the parents' attitude is positive, if there is a strong sense of closeness, of *"pulling together,"* and if there is a delight in creatively exploring entertainment that costs no money, the children can rise above what otherwise might be low self-worth.

Financial security is an integral part of emotional stability. It isn't the quantity of money that is important. What is important is the quality of family cohesiveness, love and attention in the children's growing up years. With considerable help from parents, who are themselves emotionally stable, children's emotional and physical health need not be at risk.

Differences in Female/Male Wages

FATHER'S INCOME			
	1	2	3
Bio. F.	24%	67%	8%
Sing. F.	29%	63%	7%
St. Grp.	20%	69%	8%

1. Lower income
2. Middle income
3. Upper income

MOTHER'S INCOME			
	1	2	3
Bio. M.	37%	26%	0%
Sing. M.	53%	46%	1%
St.Grp.	35%	41%	0%

1. Lower income
2. Middle income
3. Upper income

GROWING UP

FATHER'S OCCUPATION						
	1	2	3	4	5
Bio. F.	21%	36%	22%	9%	9%
Sing. F.	14%	29%	40%	8%	8%
St. Grp.	14%	29%	43%	0%	6%

1. Professional
2. Managerial
3. Trades
4. Laborer
5. Farmer

MOTHER'S OCCUPATION						
	1	2	3	4	5
Bio. M.	12%	15%	8%	11%	54%
Sing. M.	20%	13%	30%	18%	9%
St. Grp.	6%	18%	8%	12%	55%

1. Professional
2. Managerial
3. Trades
4. Laborer
5. Housewife

One woman's mother was a farmer.

THE TWO-PARENT FAMILY IS NOT THE BEST

ON WELFARE WHEN GROWING UP?

	Yes
Sing. F.	1%
Sing. M.	17%

In this study most women who had been raised by single mothers worried about finances and complained that their father's leaving, or his death, reduced the family standard of living to a level which made day-to-day living difficult. As one woman wrote, "*My father paid no child support and we were among the poorest in our community. (The worst thing about poverty is that it leaves so little room for dignity. My brother and I were deeply ashamed of being on Welfare. It left such a scar on me that I cannot imagine the circumstances under which I would seek it for myself.*" Many of the girls who grew up without fathers suffered not only the loss of that parent, but also the loss of financial security, a loss and a worry that still plagues many of them.

When their husbands died, many single women were left, not only with small children to raise for many years, but without any insurance money or significant assets. Many of those who were divorced or deserted received no child support payments and were even "*put upon*" by their ex-husbands who returned from time to time for a hand-out.

It is not unusual for women to go without child support payments. Even today with better means of enforcing support payments, over half of the fathers required by the courts to pay child support pay either less than required or nothing at all. Then too, many women who gain custody of their children are never awarded child support.

It is easy for women and children who had lived a family life free from financial stress to find themselves inching toward welfare and poverty when a husband leaves or dies. After a divorce national studies show that the average woman's income drops by 74% while the average man's jumps by 43%. Children are fully aware of their lowered standard of living, and, unfortunately, of their diminished respect from their peers. It takes about 70% of the former family income for a mother and two children to live at the same standard as before a divorce or death. That is an almost impossible transition for a single mother to make.

Asked why many fathers don't pay, the researchers from a variety of studies on child support have concluded that the greater the strife between the mother and father, the less likely the father is to pay child support. Another reason is related to power. Withholding child support payments is holding power over an ex-wife. Sometimes a mother will prevent visitation rights of the father if he has not made his support payments. Though this may bring forth support payments, sadly, this technique hurts the children.

However, it was not only women raised by single mothers who complained about economic hardship. Even women from the single father group, who seemingly should have had greater oppor-

THE TWO-PARENT FAMILY IS NOT THE BEST

tunities for financial success, were reported as being terribly poor.

Financial hardships were reported in the biological parent group and the step parent group as well, but not to the extent that they were reported by the single mother group.

One woman from the single mother group who wrote that her mother worked 75 to 80 hours a week at menial jobs while her children were growing up, began to worry about money at an early age. One wrote, "*I feel we should never allow men to abandon their children for whatever reason. They should be held responsible for adequate provisions and medical, dental and educational needs. I do not understand how a parent could turn away from their little helpless children and never look back or see them again. I found out when I was 18 that my father lived in a city 150 miles from us. I sometimes wonder how he could do it and be at peace with himself. No, I never had a desire to see him as it was obvious he didn't want us.*"

Another who has since graduated from college and has a good job, wrote, "*I felt confused and I felt like crying much of the time but I did not know why I felt this way. I hated to have to worry about money...I don't trust men because they are unreliable and they always put themselves first. I wonder if I ever can get over my fears of poverty and of being abandoned.*"

It is not just the lack of money to live like their friends that bothered these girls, but hand-in-hand with being reduced financially was the pain of having been deserted by their fathers. "*My father hurt me when he told me at age four that he was leaving my mother for another woman that he loved instead of my mother.* " Another whose father had died, wrote, "*If my Dad had lived I would have been raised in an upper class home and gone to the best schools. I probably wouldn't have been exposed to the problems of lower income families.*" Another wrote, "*My father had children in his first marriage and in his second marriage. He paid child support for the first children but not for my sister and me because he said he didn't have enough for all of us. This still hurts. I have no contact with him.*"

What, then, should a single mother do? Finding another husband may not be the best answer as indicated in the section on Close Knit Families. Step fathers may be financial providers, but many have difficulty relating in a healthy, fatherly way to step daughters. The suggestion here is that all girls be educated for job skills that will help them support a family should they need to. Women who have children and are not able to support themselves and their children are at risk.

The second suggestion would be that both mothers and fathers have adequate life insurance policies to offset the loss of income, should one of the income-producing parents die. The third suggestion is that all women should work for any legislation that will enforce child support payments. It is true that we have left behind the idea that a girl, when she marries, will be supported for the rest of her life. But even today too many girls leave themselves ill prepared for the consequences of spousal death or desertion.

Mary Ann Glendon, Professor of Law at Harvard University, in speaking with Bill Moyers, said

THE TWO-PARENT FAMILY IS NOT THE BEST

that our "*no fault*" divorce laws more or less say, "*no responsibility for the provider to support his children.*" We communicate that it's very risky for a woman to commit herself to full time child care. She never knows if her husband is going to leave her and if he does, how she will support herself and her children.

Even though happily married, women go to work for many reasons, and one reason is to ensure that they will not later have to live in poverty. The European system says to husbands, "*if you're going to get a divorce, you're going to have to be responsible for your children.*" The provider's paycheck is docked. And if the provider is too poor, the government steps in and pays a respectable amount of money, not just enough to keep people in poverty. As a consequence, Glendon says, children are better off in Europe than in the United States The proof of that is that a larger percentage of children in this country are poor -- now approximately 20% of children live in poverty.

In a Twelve Nation Survey, March, 1990, reporting on child welfare conditions in industrial countries, the United States and Australia had the highest child poverty and infant mortality rates in the group and the highest percentage of children affected by divorce. As children of divorce usually live with their mothers, and as these mothers are responsible for supporting their families, the education of girls should be especially considered by school boards, to ward off impending poverty and to protect the community's financial resources..

Also the changing family patterns need to be accepted as reality. A California Task Force on the

GROWING UP

Changing Family reported in June, 1989 that the fastest growing households in California are single parent families and that almost half of the state's households are headed by females living in poverty. Not only are these single parent households the result of divorce, they are also the result of the growing number of unwed mothers. The Census Bureau reported in June, 1989 that 40% of American mothers under 30 are unmarried when they get pregnant. The report continues that the odds are very good that these mothers and their newborns will end up living in poverty.

    Though the financial situation for the women in the single mother group in this research was difficult when they were growing up, and the extent of their financial strain may very well have been as great as that strain is for single mothers today, the number of single mothers is much greater today than before. That does not diminish the financial problems that the women in this research had to face. It is only to say that the whole country today is being affected by the scope of the single mother situation. Welfare roles will expand, taxes will need to be raised to support women and children who cannot support themselves. As stated before, as 20% of the nation's children are now living in poverty, this will have a profound effect on all social programs and most probably will not only negatively affect the well-being of these children, but the well-being of the entire country.

THE TWO-PARENT FAMILY IS NOT THE BEST

GENDER EQUITY IN THE HOME

"In our family, men, including my younger brother, were of higher status than women. We all worked hard, but the men had more freedom, and always got the first choice of chicken pieces."

Whether boys and girls are treated equally or not, will reflect on their sense of self-worth. The way the members of the family treat their children places one of the first imprints on their personality. How the most important people in their lives view them will affect the children's view of themselves. How even small tasks are relegated to family members, or withheld, can affect one's sense of self.

In years past it has been the practice to allocate household chores on the basis of gender. Tasks considered menial, such as housecleaning, have almost always been relegated to the girls in the family. The long-term effects of what is referred to as sexist treatment, both at home and at school, have resulted in an inferior positioning of women in the work of the community, the nation, and the world.

Girls growing up were counseled by parents and school counselors to prepare themselves almost exclusively for marriage, and later for *"just in case"* jobs -- *"just in case"* they didn't marry, or *"just in case"* their husband died. The lack of feeling as worthy as their brothers often resulted in lower aspirations for girls, which in turn resulted in career choices which affected their standard of living, personal fulfillment, and eventually a lower retirement income in old age.

Concerted efforts have been made since the beginning of the 1970's to change this outlook, during what was then considered the initial stages of the latest women's movement. There were conscientious attempts to eliminate stereotypical male/female roles in schools and in employment. Girls were permitted to enroll in what had heretofore been considered male classes such as drafting which could lead to courses in engineering. Boys were permitted to enroll in health care classes which could lead to careers in nursing.

All in all, the change in the way boys and girls were treated outside the home began to affect the attitude about what each gender could accomplish. There were, and are, die-hards who insist that girls should be brought up to stay home and raise the children, and not train for well paid jobs. But since more and more women are working outside the home, the wishes of the die-hards seem empty.

The questions for this research concerned the girls' treatment at home. The first issue was to determine if there had been a difference in the treatment of brothers and sisters in homes with single fathers, compared with equality treatment in the other groups. The questions were: "*If you had a brother, did he share equally in the housework?*" "*Were you and your brother treated equally?*" "*If not, what areas?*" "*Did all household members share household work?*" "*Did your mother share equally?*" "*Did your father share equally?*"

THE TWO-PARENT FAMILY IS NOT THE BEST

Of those who had brothers, more than half of the women in the single *mother* families reported more equality than in any other group. Maybe this was because there was no male role model in the home who made the brother feel that housework was women's work.

In single *father* households, less than half of the women reported that their brothers shared equally. As one wrote, *"Dad believed in a democratic home. We all had equal responsibilities in both house and yard work."*

Brother Share Equally In Housework?	
	Yes
Bio.	29%
Sing. F.	43%
Sing. M.	55%
Step	31%

In other words, in the two groups where there were *two* parents, biological and step parents, where there were male and female role models, boys did *less* housework. This was most likely because the boys in the homes where there were mothers and fathers, did not see their fathers often, if at all, vacuuming rugs, or folding clothes from the dryer. Of the boys who did share in housework, it was said that boys would help with dishes but would not dust, or do other cleaning, or laundry. To the question, *"If you had a brother, did he do household chores like* dishes, laundry, housecleaning?" one woman in the biological group answered, "HEAVEN FORBID!!!"

Another woman in the biological parents group expanded on the problem of being treated differently than her brothers. "*I could never accept a date on a Saturday night because I had to sit my younger brothers because my parents always went out that night. As I grew older I learned that the boys were allowed to do so much more than I was and were given more and better privileges. They could go out and play and I had to help Mom. I wanted to go to college and I placed very high in my senior year of high school in the college placements tests. My father refused to let me go to college, encouraged me to work and get married like all women should. My father always told me when I asked why I couldn't do the things that the boys could do, 'You are a girl and girls don't act like boys'. What he said went. I realize now as an adult that my mother was actually scared of him that if she wasn't submissive he would leave her with four kids. She doesn't have any skills to be able to offer an employer and has always been supported by my father. It was often inferred in our family that my 'intelligence was wasted on a female.'"*

Another woman in the biological parents group explained a different situation. "*I was raised in many ways like a boy as Dad had no sons and when an extra pair of hands was needed it didn't matter whose, so I helped mechanic on the cars, carpenter and helped in haying on Granny's farm. So I learned two roles in my upbringing. Mom and Dad didn't seem to be aware of what they were doing as they were shocked when I turned out independent, smart, assertive and*

THE TWO-PARENT FAMILY IS NOT THE BEST

capable and not interested in giving up my freedom to a marriage."

In each group, women said the work divisions were that boys did more outside work while girls did the housecleaning. Boys were permitted to participate in sports more, they had much more independence, especially in the biological group. One wrote about when she was older, "*My parents never bought me a car as they did for my brothers.*"

In the step parent group it was said that girls were more pampered but did more household chores. One said that her "*step brothers could do no wrong; I could do no right.*" Another step child said, "*I was punished less often and less severely.*" One with a step mother wrote, "*My step brother got special meals other than what the rest of us ate. He had his own room, and he was generally treated specially like being hugged and kissed by my step mother which she never did it to me.*"

In the single father group, those who were *not* treated equally said, "*Boys could stay out later and if they had a job were relieved of some chores, while my sisters and I were not.*" "*I was treated like a maid.*" "*I didn't have freedom to come and go as he did and forbidden to get involved in rough sports.*" "*I was expected to do more domestic chores while brothers were taught to handle firearms.*" "*I was treated like a boy and dressed like a boy but when it came to household chores I was expected to do them. I never did them out of rebellion.*" "

Another in the single father group wrote of her many chores, repeated here in its length because it represents what many others said. "*I guess the one thing that I remember most is my being expected to be the housekeeper, not chores like doing dishes or dusting; but being in charge of the house, cooking the meals, cleaning, washing clothes and doing the dishes. Being only ten years old I think it overwhelmed me but my father and brothers just accepted I should know how to take care of Women's Work and so I accepted it as part of my life. I also was expected to help my brothers with their chores feeding the chickens, yard work, washing the car, etc., and doing what I found out later (much later) was these chores were boys' work. But my father never said I couldn't do things because I was a girl. As a matter of fact nothing was too heavy for me to lift or carry. I was expected to do what my brothers did. Being raised like a boy gave a sense that there just wasn't a job I couldn't do or a situation I couldn't handle."*

She continues, "*There were many times when I was out with my girl friends and the car broke down or we were stranded and I was the one the other girls looked to to figure out how to get out of the mess, which I usually did. For one reason or another I was always amazed that I was the only one to come up with the solution, or if not the solution, the ability to get the other girls to start thinking how we could get out of our fix ourselves -- not just sit around wringing our hands. If we were out with boys and became embroiled in the same type of mess and I offered a solution to the boys, I was completely ignored unless I took one guy aside and gave him the idea for the solution without letting him know I was the one with the idea.*"

Then she adds, "*For a long time I was ashamed of other women and girls their inability to do things that*

THE TWO-PARENT FAMILY IS NOT THE BEST

I found easy. It made me ashamed of them and mystified me for I couldn't understand how or where they had been raised. Most of them went to pieces if the car had a flat tire or dead battery, hurrying to call a man to fix these very small problems."

In answer to the question, if all household members shared household work, women from single mother and single father groups wrote that in approximately forty percent of the households all shared equally. But when the question, "*Did mother share equally in household work?*" was asked about families where there had been two parents, biological and step parents, the answers were that mothers did it all. No wonder then that at a ratio of three to one, in households where there are two parents, sons follow their fathers' pattern of doing little or no housework.

In a recent study of how husbands were helping in housework when their wives worked, the results pointed out that men do help, but not enough. From 1965 to 1985 they increased their load at home from 15% of the housework to 35%. That means that women are holding full-time jobs and doing 65% of the work at home. When men help with childcare it is considered "*babysitting.*" That word is not used when mothers are caring for their children. John Robinson, the director of the study said, "*I have a sense that we have reached the limits of how much housework is possible to squeeze out of husba*nds"

It is thoroughly possible that the way we raised boys will affect how much they will participate in housework as adults. As housework needs to be done, and as few people have household help, and as most wives and mothers work, it would seem only fair that housework be shared by all capable family members. It behooves today's generations of parents, fathers and mothers, to educate sons as well as daughters to do their fair share. Sons should not expect their future wives to pick up their dirty socks and take full responsibility for emptying the dishwasher, changing the bag in the vacuum cleaner, cleaning the refrigerator or dusting behind the sofa. Chances are his wife will also be weeding the flower garden on Saturday and stopping at the gas station with a car-load of children on the way home from school to make an appointment for a lube job.

Women today are taking on too much work. Though they probably cannot get much more help from their husband's now, they can raise their sons differently than previous generations did. This applies especially to women in the two-parent families who are less apt to train their sons to pick up after themselves, leaving the menial tasks to their mother and sisters.

In this study where there were no male role models of men who did no housework, more boys participated in the necessary tasks. There is probably not much chance today, where there are fathers, that these fathers will lead their sons to do work that they themselves won't do. It's up to this generation of mothers to teach their sons to help, to take the load off of future wives and mothers.

RESPONSIBILITIES

THE LITTLE MOTHER

"If a child in my care was hurt, I was held responsible. I had to think for all of us while my mother was at work."

A little girl who had lost her mother might easily slip into the little mother role. Wanting to make things easier for her father and possibly younger siblings, she could become the person who looked after the safety of the other children, called them in from their play, made sure they ate their meals and did their homework. Little girls in this situation could also become the little wife, doing the laundry, dusting the furniture, and preparing the meals. And any father left with the responsibility of raising a family by himself would welcome and encourage help from his children. But does this kind of help from children happen often? And does it happen in other families as well, that is, single mother families, families with both biological parents, and step parent families? And if so, what is the effect on the children?

Two questions were asked of women raised by single fathers: "*Were you the little mother?*" and "*Were you the little wife?*" These questions were also asked of women raised by both biological parents and by step parents. Women in the single mother group were asked, "*Were you the little mother?*" and "*Did you take on some of father's role?*"

It was expected that there would have been more "*little mothers*" in the single father group. However, that was not the case. The highest percentage of women answering "*yes,*" to this question, was in the single *mother* group.

The next highest percentage of women who said they were "*the little mother*" was in *step parent families*, followed by women in the single father families and then by women in the biological parents group.

WERE YOU THE LITTLE MOTHER?	
	Yes
Bio.	32%
Sing. F.	38%
Sing. M.	52%
Step	41%

THE TWO-PARENT FAMILY IS NOT THE BEST

	OF THOSE ANSWERING "YES"				
	1	2	3	4	5
Bio.	81%	12%	4%	4%	0%
Sing. F.	40%	10%	33%	10%	6%
Sing. M.	52%	6%	21%	15%	6%
Step	50%	28%	11%	5%	0%

1. Child care
2. House care
3. Both child and house care
4. Care of parent
5. Care of parent and sibling

Step Parent Families

One of the women in the step parent families who said they were *the little mother* wrote, "*I had to do all the work in the house.*" Another wrote, "*Two children were born to my step mother. They slept with me. I dressed and fed them and was responsible for their care until I was 18.*" And another, "*I took care of my younger sister more than anyone else.*" "*I was the eldest child. I had one sister younger than I and then three children were born to my step mother. I took care of them.*" Others indicated the same kind of child-care responsibility. "*I cared for my baby brother all summer, after school, evenings, and week-ends.*" "*I took care of my younger sisters not only physically but emotionally as well.*" "*Since I was the oldest of seven children it was only natural that I should help.*" "*I *started taking care of my younger sisters and brothers when I was very young. Even though I had a step mother, my younger siblings gave me Mother's Day cards but they didn't give them to our 'mother.'" "I felt burdened by caring for my siblings, but in retrospect it wasn't that bad.*" Another woman who had multiple responsibilities wrote, "*I took care of the house and my parents when they were drunk. If I didn't do the housework and have dinner ready when they stumbled in, I got beaten.*" Another woman was the child-peacemaker. "*I am the one who made peace and tried to get everyone to get along.*"

Single Mother Families

Women who responded from the single mother group that they were *the little mother* wrote, "*I was often left with my little sister, responsible for making sure the house was cleaned, that we had meals, that we went to sleep on time, that laundry, etc. was done.*" Several felt that they were not only mothers to their siblings, but also to their mothers."*I helped bring up my brothers, I took care of my mother.*" "*I felt I was my sibling's mother and my mother's mother.*" Others added, "*Being the oldest in the family and having to be away from home so much, my mother depended upon me to see that our home work, chores, meals, laundry were done properly and to be in charge of the younger children.*" "*Raised my sister from infancy.*" "*When my mother drank, I parented her by ...calling her jobs, caring for her, seeing that she ate and did not disgrace us openly.*" "*I did most of the cleaning,*

THE TWO-PARENT FAMILY IS NOT THE BEST

cried most of the time and got little recognition...A TRUE MOTHER!"

When fathers die, or mothers divorce their husbands or are deserted by their husbands, the mother almost always needs to go to work. That means, if there are no other child-care arrangements, the children have to learn how to care for themselves. As these statements from women who were obliged to care for their younger siblings indicate, it was understood that when mother went to work, the oldest daughter was responsible not only for the other children, but also for many of the household chores. This work was not necessarily resented, or at least not by all. As one wrote, expressing the feelings of several women, "*All of us were called upon to help and nurture our younger sisters.*"

Single Father Families

Women who responded from the single *father* group that they were *the little mother* said they were obligated to take care of their younger siblings. "*I raised my sister from the time she was seven until she was fourteen, and then I left home.*" "*My brothers told me their problems and I tried to help.*" "*Sister said she was too little, brother said he was a boy and shouldn't have to do girls' work and I hated to be punished so I did it all. Being shy it was easier than fighting them all and Dad wouldn't listen anyway.*" "*My brother was born when my mother died. I took care of him.*" "*My older sister left home when I was twelve; then I became the 'mother.'*" "*I was mother to the world that never gave me one." "While my friends were still playing with dolls and acting goofy, I was tending real babies, handling the household laundry on a wringer washer at first, cooking complete meals, scrubbing floors, etc. I was proud of what I could accomplish and secretly felt superior to my peers. At the same time I was a kid and wanted to be goofy and carefree and normal. I wanted to fit in and not be an oddity. This conflict went on all through my childhood and adolescence."*

THE LITTLE WIFE

"I felt determined my family would not miss Mom so I tried to do everything she did."

As to the question, *"were you the little wife,"* the only significant percentage of answers was from the single father group. About one-third answered that they had taken on the wifely chores. They wrote: "*I had to do all the things a mother did, more than I was capable of doing.*" "*I cooked supper, took clothes and washed them, discussed 'our child,' my sister, cleaned up dishes, watched TV with him until bedtime, and then started the same cycle the next day. Saw him off to work before waking my sister up for school.*" "
"*Dad told me I was the woman of the house and taught me cooking and sewing.*" "*Once he taught us everything he expected his meals promptly, his clothes cleaned regularly. I listened to problems and offered him soothing words.*" "*More like a maid actually. When I got out of my father's house I swore*

THE TWO-PARENT FAMILY IS NOT THE BEST

I'd never be another man's maid." "Expected at eleven years to cook, clean, sew, take complete care of house and family." "In my teens I found myself as a caretaker, cooking, cleaning, and protecting Dad."

"I took care of the house, plus went to school, plus worked from age fourteen." "I was a cook and cleaning person." "I did everything a wife would do except sleep with him." "Did help some with two younger sisters but we were all responsible." "I had to do a lot more for my brothers and when my father got sick I had to baby him." "People chuckled, but I really worried and felt responsible. I had all the work and no authority."

WERE YOU THE LITTLE WIFE?

	Yes
Bio.	10%
Sing. F.	29%

IN WHAT WAYS, THE LITTLE WIFE?

	1	2
Bio.	63%	37%
Sing. F.	73%	27%

1. House and sibling care
2. Dad care

TAKE ON THE FATHER'S ROLE?

"I did the lifting, the yard work and fixed things."

Single Mother Families

Did any of the girls growing up in a single mother home take on some of the father's role? Many said they didn't know what a father's role was.

NO ONE IN THE SINGLE FATHER GROUP SAID THEY DIDN'T KNOW WHAT A MOTHER'S ROLE WAS.

The women in the single mother group, who said they did take on some of a father's role wrote, *"I was protecting my mother." "I disciplined my siblings and taught my brothers how to fish." "I confronted difficult neighbors and troublesome men." "I became the decision-maker in the family." "My mother did not like to make decisions. I had to make a lot of inappropriate decisions, for example, what kind of a car to buy." "I always found missing things, fixed things." "My mother often discussed business details and relied upon me to carry some of these for her. I felt very ill prepared for some of these things and overwhelmed by some of it on many occasions." "I ran the house and yard and paid the bills."*

THE TWO-PARENT FAMILY IS NOT THE BEST

TAKE ON FATHER'S ROLE?	
	Yes
Sing. M.	39%

Note that girls in both the single father and the single mother families mention protecting their parent -- in a sense taking on a parental role.

Biological Parents Group

Children, at an early age, in *all* groups in this study were called upon to carry out what could be considered adult responsibilities, beyond simple chores allotted to children. These responsibilities included a major share of taking care of the house and children. Women in the biological parents group also indicated that they were the *little mother*. They were just as aware of being overloaded as were women in the other three groups. *"Mother would yell at me to get younger siblings to do such and such and I'd pass the command and the emotions. I was often in charge of the younger kids." "When my mother was sick I learned how to cook and take care of the house. This continued when she was well and busy with her own things." "My mother opted out of most traditional mothering activities; I took them on, and I was her nurturer at least as much as she was mine." "I took more care of them than they of me." "Often I felt like a mother to my mother." "When my brother was born, her third child, Mom was depressed. I was ten. He was mine so to speak." "Both parents worked. As oldest girl I assumed household and parenting duties." "I tried to protect my younger brother from my parents' arguments. Mom says I brought him up. She worked. I started changing his diapers when I was seven years old." "I was expected to do a lot of the housework which I always resented but could not speak out against." "I cooked dinner every day from 6th grade to high school graduation."*

On the whole, the oldest girl in the family, regardless of which group, was obliged to take on a great amount of child care responsibilities.

Of the women in the biological group who said they were considered the *little wife,* which was only 10%, one wrote, *"When my mother went through a period of agoraphobia, I often accompanied my father on business outings."* And another said she felt like *the little wife, "When my father would say something like, 'Your butt wiggles just like your mother's,', or when he'd complain to me about my mother."* One woman who had been sexually abused by her biological father wondered if she was in the role of the *little wife.* Another said, *"It was always obvious that the marriage was bad and Dad looked to me for support and comfort."*

Sometimes it is not possible for parents to get outside household or child-care help, and they need to rely on their children. But since many of the voices here carry resentment about the amount of work they did, this means there probably was not enough compensation in terms of appreciation for doing adult work, or there was too much expectation and not enough play time arranged for the child.

THE TWO-PARENT FAMILY IS NOT THE BEST

In today's families, especially as so many mothers are working, women need all the help they can get and may too often put excessive demands on children's time. This may not be offset by permitting free time for play or other childhood activities. A balance should be possible and children should have some family responsibilities. But they should not be taken advantage of by adults.

Children need not grow up resentful or anxious to leave home to escape housework and child care, if parents can let up from time to time on their demands. The saying, *"all work and no play makes Jack a dull boy,"* is quite apt. Children need to play.

Parents may feel that child's play is a waste of time but it is a necessary basis for personality. The child over-burdened with work, not balanced by free, exploratory play periods, may very likely have few interests, limited aspirations, few friends and considerable loneliness.

OLDER THAN ONE'S YEARS

"I faced an adult situation at the age of six."

Though not all were *"little mothers,"* or *"little wives,"* or took on a *"father's role,"* enough children did to indicate they carried responsibilities beyond ordinary childhood tasks. Because of these early responsibilities, did the women in this research, as they were growing up, feel *older than their years*?

Could *"feeling older,"* be related to the responsibilities just mentioned, i.e. being *"the little mother,"* or *"the little wife"*? Not so with the single father group. *Though almost three quarters in that group said they "felt older than their years,"* only about one-third had said they were *"the little mother."*

However, in the single *mother* group, where it appears more children had greater responsibilities than did children in the single father group, almost two-thirds said they felt *"older than their years."* It seems that in the single mother group the responsibilities may have influenced the girl's feeling older. But for the single father group, there must have been more reasons than responsibilities for the women to feel *older*.

Could it be that fathers, not being stereotypically as protective as mothers, do not nurture and/or "baby" their children to the degree that mothers might be inclined to do and so the children *"feel older."*? A girl growing up in a single father household could compare the treatment she receives with that of her peers and conclude, that she is more

THE TWO-PARENT FAMILY IS NOT THE BEST

mature. By contrast, a mother might, for instance, ensure that her daughter leave for school in the morning with her books and lunch, whereas a father might assume his daughter knows she should be prepared for the school day and not feel the need to remind her of what she should bring. Also, on a different tone, fathers do not generally tolerate what they might call "*whining*," so girls in single father homes may more easily learn to work out their own problems. Mothers generally "*placate*" more than fathers and are often known for wanting to "*make things better*," and to mediate.

But what of the women in the other two groups? Almost sixty percent of women growing up in two parent families, that is, women in both the biological parents group and women in the step parent group *also* felt older than their years. How does this correlate with childhood responsibilities? Though approximately the same number of women in each of the two-parent groups said they "*felt older*," fewer women in these two groups had said that they were "*the little mother*," or "*the little wife*."

DID YOU FEEL OLDER THAN YOUR YEARS?	
	Yes
Bio.	58%
Sing. F.	71%
Sing. M.	64%
Step	57%

Conclusion

Except possibly in the single mother group, it appears there is no definite connection between childhood responsibilities and feeling older. Why all women in all groups felt older than their years is unclear except, maybe, all children feel that way. Maybe all people feel they did not have enough of the kind of caring which they vaguely remember from their earliest years. There may be a nostalgic longing for that early cuddling, and the protection from the outside world.

But what of *feeling older than one's years* in itself? Is this a sad situation for a child? Possibly we tend to think so. Possibly we feel that if the child is not playing out her childhood in childish ways -- that somehow the child is being cheated. But is that so? One woman in the biological parents group wrote that she felt older because friends came to her for advice and she liked that. Another in that group said she felt *younger* than her years because her parents were over-protective, indicating resentment that she was not permitted to mature as she would have liked.

It seems *"feeling older than one's years,"* is not necessarily y harmful to a child and may be even good. If there is resentment, that would not be healthy, but not all women who had heavy responsibilities and *"felt older"* were resentful. Several were proud of *"feeling older"* and proud of their carrying out responsibilities.

Today's parents need only to ensure that their children who are obliged to do many family chores,

THE TWO-PARENT FAMILY IS NOT THE BEST

have play time, and, if they do "*feel older*" than their peers, that they not be ridiculed or ignored.

LOST CHILDHOOD

"I had too many responsibilities. I was forced to find a job at 12 years old. My mother's line was 'either row or get off the boat.'"

It appears that, except for some women in the single mother group, there is little correlation between childhood responsibilities and the child's feeling older than her years. Even though the majority of women in *all* groups felt older than their years, there seems to be no sense of regret or loss that they *did* feel older than their years. In fact, some were proud of that maturity. But, if the question is asked, did they feel because they had *lost a parent* that they had *lost their childhood*, would there be a sense of regret?

There is a pathetic ring to the phrase, "*lost childhood.*" One can lose other things and there is the possibility of later retrieval, but not for a childhood. For a child to lose a parent is tragedy enough, but to feel, in adult life, that the loss of the parent caused the loss of her childhood, that is truly sad. For how many people does this happen? Is it possible to lose a parent and have the surviving parent supportive enough and emotionally healthy enough so the child can live out her childhood, free of excessive responsibilities and lovingly cared for? In many cases this was true, but for many this was not so.

THE TWO-PARENT FAMILY IS NOT THE BEST

Single Father Families

There is definitely a sense of loss in over half of the women in the single father group who said that as a result of having lost their mother they had lost their childhood. Their most cited explanation was that they had to grow up too fast.

As previously mentioned, fathers are not as stereotypically solicitous as mothers, and that, combined with the girl's having too many responsibilities would tend to leave her feeling that she had lost her childhood. For these girls, playing outside in the neighborhood was probably often interrupted by fathers calling to their young daughters to come home to fix dinner, if she even had time to go outside and play -- something for which all children yearn.

Comments from women in the single father group included, *"Expected to take care of myself when I was only a child." "Had to take care of myself without running to Daddy a lot." "I lost some steps girls go through with mothers." "Feelings had to be suppressed. With my father I wasn't allowed to ask questions or to cry." "Other children had their hair curled. I had to have my hair cut short like a boy's because Dad didn't have time." "I had to quit all my classes in ballet, piano and help take care of myself and father." "Couldn't do after-school things because too much housework." "Saw other girls being fussed over by their mothers on things I had to do on my own."*

Single Mother Families

Fewer women than in the single father group, but still almost half said that as a result of having lost their father they had lost their childhood. They, too, cited *too much responsibility* as their explanation. Their comments reveal a sense of loss, such as, "*Maybe I've lost that thing about being Daddy's little girl. but since I don't know what that was...*" Other comments include, "*When my father was alive he'd take us to 'fun' places on his visiting days. We went to fairs, beaches and to our cousins.*" "*I wasn't allowed to be a child. Mom had no patience with me.*" "*In a way I felt more responsible for my mother.*" "*I couldn't do things with my 'family' other kids did. I felt grown up.*" "*I didn't have a 'normal' family life.*"

Step Parent Families

In the step parent group, of those who had grown up with their biological mother and step father about one-third said they had lost their childhood compared with *two-thirds* of the women who had grown up with a step mother. In step parent families, where the biological mother is present, the girls appear to be happier. A few women praised their step mothers, but mostly step mothers come in for derisive complaints, such as "*I lived in constant fear and trembling from the day she came.*" "*When my step mother came, I was no longer permitted to be a child any longer. I was seven. My environment changed from free and open hugging to the opposite.*" "*My

THE TWO-PARENT FAMILY IS NOT THE BEST

childhood was spent on how to cope. Not how to have fun." "I was a nursemaid to the family. No childhood."

Women who had step *fathers,* who said they had lost their childhood commented, *"My biological father was a kind man before he died. My stepfather never was kind or showed love." "If my stepfather had had better parenting and husbanding skills I probably would have not felt so rejected and abused."*

The following chart separates biological mother in the step group, and step mother in the step group.

LOST YOUR CHILDHOOD?	
Yes	
Sing. F.	53%
Sing. M.	43%
Bio. M. St. Grp.	30%
Step M. St. Grp.	58%

SINGLED OUT AS DIFFERENT?

"Ostracized immediately after my mother's death. Didn't fit in in conversations about mothers. Lacked certain social skills."

Did girls raised in single parent homes, or step parent homes, feel different? As they could compare themselves with other children growing up with two biological parents in what was considered a *normal* family, how did they see themselves in this comparison? How did they see other people's reaction to their situation. The question asked was, *"Did you feel you were singled out as being different?"*

As the women in this research were growing up years ago when divorce was rare and often frowned upon, and single parent homes were most unusual, especially single *father* homes, it would appear quite likely that the children would have felt some stigma regarding their home situation and many did. However, a high percentage of women in *all* groups felt that they had been singled out as being different, including women in the biological parents group.

THE TWO-PARENT FAMILY IS NOT THE BEST

SINGLED OUT AS DIFFERENT?	
	Yes
Bio.	50%
Sing. F.	56%
Sing. M.	48%
Step	57%

Single Father Families

"*I envied my girlfriends who had mothers -- even when they told me the problems they had with them.*" "*My girlfriends were controlled more than I was.*" "*I learned to be independent and self-sufficient in my young years because we didn't have a mother to run and cry to. My brother and I were very close because of this.*" "*They said I was too independent. Very self-reliant. I can be aggressive and opinionated, sexually free. No double standard.*" "*People saw I could handle my upbringing myself.*" "*It's unnatural not to have a mother.*" "*I've escaped a lot of mother hang-ups, feminine rivalry.*" "*People either excused or blamed our behavior on having no mother.*" "*Not included in mother-daughter activities.*" "*I tried to not let people know I came from a one-parent family.*" "*Always compared to classmates who had 'both' parents, by teachers.*" "*In small community, our family was the only one where there was no mother.*"

"*On Mother's Day in church each child was given a carnation. Red if she was living, white if she was* dead. I was the only child wearing white." "Dad came to Campfire Girls. I was a tomboy and enjoyed male activities." "We were considered 'strange' being raised by a man." "Considered 'bad apple' because no mother." "Sometimes people with two parents looked down their noses." "Small town Midwest parents looked upon a single parent family as possibly unsafe for their children." "I always felt I was lower class because I didn't have a mother to teach me proper ways of things." "Had no outside interests because I had to be a mother to my little sister, and also 'housewife'." "Singled out because fathers shouldn't be raising little girls."

"Our family was held at arms length by the community." "Community felt we would amount to 'no good' growing up without a mother." "I remember when I first discovered that other children had two parents! It was good to be raised by my father. Those years were influential ones and serve as one of the most stabilizing forces in my life. Nevertheless, I remember feeling strange as to why my father was raising me." "Growing up in Utah, being raised by my father, I felt strange. This is, because of the Mormons, a very family oriented type of society. To be a young girl growing up without 'Mommy' in this kind of community often left me feeling estranged and left out. But as an adult, I can only now appreciate the strength and self-reliance I have because of this experience."

THE TWO-PARENT FAMILY IS NOT THE BEST

Single Mother Families

"Were you singled out as being different?"

"Yes. I didn't have a Dad." "There were a few other kids of divorced parents, but I think our neighbors pitied us." "Because my mother was alcoholic, the area of town we lived in was shabby, I had to prove myself daily to the better-off kids I insisted on being with." "Yes. Because we were very poor." "Because of my upbringing I am assertive and a bit domineering. Society says that those are not qualities women are supposed to have." "Yes. Often in school." "I was one of two students who lived in an apartment instead of a house." "I was applauded and rewarded too much as a sop to my being 'orphaned,' father died and mother worked."

"We were considered a 'troubled' family with no dad to discipline us." "I was awkward when someone would try to arrange father/daughter events with me." "I never wanted/needed a dad, but I used to wish my mom would do all the 'PTA' stuff kids with homemaker moms would do." "Raised Catholic. My parents divorced and were excommunicated." "If you had no father you were different and were made to feel different." "Because I had no father, people were critical of me." "Constantly identified as 'having no father'" "I never tried to fit in and I enjoyed being singled out." "I was singled out as being different and I am different than women who had fathers, but I'm okay."

Step Parent Families

From women who had step *mothers*: *"When I went to a grammar school I was the only one without a mother and later one of only a few with a stepmother." "As a child we received no love and that has left scars. One is different." "I was told that I was not pretty and that I was bad." "Yes I was singled out because my stepmother refused to let us visit relatives and because she was so strict with us that the neighbors talked about us." "My school mates were uneasy about the death of my father and stayed away at first." "Kids wanted to know why I didn't look like my mom (who was my step mom) and why I was afraid to get dirty and why I didn't ever have any new clothes."*

From women who had step *fathers*: *"I wasn't allowed to do activities other children did." "We were poor and dressed and ate differently." "Having a mother with a step father when other kids had two parents. Then my mother divorced my step father when I was in a Catholic school and divorce was considered taboo."*

Biological Parents Families

It is understandable that women in this group would not have been singled out because of their lack of one parent. But they were singled out for other reasons, such as, *"Health problems." "I was a vegetarian." "For religious reasons." "I didn't dress, talk, or act like other girls my age." "My mother is foreign. Other classmates' parents taken aback." "Because I* was overweight and children are cruel to other children." "Because I was gifted." "I was singled out by classmates because I chose the friends I wanted, not just those that were popular. Also I liked to read and learn and in junior high school that is instant death." "My parents were immigrants." "

Conclusion

It could be that children generally harbor feelings that they are being singled out as being different when that may or may not be the case. This may be somewhat akin to children "*feeling older than their years.*" In both cases, one might assume that the children growing up in unusual households or having unusual responsibilities would be more apt to "*feel older,*" and would be more likely to consider themselves "*singled out as being different.*" But that does not explain why children in the biological parents group also, almost to the same extent, also felt older and also felt singled out, although for different reasons. Though comments from the women in the biological parents group do not seem as poignant as those from the other groups, they do reflect childhood pain.

Again, the best antidote for childhood pain inflicted from outside the family, is the family unity. If that is strong, it not only provides a refuge, but it also imbues children with the strength to go forth again after what might be perceived as an attack.

WHAT PEOPLE SAID

"*I was expected to amount to no good.*"

Living in an unusual family situation, leaves children vulnerable to hurtful comments. Was there a difference in kind or degree of remarks made to girls in each of the four groups? It is always said that children can be cruel to each other, but what about cruelty of adults to children?

Single mother homes are not unusual today, but single father homes are still somewhat rare. What are the remarks that children growing up in these circumstances are subjected to? The number of step parent families is on the rise, but do the numbers make it any easier for children who hear disparaging remarks about their situation? And then, what of the children growing up in families with two biological parents? These families are considered the 'norm.' Are the children any less immune to unpleasant remarks? The questions was asked of the single mother/father group, "*If you lost your mother/father when you were in grammar school or before, what do you think people were saying about you: (friends, friends' parents, teachers, neighbors).*" Of the step parent and biological parent group the question was the same except it does not mention losing a parent.

Surprisingly more women in the biological parent group wrote that they were the subject of disparaging remarks than did women in the other three groups.

Women from single parent families were the recipients of comments which pitied them. Pity sets up a relationship hierarchy with the person pitied in a lower status than the person who pities. The pitier presumably is in some way better off by comparison. The pitier sets herself above the pitied and the one pitied often feel this as a denigration. While there may be some material benefits to being pitied, as for instance, receiving sympathy or money, to be even temporarily denigrated as "not as good as," can be harmful. No women in the biological group wrote of being pitied.

IN GRAMMAR SCHOOL, WHAT SAID ABOUT YOU?				
	1	2	3	4
Bio.	40%	0%	47%	3%
Sing. F.	6%	35%	34%	4%
Sing. M.	5%	30%	21%	10%
Step	31%	22%	33%	2%

1. Pride in me
2. Pity for me
3. Disapproval
4. Miscellaneous

Single Father Families

Remarks were both positive and negative from women growing up in a single father household: "*I felt they were saying I was not normal*

GROWING UP

and should be avoided because my mother was not in the household. In many ways at this time I was ostracized." "Neighbors felt sorry for us." "My friends thought I was strange because I didn't have a mother." "Most people were sympathetic. Extended family was helpful. My father was protective and if anything had been said he would have questioned it." "Those poor little kids. They're so ragged and wild. The girl needs a mother to show her how to act properly." "My Dad's parents didn't want us around and told him he should put us in an orphanage." "People were fascinated that my father had done a good job raising me and they were surprised how well adjusted and accepting I was of the situation. They saw strength in my acceptance and realized that I was mature for my age." "Older people felt sorry for me. It only made it worse for me and I was treated differently." "They were sympathetic with my dad's situation and admired him for his courage and devotion." "Poor thing -- she'll have to be the mother now." "Poor motherless children."

Single Mother Families

"I was told I was an 'orphan'! I felt pitied because mother went to work." "Coming from New York was a stigma because there was only one grounds for divorce -- adultery." "People thought I was weird since I always insisted I never had a father. I remember an angry teacher because of this reply." "I think older people feel sorry for children who have lost a parent. Young friends don't understand the absence of a parent and call names like 'bastard'. At the time I was

THE TWO-PARENT FAMILY IS NOT THE BEST

angry and confused." "I often felt that people were pitying us, saying our family was incomplete, that my sister and I did not have what was needed -- a father." "I think people pitied us to a certain extent, but mostly considered us an aberration of some sort -- distinctly inferior in quality." "My mother made me feel a bit damaged -- as though I and my sister were less strong than others." "'Poor girl, growing up without a father' something like that." "I think they thought I was strange, odd, different, not as good as they." "That we were poor now that my father had left." "People said it was a shame I had no father but look how mature I was 'under the circumstances'." "I was raised in a Catholic neighborhood. There was something shameful about divorce and the 'loose divorcee.' My sister and I were told not to tell people that my mom was divorced. I felt like a freak somewhat." "Poor child." "They felt something must be wrong with my mother to have my father leave her." "My mother said if I'd been a boy my father would never have left."

When these remarks are compared from single father group to single mother group it is revealing that many disapproving remarks from the single father group are directed at the *child*. She is either wild, or expected to be bad, or "*amount to no good.*" In the remarks from single mother groups, the remarks are often directed at the *mother* -- bad for a woman to leave her husband, or she must have been bad or her husband would not have left her, and, it was bad to get a divorce.

In one situation where the girl was in a Catholic school, her mother was not allowed in the PTA because she was divorced. This was all a few years ago. The number of divorced women now has changed the attitude to one of more acceptance. If mothers had left their husbands, the mother must be "*out of her mind,*" or if the fathers had custody of their children, it was rumored that that must be because the mother was an unfit mother.

Step Parent Families

Most of the women in the step parent families who had *biological mothers* wrote of positive remarks people were saying about them. Other than a few negative comments like, "*She's too fat,*" "*They didn't know why my mother was mean to me,*" "*She's stupid,*" most comments were about good things people said about them.

Of the women who had *step* mothers, there were also numerous complimentary remarks made about them. But there were more negative remarks directed at these girls who were growing up without her "real" mother, than there were for girls who had their biological mother. Once again, a girl without a mother is looked on as someone who is going to "go bad." "*Odds are not in her favor. She'll end up in a bad way.*" "*She's bad, stupid, not right.*" "*Some made fun of me, some appeared to feel sorry for me because I had lost my mother and was poorly taken care of.*" "*Look at that poor little girl who has lost her mother.*"

THE TWO-PARENT FAMILY IS NOT THE BEST

Biological Parents Families

More women in the biological parents group, than in the other three groups, wrote that comments about them were of approval. These comments included such things as "*I was a good girl.*" "*She comes from a 'good' family.*" "*She has nice clothes.*" "*What a fine, conscientious girl.*"

As mentioned previously, women in the biological parents group reported the highest percent of complimentary remarks, but they also reported the highest percentage of disapproving remarks. Since these girls were growing up with their two biological parents it was unlikely their family situation would be criticized. Comments related to other things. "*She thinks she's better than us.*" "*Fat and stupid.*" "*Slow in school and 'bossy'.*" "*There's that 'snooty' so and so.*" "*Fat, poor, bad family life.*" "*Shy, no confidence, fat.*" "*Smart student but really dumb in math.*" "*Country 'Hick'.*" "*Mean, disrespectful, lazy, underachiever.*" "*Clumsy and not good at sports because of poor eyesight.*" "*Spoiled.*" "*What a weirdo!*" "*Negative things.*" "*Teachers considered me unimportant because poor people aren't supposed to make 'A's'.*" "*They said I was anti-social. A bookworm.*" "*Too tall, too skinny, dumb.*"

Conclusion

Even though there are now many more divorced women with children, and the attitude about divorce has softened, it would be unwise to say that what was said in years past is not now relevant. Children living with one parent today suffer some of the same stigma as in past years. It is still believed that the two-parent family is the "*normal*" family and many children growing up without two parents feel cheated. One example of how an eight year old boy living with his father and mother has an undeniable belief that he is somehow better off than his young friend who lives with his single mother occurred when they were both fishing with their fathers. One father was spending his visitation day with his son. When the boy with the divorced father caught a large trout, the other boy became obviously jealous. He blurted out, "*I don't care about your fish. Our father lives with us.*"

It would be helpful if children of single parents could know that, though they may hear disparaging remarks about their family situation, children of two-parent families are also victims of unkind remarks.

The larger message is that the two-parent family is, as a group, no better and no worse than other family groups. If children and parents in single families could realize that the single family situation, on average, is just as healthy for raising children as the two-parent family, they would not be so vulnerable to innuendos about their family's supposed inadequacies.

OTHERS PERMITTED TO PLAY IN YOUR HOME?

"Not right for children to play with a girl child who was living alone with a man."

Whether or not childhood friends are permitted to interchange playing in each others homes is important because it means the host child can share equally with her friends. The child whose friends are *not* permitted in her home may feel, that her home is not good enough, or that *she* is not good enough, or that there is a suspicion of something wrong with her family. It is understandable that in homes where there is no adult, as for instance in homes where there is a single parent who works, or where both parents work, neighboring parents would not want their children in these homes, beyond their supervision. Even if the child is told all the reasons why her friends can't play in her home, this does not diminish the stigma that somehow *she* is off-limits.

In the ever-increasing number of single parent families, a reasonable method of eliminating some of this stigma would be for the parent to encourage the child's friends to come and play when the parent is *not* working. True, working parents arrive home after a day's work, tired, needing to prepare supper, help their children with homework, and a multitude of other things. But because the exclusion of their child's friends from their home is painful for the child, efforts should be made to make their home, however humble, a place where their child can welcome friends and share toys.

There will still be the hurdle of permitting a girl child to play with another girl child in a home where there is a single father. Many people believe this is too risky, and in some cases it is. However, if the single father could make arrangements for a woman to be present when his daughter is expecting friends, that should help to allay fears of the father's possible misconduct with the girls. This is a difficult problem for a single father, but one worth attempting a solution since it is significant to his daughter's development and perception of herself. Not that one has to have the same number of parents as others to grow up with self-esteem. But when parents discriminate, even wisely, as to whose homes their children may not play in, this hurts the would-be host child. Discrimination, even though understood intellectually, is emotionally painful. With effort, parents can ease this pain.

OTHERS PERMITTED TO PLAY IN YOUR HOME?	
	No
Bio.	8%
Sing. F.	34%
Sing. M.	14%
Step Grp.	33%
Stp M. Bio. F.	24%
Stp F. Bio. M	46%

Single Father Families

The question asked was, "*After you lost your mother/father were neighborhood children permitted to play in your home?*" Comments from the single father group were, "*No woman in the house.*" "*They felt nothing good could happen in our house.*" "*Other parents were afraid of our situation.*" Others mentioned specific worries. "*I was afraid to invite my friends in, in case my father fondled them as he did me.*" "*It was always a cluttered dump.*" Several were worried because their fathers were alcoholic.

Single Mother Families

The fear of not letting their children play in homes where there was a single parent, related mostly to homes where there were single *fathers*. Parents permitted their children to play in single family homes if the single parent was a woman. Only 14% from the single mother group reported that other children were not permitted to play in their homes. Their comments: "*My mother worked full-time. We were not allowed to have company nor go play elsewhere.*" "*There was always some fault my mother saw in them.*" "*No one to supervise.*"

A woman whose mother was divorced says, "*Children who were my father's relatives were not allowed to come to our house, nor could we go to theirs.*" "*Only if my mother was home.*" "*Some didn't care to come into our house or play with us due to the absence of supervision and the condition of our house.*" On the questionnaire, explanations were asked only if the answer had been that other children were not permitted to play in their home. One woman wrote, "*Yes, they could come in and play but only one at a time when my mom was at work but I let more in.*"

Biological Parents Families

Since few women from the biological parents group indicated that their friends were not permitted to play in their homes, there were few comments from these women. Of those, comments varied. "*Parental fear that they would steal or cause trouble. We did live in a very 'bad' neighborhood.*" "*Yes but very infrequently.*" "*Visitors not permitted unless home was spotless.*" One whose parents were both alcoholic wrote, "*They were permitted to, but I didn't want them to see my lifestyle.*"

Step Parent Families

Children least likely to have their childhood friends play in their homes were those in the step parent group who had a step father and a biological mother. Almost half of this group were not permitted to have children play in their homes. "*My mother never reciprocated that way. I would have been embarrassed if there had been an outburst.*" "*Either our house was 'too clean' or 'too dirty.'*" "*My step father did not like company.*" "*They would be messy and noisy.*" "*My step father was a pain in the ass. He made my friends feel uncomfortable and there were too many*

THE TWO-PARENT FAMILY IS NOT THE BEST

rules." "*Mom usually had a headache.*" "*My mother was jealous and did not like my friends.*" "*Stepfather's moods unpredictable.*" "*No one's kids could meet my folks expectations. So better not to have any around.*" "*I had too much work to do.*"

Women who had step mothers wrote, "*We had chores to do. When my stepmother was out, no one was allowed over.*" "*I wasn't allowed to play much in the house.*" "*That was a rule and the house was usually a mess.*" "*The nearest neighbor was five miles away.*" "*She would not allow me to have a friend.*" "*No. Stepmother never home.*"

Conclusion

It could be considered a minor thing to prevent one's child from having friends come play in her home. For children who grew up in two-parent families where there was often a mother present, this was probably not a problem. But it is, however else it is said, a form of discrimination against the child in a single parent home.

Today, with the ever-increasing number of single-parent families and working parents, this is still a problem for many children. But all parents, single or married, with time and planning and effort can make arrangements for their children to play host to their friends. It is not good for children always to be the guest in their playmates' home. Sharing status is important to their relationship with their friends and can translate in later life to successful adult relationships.

ON YOUR OWN?

"Made my own decisions, drew my own conclusions, developed my own values."

It could reasonably be expected that children in single parent families would be on their own more than other children, which was true for over three-fourths of the single mother and single father group. But two-thirds of the step parent children were also on their own as were almost half of those in the biological parents group. Was being on their own harmful, or was it harmless, and maybe even to a degree beneficial?

Over half of the women who had been on their own more than other children said this made them independent. Though loneliness was mentioned by women in all groups as a consequence of being on their own, it was mentioned most often by women in the single mother group.

ON YOUR OWN MORE THAN OTHER GIRLS?	
	Yes
Bio.	49%
Sing. F.	85%
Sing. M.	87%
Step	67%

THE TWO-PARENT FAMILY IS NOT THE BEST

OF THOSE ON THEIR OWN, WHAT EFFECT?

	1	2	3	4
Bio.	58%	10%	13%	19%
Sing. F.	60%	15%	11%	13%
Sing. M.	52%	13%	24%	10%
Step	55%	12%	6%	26%

1. Independent
2. Resourceful
3. Lonely
4. Miscellaneous

Single Father Families

Comments from the single father group who wrote that they were on their own more than other children included, "*It made me independent, resentful of authority.*" "*Made me a loner,*" "*Very big sense of responsibility.*" "*Made me a solitary person.*" "*Made me mature faster and more at ease with myself.*" "*I was not fearful of being alone.*" "*More time for introspection, more responsibility and freedom, but also lonely, longing for fantasy family on T.V.*" "*I feel I can manage a life better than most.*" "*I became a loner with imaginary friends and I read voraciously.*" "*I need a lot of 'alone' time. Also a bit socially awkward.*" "*Fierce sense of independence.*"

Single Mother Families

A few of the many comments from the single mother group who said they were on their own more than other children include: *"More independent, self confident, able to take care of myself." "I learned early to be self-reliant." "I was lonely most of the time." "Made me very independent and somewhat of a loner." "Felt lonely but made me more creative." "Made me feel grown up. I thought I was neat." "Made me more responsible and self-reliant."*

Biological Parents Families

These are a few comments from the 49% of the biological parents group who wrote of being on their own. *"I was on my own by my own choice. There were no children or friends my age in my neighborhood. The effect of this is that I felt very awkward and self-conscious in interpersonal relationships. Very shy!" "It made me very independent at a very early age." "I have a difficult time trusting and being close to people." "Made me responsible." "Loneliness." "Yes, I was on my own because my brother married when I was 5 years old and I couldn't really discuss things with my parents without getting lectured. This forced me to turn to outsiders for feedback about ideas of life, etc." "Made me independent and self-reliant." "It made me feel that my 'self' was worthwhile." "Made me able to like being alone." "Had to achieve my own confidence in myself."*

Step Parent Families

Over two-thirds of the women in the step parent families said they were on their own more than other children. Some of the comments from the women with step *mothers* were, "*I was very independent in going out with friends.*" "*I am very independent, can go anywhere alone.*" "*Unloved, unwanted.*" "*I became independent with a job and ability to run a household at age 15.*" "*Gave me a sense of responsibility and self-reliance.*" "*I became overprotective of my two 'real' sisters.*" "*I didn't feel acceptable to anyone or responsible to anyone.*" "*I learned self-sufficiency and how to entertain myself.*" "*Introspection. Made me a writer.*" "*Lazy, unmotivated. After Mom died I had lots of free and empty time.*"

Some of the comments from women with step *fathers* were, "*I became self-reliant and independent.*" "*I can handle emergencies.*" "*Felt isolated, not part of family -- an outsider.*" "*I became a loner, dependent on myself.*" "*I am content to be by myself and can always find things I enjoy doing.*" "*I am not afraid to be alone.*" "*No fond memories of my childhood.*"

Conclusion

Many women in all groups mention that being *on their own* caused them to be independent, resourceful, responsible, self-reliant, and able to be alone. In the answer to several questions there have often been differences among groups, and also differences in the answers between women who had step*mothers* and those with step*fathers*, but for this question the answers from women in all groups are more similar.

Except for "*loneliness*" which is mentioned several times and in different ways, most explanations are positive. Nobody mentions the physical danger of being on one's own, or fear of the unknown. The results of being, to a degree, *on one's own*, appear to be more positive than negative. If that is so, children in single parent families would seem to have more opportunity to develop independence, self-reliance, and responsibility. But the results of this study indicate that many children in families with two parents are also often on their own. They too, believe the results of that experience have made them independent and resourceful.

It needs to be said that the world in which these women grew up might have been safer as compared to today's dangerous world. Now there are frightening statistics of the number of child abduction and child molestation cases. A parent who allows a child to be too much on their own might be accused of child endangerment. If being on one's own is important in helping a child develop independence and resourcefulness, which it appears to be, then it behooves parents to find ways to permit safe, free time for their children.

RISKS

"I believe I was more willing to trust my children to try out things on their own than I might have been had my upbringing been different."

Because the women in all of these groups said that they spent considerable time *on their own*, the question arises as to whether or not these women, when they were children, were permitted to take more risks than other children -- risks permitted by either their mother or their father.

This discussion refers to the answers on the questionnaire, which asked, "*Do you believe your mother/father permitted you to take more risks than your friends' parents permitted?*" Unquestionably, single parents, whether they were mothers or fathers, permitted their daughters to take more risks than did other parents. As single parents are generally not at home as much as parents in two parent families, children of single parent families were probably permitted more risks, among other reasons, because of a lack of consistent supervision.

A somewhat higher percentage of single *fathers* permitted risk than did single *mothers*. This compares with the biological parents group where more fathers than mothers permitted risks. The opposite is true in the step parent group.

FATHER PERMIT RISKS?	
	Yes
Bio.	32%
Sing. F.	58%
Step	29%

MOTHER PERMIT RISKS?	
	Yes
Bio.	27%
Sing. M.	51%
Step	39%

As one question often gives rise to another question, one that could be asked next is, "*How does this permission of risks relate to whether or not their mothers were working?*" It is assumed that fathers in the single father group were working, but what of the *mothers* in the other three groups? Whether or not mothers permitted risks was correlated with whether or not mothers were employed.

Almost all of the women in the single mother group had mothers who worked outside the home. Almost half of the biological parents groups' mothers worked, and slightly less than half of the step parent group. How did their employment relate to whether or not they permitted risks?

It might also be assumed, because of the necessity of their absence, that mothers, even today, who work outside the home, permit more risks than mothers who are homemakers. This was true for the biological parents group and the step parent group. A higher percentage of those who worked permitted risks than those who did not work. But working or not, this made no difference in the single mother group. Those few who did not work were as apt to permit risks as those single mothers who worked. Possibly the single mother is a risk-taker herself and encourages this in her daughter, or at least does not discourage it.

PERCENT OF MOTHERS WHO WORKED	
Bio.	49%
Sing. M.	91%
Step M.	28%
Bio. M Stp. Grp.	14%

OF MOTHERS WHO WORKED AND PERMITTED RISKS	
	Percent
Bio.	33%
Sing. M.	54%
Step M.	71%
Bio. M. Stp.Grp.	71%

GROWING UP

OF MOTHERS WHO DID <u>NOT</u> WORK AND PERMITTED RISKS	
	Percent
Bio.	19%
Sing. M.	56%
Step M.	18%
Bio. M. Stp. Grp	31%

An extreme case of a biological mother in the step parent group not permitting her daughter to take risks was written by a woman now in her fifties. *"She tried to teach me to jump rope indoors so that neighbors wouldn't see me failing. When I was unable to perform as she wanted, she made me throw the new rope into the fire and watch it burn. For many years I was afraid to try new things because I knew I would fail."* The right and the opportunity to fail should be in the Children's Bill of Rights. How else do people learn to accept their failures as well as their successes?

Not placing boundaries on children's activities can be as painful for a child as placing too many restrictions. The following comment from a woman in the step parent group who had a biological mother seems to suggest that the parent doesn't care. That may not have been the case, but it was the child's interpretation. *"The thing I remember most (about growing up) is that I was never told I had limits. As long as I didn't rock mother's boat it was all right. So I did a lot of unhealthy things, too much sex too early, not enough communication or interest in me by* mother. *I can remember being lonely even if I was with large crowds. I was loud and even obnoxious. I always felt like I wasn't really there. It felt like I lived without feeling or thinking. I can remember being in my bedroom at around 11 or 12, looking into the mirror and crying for someone or something."* Because this girl could do anything she wanted to do, she seems to feel hollow.

Unsupervised child's play can, at the worst, be dangerous. But, at best, it can be creative. It would seem from the comments in the questionnaire, that the child who can create her own wholesome activities and find them satisfying, develops self-confidence and self-esteem. The child who responds primarily to direction and encouragement from an adult, and constantly is told not to do certain things for fear of getting hurt, may not be taking any risks or making any mistakes, but she may not be learning to develop her ability to think and plan for herself. As someone once said, *"A little benign neglect is necessary for the child to become an individual..."* It is also said that in order for the child to grow up, the parent needs to grow up too, by letting the child wander out into the world and take her chances, with, of course, reasonable protection depending on the age of the child.

As fewer mothers in the biological group permitted their girls to take risks, we might surmise that, as compared to the other three groups, these girls did not have the same freedom to develop the adventuresome creative aspects of their personality. Nor were they exposed to as much danger, real or potential. One wrote, *"My parents seemed to be afraid to allow me out on my own because I might 'make an ass' of myself and that would bring shame on them. I was not even allowed to stay home alone."*

The results of this question "*Did your father/mother permit you to take more risks than other girls' parents?*" were compared with the results from the Gough Adjective Check List which was mentioned in the Introduction. This is the list of 300 adjectives which the respondents were asked to check if the adjectives described the respondent. These adjectives include such words as "*ambitious, efficient, conscientious, interest wide, optimistic, reflective, daring, gentle,. artistic, inventive, original.*" Specifically the results from the Creative Personality Scale of the Gough Adjective Check List, were compared with the results of the question about risk-taking on the questionnaire. More of those who were permitted risks saw themselves as creative than those who were <u>not</u> permitted many risks.

The original questionnaires were answered approximately two years before the Gough Adjective Check List was answered. It is unlikely any conscious connection was made between the questions asked in each. In the Adjective Check List there are groups of adjectives scattered throughout the list which comprise one aspect of personality. Different groupings describe different aspects. The respondent is likely not aware of which adjectives fall into any groups, or that there are groupings at all.

The Creative Personality Scale is described on the Description of Scales for the Adjective Check List as, "*The high scorer on the Cps is venturesome, aesthetically reactive, clever, and quick to respond. In-*

tellectual characteristics such as breadth of interests, cognitive ability, and ideational fluency are also apparent. The low-scorer is more subdued, less expressive, more conservative, and less inclined to take action in complex, ill-defined situations."

The women who answered from the original questionnaire that they were permitted more risks, checked adjectives which formed the group on the Adjective Check List for the Creative Personality. For each group of women, the percentage scoring in the upper 60th percentile range of the Creative Personality Scale was higher for women who were permitted risks, than for women who were not permitted risks.

Conclusion

Children from single parent families are permitted more risks than children with two parents. It makes no difference whether these single parents are working or not, or whether two parents are the biological parents or step parents. Children with working mothers permit more risks, except if the working mother is part of a two biological parents family. A higher percentage of children who are permitted more risks than others, score higher on the Creative Personality Scale than children who are not permitted risks.

What does this information about permitting risks portend for the future? With more single mothers, more single fathers, more working mothers than there were when the women in this research were growing up, how can this information help other families now and in the future?.

There are more unsupervised children today than there were when the women in this research were growing up, and there will be more in the future. There will be more and more "*latch key children*," a new term for this generation, than there have been before, as currently 65% of mothers are employed. As a result there will be more children "*on their own*" and more children "*taking risks*."

There can be, and there are, harmful results of children being unsupervised too long. Adequate supervision is vital for children to grow up out of harm's way. But it seems evident that supervision should not be too restraining. Almost all the women in this research who have been "on their own" have stressed the positive results, especially independence and resourcefulness. Most of the women who have been permitted to take "risks," believe in their own creativity. Only the women in the biological parents group were less free to take risks, whether their mother worked or not, but those who *could* take risks scored high on the Creative Personality Scale.

Whether mothers are single, whether mothers stay home or not, whether girls are raised by fathers, or with step parents, children do not need to be at risk. With a combination of good supervision and considerable safe, even sometimes, solitary exploration time, children are free to explore aspects of their personality which then help them develop their own identity which can help them make mature choices for their future.

ENCOURAGED IN THINGS OTHER GIRLS WERE NOT?

"Woodworking, auto mechanics, getting my own career, having the right to say 'I don't wish to marry and raise children.'"

Mothers in the single mother group encouraged their daughters in things other girls were not, more than did parents in any other group, though single fathers followed closely in the percentage of women encouraged by their parents.

The activities in which the girls were encouraged were separated into four categories: (1) either DEEP FEMININE meaning having stereotypical characteristics attributed to women such as being *empathetic, understanding, giving, caring, a mediator;* (2) SUPERFICIAL FEMININE such as being *beautiful, good housekeeper, good cook, seductive, talkative, frivolous;* (3) DEEP MASCULINE meaning having stereotypical characteristics attributed to men such as being *cool headed, rational, independent, a decision maker, financially able, stoic, intellectual, self-reliant*, and (4) SUPERFICIAL MASCULINE such as being *handsome, sports-minded, mechanically inclined.*

ENCOURAGED IN THINGS OTHER GIRLS WERE NOT?	
	Yes
Bio.	54%
Sing. F.	60%
Sing. M.	67%
Step	49%

ENCOURAGED IN WHAT THINGS?				
	1	2	3	4
Bio.	37%	13%	4%	1%
Sing. F.	34%	18%	5%	0%
Sing. M.	48%	11%	4%	3%
Step	20%	22%	4%	2%

1. Deep masculine
2. Superficial masculine
3. Superficial feminine
4. Deep feminine

Single Mother Families

As women in the single mother group reported the highest percentage of women who were encouraged in "*deep masculine*" activities, such as becoming financially capable, independent, self-reliant, the mothers of these girls were either consciously or subconsciously preparing their

THE TWO-PARENT FAMILY IS NOT THE BEST

daughters to be ready to make a living and to do it by getting educated, taking risks, solving problems and, if need be, being stoic. "*My mother encouraged me to be independent.*" "*She encouraged me not only to learn carpentry but to do well in math/science studies.*" "*To go for what I wanted on my own, rather than expecting everything to fall into my lap.*" "*To go to college, have a career.*" "*Helped me develop the ability to live alone and support myself.*" "*To go to college and graduate school and not think about marriage until later in life.*" "*To build my own life and not rely on anyone else.*" "*To be self-sufficient, to be somewhat aggressive, to be competitive.*" "*Encouraged in eclectic reading.*" "*To not get married early, to have a career, to be intellectual, to be artistic.*" "*My mother encouraged me to think for myself on certain subjects. Other children were told how and what to think about.*" "*Anything that I wanted to do that was considered 'masculine,' she urged me to go past that image.*"

Only four percent of the women in the single mother group said they were encouraged in "*superficial feminine*" things such as housekeeping, cooking, working toward typically feminine careers.

Single Father Families

Of the women raised by single fathers who were encouraged in things other girls were not, most, as with the girls in the single mother group were encouraged in the "*deep masculine*" things. A few of the comments follow: "*Reading and mathematics.*" "*Judo, boxing, arm-wrestling.*" "*Cooking and housework; to *get an education so I could support myself." "To explore new things. Be assertive." "Athletics was always important to my father. He pushed me to succeed." "The use of hand tools to take things apart and put other things together." "I was the only one in my high school class to go to college that fall." "Sports. Independent thinking. Ability to rely on myself." "To think, to be honest and to be realistic." "I was encouraged in reading and mathematics." "To be independent, to believe in 'I CAN' and to stick up for myself." "I was encouraged to think about intellectual matters." "To get an education so I could have a career."*

Many women in the single father group reported that they were told by their fathers they could do anything they set their mind to. Being raised by a father, they were probably exposed to more masculine activities than girls in the other groups. For instance, one said her father was a "Ham Radio Operator," and helped her to learn to receive and send the Morse Code. She added, "*I'm sure my father was aware of the restrictions placed on women but he never told me I couldn't be anything I wanted to be. When I announced that I wanted to be a doctor and the following week an air line pilot, he never laughed or told me I had to become a nurse or a flight attendant instead. My father was a great help in making me feel normal in a non-traditional environment.*"

The following poem by Laura Craig sums up a girl's life, encouraged in things many other girls were not.

THE TWO-PARENT FAMILY IS NOT THE BEST

My dad taught me to swim
Hit a baseball
Sing, read music
Play the piano
Change a tire
Cook, iron
Plant a rose bush
Fix a faucet
Catch a mouse
Use a telephone
Get up on stage
Get a laugh
Play Pinochle
Do the Charleston
And be alone.

Biological Parents Group

Over half of the girls with two biological parents were encouraged in things other girls were not. As with the single parent groups, these girls also were mostly encouraged in the activities which were stereotypically "*deep masculine,*" such as getting an education and taking care of themselves.

A few of their comments include, "*Hunting, fishing, and making money.*" "*Non-traditional job occupations -- taxi driving.*" "*All types of sports, hockey, lacrosse, ringette, soccer.*" *Political volunteering, mathematical pursuits, reading anything I wanted to read.*" "*Sports.*" "*Continuing my education. Going out on my own after college." "My mother encouraged me because she was an early advocate of equal rights for females." "Business leadership." "Intellectual pursuits." "Things that were stereotyped for boys like carrying heavy boxes. Dad said I can do it." "To be independent, get an education, have a career." "Taking risks. Sports, Fishing." "Getting an education; learning things; staying single and at home." "

Step Parent Families

Those who had the lowest percentage of women who had been encouraged in things other girls were not, were women in the step parent group with not quite half saying they had been encouraged. A slightly higher percentage of these women were encouraged in the "*superficial masculine*" things than were encouraged in the "*deep masculine*" things. Most women from the step mother group were encouraged by their biological fathers. They wrote they were encouraged in "*Fixing things, building things.*" "*My father had me run machinery and do almost everything in his office and machine shop.*" "*To enjoy math. Be aggressive.*" "*Being athletic and participating in sports.*" "*Hunting and fishing.*" "*Father wanted us girls to be independent and be able to support ourselves if need be.*" "

Women in the *step* father group were encouraged mainly by their biological mothers. They wrote: "*To be on my own. Select courses from the curriculum that would lead to college. Have a job.*" "*Don't get locked into a female role.*" "*Had a motorcycle.*"

THE TWO-PARENT FAMILY IS NOT THE BEST

"Skills in science, math, assertiveness." "Music and belonging to Scouts." "Athletics, a career, spiritual life." "I was encouraged to do things like painting and minor carpentry with my brothers." "Encouraged to explore my interests."

Conclusion

More women in the single mother group received encouragement in things other girls were not, than did women in any other group. Fewer women in the step parent group received encouragement than women in the other groups. Women in all groups were encouraged to get an education and a career, but more women in the single mother group were encouraged to be independent, and self-reliant than were women in other groups. More women in the biological parents group were encouraged in "*superficial feminine*" things such as cooking, housecleaning than women in other groups.

There were a few women in all groups who said they were never encouraged in anything and a few said they were actually discouraged in anything they wanted to try. In the biological parents group, both parents encouraged their daughter. In the step parent group, it was almost always the biological parent in that family who encouraged the daughter.

Women in this research appreciated the encouragement they received and from which they probably profited. What does all this tell us for the girls we are now raising? Though independent, self-reliant women can be threatening to some men who

GROWING UP

prefer more stereotypical females who are subservient, submissive and dependent, these independent, self-reliant traits have obvious advantages for women and their children. Since the trend in families is toward more and more single women with children, the traits of self-reliance they encourage, in their daughters particularly, can decrease reliance on a welfare system as well as increase the self-respect and self-worth of children growing up in this country.

ROLE MODELS

"My grandfather contributed to my having, as an adult, some good feelings for men and was an antidote to harsh scolding by my father."

Grandparents should take heart! They figured significantly as role models for their granddaughters, whether it was a male role model for the girl without a father, or a female role model for a girl without a mother. Grandparents were even good role models for parents in the home who were not good role models themselves. The question asked was: "*If you had a male/female role model, who was she/he?*"

DID YOU HAVE FEMALE ROLE MODEL?

	Yes
Sing. F.	66%
Step	28%

DID YOU HAVE MALE ROLE MODEL?

	Yes
Sing. M.	58%
Step	40%

FEMALE ROLE MODEL

	1	2	3	4	5	6
Sing. F.	33%	15%	9%	14%	9%	20%
Step	29%	14%	0%	43%	0%	14%

1. *Grandmother*
2. *Sister*
3. *Friend's mother*
4. *Other relatives*
5. *Neighbor*
6. *Other*

THE TWO-PARENT FAMILY IS NOT THE BEST

	MALE ROLE MODEL					
	1	2	3	4	5	6
Sing. M.	32%	16%	9%	16%	22%	5%
Step	15%	10%	0%	60%	15%	0%

1. *Grandfather*
2. *Brother*
3. *Friend's father*
4. *Mother's boyfriend or her husband*
5. *Other relatives*
6. *Other*

Those in the single father group who listed "*other*" as role models wrote: "*Good qualities in many women.*" "*Girl Scout Troop leader.*" "*Grandmother, but she died when I was seven.*" "*Mothers in the neighborhood -- they all shared taking care of us.*" Grandfathers also were significant for girls raised by single fathers if the single father were not a nurturing type man.

From the single mother group, women wrote kindly of their male role models. "*Two uncles, both living far away but both attentive and kind. My mother's brothers.*" "*An Uncle, a brother of my mother.*" "*My sister's Sunday School teacher.*" "*Best friend's father.*" "*To a degree, my brother, eight years older.*" "*Pastor.*" "*Various school teachers.*"

From the step parent group, women wrote of grandmothers, friend's mothers, uncles, live-in housekeeper, and of those in the step parent group who had *step* mothers, many wrote that their female role model was their step mother. One who had lost her mother wrote, "*No role model but a fondness for one of my friend's mother who was especially nice to me.*"

Of the women in the step parent group who had lost their father, many wrote that their male role model was their step father. Also mentioned often were grandfathers, uncles, and older brothers.

Grandparents should take pride in their helpfulness to their granddaughters when they have had great need. To be pointed out as a role model is to receive a compliment. Two generations older than the child does not matter to her. It is that these role models had good character which their granddaughters appreciated.

Grandmothers and grandfathers, especially if they are retired, often have less hurried and less harried time to spend with their maturing grandchildren. This time spent can make a good difference in a child's personality. But whether it was a grandparent or an uncle, an older sibling, a friend's parent, or a neighbor, these role models are remembered with fondness. No doubt many women in this research now emulate the best characteristics of their role models.

THE TWO-PARENT FAMILY IS NOT THE BEST

FANTASY MOTHER

"*Beautiful, patient, never hollered, did all the housework.*"

For young girls growing up without a mother it is conceivable that they would day-dream about what it would be like to have a mother. This would help to fill the void. Imagination steps in where reality fails. The questions were, "*Did you have a fantasy mother? If you had a fantasy mother, what was she like?*" But what of the girls who *had* a mother or step mother in their families -- did they also have fantasy mothers? All groups, except the single mother group, were asked this question.

Women in all groups answered that they *had* fantasy mothers including women who had mothers.

FANTASY MOTHER	
	Yes
Bio.	29%
Sing. F.	49%
Step	56%

(In the chart above, the women in the step parent group who had fantasy mothers were in the group which had *step* mothers.)

What was that fantasy mother like? Invariably she was the traditional female type. She was "*dependable, loving, caring, forgiving,*" "*Pretty and helpful." "Supportive, loving, encouraging, interested." "I have never thought about it before, but she would be a Christian, soft spoken, and content. She would sew and have a love for knowledge, be honest always, and have common sense." "All sweet and loving -- contented." "She would take me shopping and spend lots of time with me." "Just a kind, strong woman to hug me and rock me." "She wouldn't escape by taking naps and wouldn't always be depressed."*

In those comments there is a deep longing for what represents "*mother*." Women who didn't have mothers wanted the traditional, beautiful, loving, caring, listening housekeeper who bakes, sews, is never depressed, never yells, and is always home. Some women from single father homes said they fantasized about a mother who was, "*like a fairy godmother.*"

Women from the biological parent group used the same descriptions as women in the single father group, like, *pretty, affectionate, warm, caring, beautiful, did all the housework in addition to baking,* and some mentioned that she would be sober. Others in the biological parent group said their fantasy mother would *teach them more about social graces and would be approachable.*

In the step parent group, *no* woman who was living with a *step* father and her *biological* mother had a fantasy mother. But where there was a *step* mother, over half had fantasy mothers. What was that mother like? "*Kind and loving.*" "*Nurturing, a good listener, my best friend, someone to do things with like shopping and traveling.*" "*Entirely nurturing.*" "*She was very up-to-date, not old fashioned. She liked everything I did and she was proud of me." "Beautiful, gracious, wise." "Sober, kind, caring, would listen, would explain things to me, let me be a kid." "Physically comforting." "Perfect -- loving." "I didn't have a fantasy mother but I kept hoping my real mother would come back to life."*

WHAT FANTASY MOTHER WAS LIKE			
	1	2	3
Bio.	76%	14%	10%
Sing. F.	82%	16%	2%
Step	100%		

1. Traditional female
2. Androgenous
3. Worldly

Conclusion

Presumably, fantasy mothers replaced what the girls did not have. In the single father group, there was a yearning for someone to take over the role of nurturer and keeper of the home, to help with the housework and cooking. Mothers today might take note that little girls need and appreciate hands-on living from their mothers. And in their growing up, aside from the teenage times when they are ambivalent about even been seen with their mothers, they want mothers to be their friends, they want to go places with their mothers and they want to talk with them.

FANTASY FATHER

"Protective, loving, caring."

Did girls who had no father have a fantasy father, and if so, what was that father like? The question was asked of all groups except the single father group. Women in all groups said they had a fantasy father, and some in each group had fantasy fathers with softer, more traditionally feminine qualities such as being warm, understanding, not quick to let their temper go.

FANTASY FATHER	
	Yes
Bio.	26%
Sing. M.	41%
Step	42%

In the chart above, the women in the step parent group who had fantasy fathers were in the *step* father group. The question asked was, *"If it was your father you lost, did you have a fantasy father?"*

Single Mother Families

Girls without fathers imagined fathers who were compassionate and understanding, like the father as one said, in the T.V. show, *"Leave it to Beaver."* One woman whose mother was divorced

THE TWO-PARENT FAMILY IS NOT THE BEST

when her daughter was five years old said her fantasy father was "*My own father, re-united with us, happily ever after.*"

More than the other groups, women in the single mother group had fantasy fathers who made money. Many single mother families had difficulty financially, especially after a divorce, and more especially when there were no child support payments. The fantasy father fulfilled the dream for the little girl who wanted to live better and wanted to see her mother free of money worries.

What kind of fathers do girls want who don't have fathers? Mostly they want men with what are known as feminine qualities but with a little "masculine" strength and financial capabilities mixed in. "*Kind, loving and PROTECTIVE!*" "*Tender, humorous, well-off, upstanding, honorable and intelligent.*" "*A man I could talk to - who would listen.*" "*A cowboy, a famous singer, strong, gentle, attentive.*" "*Like my dear uncles with some FDR mixed in!*" "*A friend's father. He was sort of sweet and kind - intelligent.*" "*Clark Gable.*" "*My fantasy was my father, still alive and healthy, outdoors type, caring, loving.*" "*He would be reliable and hard-working.*" "*Like the father in the old 1950's T.V. shows like 'Father Knows Best.'*" "*Like my father, warm, loving and caring.*" "*Physically strong, sensitive to all family members, handsome and wealthy.*" *Wanted all the best for his family.*" "*He was all-understanding. He was going to rescue me. He was like a lover.*" "*Intelligent, loving, dependable, like Robert Young in 'Father Knows Best.'*" "*Ben Casey! Handsome, wealthy, he'd let me sit on his lap.*" "*Young, strong, handsome and loving - an almost sexual fan-*

tasy father." "Wise, very smart and very attentive. A lot like the men in 'Star Trek'." "He was just the memory of my own father. Strong, kind, loving, gentle, and fun to be with." "Big, strong to hold me." "Like my grandfather: loving, supportive, non-critical. The only person in the family who treated me like a child, appropriately." "He was there physically and emotionally and would support me in my mental and physical endeavors." "He would rescue me if I called to him." "Loving, sure of himself, willing to share." "Kind, non-yelling, big, tall,well-built."

One woman in the single mother group wrote that she "*blacked out all thoughts of a father.*" And another said, "*I had a fantasy 'family,' but the father's role was very indistinct and blurred.*"

Biological Parents Group

Though they already had fathers, more than one quarter of the women in the biological parents group said that they also had fantasy fathers. Most of those expressed a need for a man who was home more than their real father, had better behavior, that is, he was not sarcastic, didn't hit and he treated his daughter as fairly as he treated his son.

"*One who spent time with me alone. One who I could talk to, have fun with. My father spent all his free time with my brothers.*" "*Warm, encouraging, didn't favor his sons over me.*" "*One who talked instead of hit; one who was kind instead of sarcastic.*" "*He didn't smoke. When he told me 'No,' about something he'd give me reasons, not just say, 'because I said No.'*

THE TWO-PARENT FAMILY IS NOT THE BEST

He didn't have to work so hard and so long." "Wise, understanding." "He was at home more often and accessible for discussions." "One who was stable, held a job, advanced in career potential, protected me." "He wouldn't spank me; he'd always hug me and say nice things and never criticized me!" "I used to wish that my uncle were my father. He was openly fond of me and took me places, bought me gifts and taught me to reason clearly." "A father who did things with his kids." "He was strong and courageous. There was no one who could get to me through him." "A father who took us places and didn't drink." " He paid attention to me and played games with me, which my father didn't do when I was growing up." "Non abusive. Fair." "He would be non-threatening and would encourage my academic achievements and intellectual pursuits."

One woman wrote that she had no fantasy father because she was very happy with her father while growing up. It is not certain whether all women who had no fantasy fathers were necessarily happy with their fathers, but it does seem that fantasy parents replace real parents, or what is missing in the real parent. Some recognize now that they fantasized their biological father into a perfect father. *"I do think the view I had of my dad made him my fantasy father for I idealized him and overlooked even major faults."*

Many women in the biological parents group wrote about wishing their father had been home more. That is something only barely mentioned in the other groups. A few women in all groups wished that their mother or father did not have to work so hard or so long. As one in this biological parents group wrote about her fantasy father, "*He had more money so that we could do 'fun' things like go to the beach, or go for ice cream, etc., instead of needing to do garden work to sell vegetables, or chop wood.*" Then there is the one woman in this group whose fantasy father was just like her uncle, "*Very macho. He cursed, drank, gambled, had fist fights and could not be pushed around.*"

Step Parent Families

Not quite half of the women in the step parent group who had *step* fathers had fantasy fathers. A few expressed a longing for the father they had lost. "*He was exactly like my real father, only healthy and wealthy.*" But most women expressed the need for the feminine side in a father along with the so-called masculine strengths, which are invariably mentioned secondarily. "*Affectionate, warm, gentle, a pillar of strength. Someone I could turn to and count on.*" "*Caring, loving.*" "*Very intelligent, warm, indulgent, tolerant.*" "*Handsome, caring, loving.*" "*Kind, friendly, humorous, intelligent, loving, athletic.*" "*Warm, caring, protective, good provider.*" "*Kind, loving, accepting.*" "*Like my grandpa -- kind, loving, accepting.*" "*Kind, sweet, huggable, caring, understanding, sense of humor.*" "*Could do no wrong.*"

THE TWO-PARENT FAMILY IS NOT THE BEST

WHAT FANTASY FATHER WAS LIKE						
	1	2	3	4	5	6
Bio.	22%	19%	30%	22%	7%	0
Sing. M	2%	2%	50%	26%	10%	10%
Step F.	9%	0	55%	27%	0	9%

1. *Physically present*
2. *Good behavior*
3. *More feminine qualities*
4. *Good masculine qualities*
5. *Superficial masculine qualities (handsome)*
6. *Androgenous*

Conclusion

In single mother and single father groups it is understandable that girls might day-dream about a parent they did not have. They could create someone in their fantasy who filled the void in their lives.

But of the girls in the two groups who *had* two parents, what was the purpose of the fantasy if it was not also a substitute for a void? The girl who had a mother, whether in the biological or step parent group, who fantasized about a mother who is warm, loving, affectionate and caring, must be longing for those characteristics which are missing in the mother she has. This same reasoning would apply for the girls who had fathers, yet who fantasized about a father who was understanding, supportive, caring. It would seem to be an imaginary substitute for the certain traits their parent did not have.

This is not to suggest that the child who did *not* have a fantasy parent was pleased with the parent she had, but it does suggest that those who did have a fantasy mother or father might have been deprived of some need from one parent.

Fathers today might take note that their daughters yearn for, not only the feminine side of their mothers, but also the feminine side of their fathers. Girls want their fathers to be protective, but they also want them to listen, to be emotionally supportive, to be kind and loving. With a different method of raising little boys it would be possible to have fathers who are both protective and sensitive.

FACTS OF LIFE

"Neither my step mother nor my Grandmother explained any 'facts of life' to me. I started to menstruate at age 13 and knew nothing of what had befallen me!"

Single fatherhood presents several questions, especially if the father is going to raise a daughter. One of those questions is who is going to tell her the facts of life? The answer from this research is that, while a few fathers told their daughters about human reproduction, most girls were told by female relatives. Several in all groups said that no one had told them about sex. But where there were mothers, it was the mothers who most often educated their daughter on this subject.

The highest percentage of women who said no one had told them about the facts of life was in the step parent group. As one step child wrote,. "*A girl friend's mother told me about menstruation. When I started my period I went to her for help, scared to death.*"In the step parent group, the answer, "*No one,*" was evenly divided between girls who had step mothers and girls who step fathers.

Other than the *"facts of life,"* which girls needed to know, there were other very personal situations confronting girls as they matured. For the girl in the single father family this might have presented a problem. One woman wrote, "*Shopping for my first bra with my dad was a bit embarrassing at the time, but it's probably one of the reasons that I am not very modest today."*

WHO TOLD YOU THE FACTS OF LIFE?

	1	2	3	4	5	6	7
Bio.	3%	36%	7%	17%	8%	11%	15%
Sing. F.	10%	13%	21%	16%	17%	12%	10%
Sing. M.	1%	48%	7%	18%	9%	10%	7%
Step	2%	37%	4%	22%	10%	18%	6%

1. Father
2. Mother
3. Female relative
4. Peers
5. School
6. No one
7. Other

Conclusion

For single fathers today, and for all parents, there are many helpful methods for passing on this vital information, such as in books and in school units of study. With the rise in teenage pregnancy and the threat of Aids it is imperative that children *do* learn the facts of life and that they learn from reliable sources. Learning the facts of life correctly may actually be the difference between life and death.

PARENTS' DATING

Did single fathers have girl friends? Did single mothers have boy friends? Did they bring their girls friends or their boy friends home? If they had girl friends or boy friends, how did this involvement affect their daughters?

DID SINGLE PARENTS DATE?	
	Yes
Sing. F.	68%
Sing. M.	73%

Conclusion

If there is some fear that a single parent's romantic involvement might cause problems in the relationship with their children, the results in this research indicated that parental dating doesn't affect the parent-child relationship. Though most single parents dated, it was something toward which their children were relatively indifferent.

PARENTAL REMARRIAGE

"When my mother remarried I felt in some way that I was losing her."

While dating of their single parents didn't bother the children, often a remarriage did. For some it was joyful, but for many it was traumatic.

Though slightly more mothers had boy friends than fathers had girl friends, this led to marrige more often for the single fathers than for the single mothers. Not only did more fathers remarry but more fathers than mothers remarried more than once.

It is often reported that the single male, whether he be recently divorced or widowed, is sought after by single women and by people anxious to play matchmaker. The same does not hold true for the single woman. Often after a divorce, the man is deluged with invitations for social events, whereas the woman is ignored. She is not only often left with the children, less money, but also with the need to build a new circle of friends.

After remarriage, though, the question remains, how did the daughters from these various groups get along with the new parent in their home? That depends on whether the new step parent is a step*father* or a step*mother*. It appears that daughters generally do not get along as well with step mothers as they do with step fathers. It may be that in a study of boys whose mothers remarried, they might not get along with their step fathers. It could easily be a matter of jealousy.

HOW MANY TIMES PARENT REMARRY?					
	1	2	3		
Sing. M.	70%	20%	8%		
Sing. F.	53%	34	5	13	5

1. Never
2. Once
3. Two or more times

Single Father Families

If a single father did remarry after many years of raising his daughter by himself, the daughter may resent her new step mother. One woman whose father remarried said he couldn't have picked a worse mate than if he'd placed an ad in a newspaper which read, *"Wanted, step family. Must be experts at innuendo, critical, pompous, self-centered, violent, and have at least a grade-school education."* She added, *"From the minute they walked into our house, we became spectators in our own lives."*

Step Parent Families

Apparently step *fathers* are easier to get along with than step *mothers*, or the daughters do not have as much association with their step fathers as other daughters do with step mothers. It is possible, with the high percentage of daughters in the single father group who did not get along with step mothers, that these daughters had been "*in charge of the house*" for sometime before their step mother came in and took over and this caused resentment.

But in the step mother/biological father group, the biological mother had died before the child was five years old. There was no girl-child "*in charge of the house*" in that group. Though many women told of how they loved their step mothers, almost twice as many wrote of their anger and hostility toward their step mothers.

One, in writing of her biological mother marrying her step father, wrote, "*When my mother married my step father, although I was only five years old, I distinctly remember feeling uncomfortable about my new father. I didn't want to kiss him goodnight and I worried about offending him if I just kissed my Mom. My step father's typical scoldings when I was young (age 6-10) -- long lectures, poking his finger in front of my face and keeping at it until I was crying. I also remember many, many times having to write 100 times, 'I will get my dishes done on time.'*"

In the following charts a few women in the Single Father and Single Mother groups eventually had a step parent when their remaining parent, after many years, remarried.

THE TWO-PARENT FAMILY IS NOT THE BEST

GET ALONG WITH STEP MOTHER?			
	1	2	3
Sing. F.	25%	45%	30%
Step	23%	32%	45%

1. Well
2. Moderate
3. Not at all

GET ALONG WITH STEP FATHER?			
	1	2	3
Sing. M.	17%	69	14%
Step	29%	42%	29%

1. Well
2. Moderate
3. Not at all.

Single Mother Families

When single mothers remarried after a long period of raising their daughters by themselves, there was not as high a percentage of those whose mothers remarried reporting not getting along with their step fathers. Most of these remarriages occurred when the daughters were in their late teens. Their contact with their stepfather might have been minimal or their own lives so well set that new family arrangements had little influence.

Conclusion

Step mothers do present a problem for daughters. Before single fathers consider remarriage it would be wise to seek counseling for themselves and their children as a group. Two thirds of the women who had step mothers had unhappy childhoods and they blame that unhappiness on having a cold, even a cruel step mother. Many said their step mothers were sweet to them until they married their father. So it would be difficult to determine before a marriage if a woman would be a kind, loving step mother. But all efforts should be made to try to determine what is best for the children. Childhood lasts only a short time and continual unhappiness during that time can damage a child, possibly for the rest of her life.

THE TWO-PARENT FAMILY IS NOT THE BEST

WHY PARENTS DID NOT REMARRY

"I didn't want him to."

Single Father Families

When daughters of single fathers were asked why their fathers had not remarried, most said their fathers were concerned with the responsibility of the family. Many said their fathers idolized their mothers and could not bear to think of marrying another woman. Some said their fathers were angry at women. A few said that as children they didn't want their father to remarry and they asked him not to.

Comments from single father group as reasons for not remarrying included: *"He didn't believe in second marriages and was busy making a living for family with help of children." "Partly because we ran away from Mom when we got a stepfather." "He is basically a hermit -- also poverty." "He wasn't divorced. My father gambled, my mother took a job that required traveling and she didn't take me." "My sister and I told him we wouldn't like it. I didn't know this until later." "He enjoyed being not married." "He loved my mother too much. She had died." "He says he hasn't found anyone but I think he's afraid to." "Was totally devoted to my mother and devastated by her death." "It was easier not to. He didn't have to extend himself in any way if he stayed unmarried." "He always*

GROWING UP

blamed it on us, but in reality he was a loner. He built a wall around himself and no one could get through it." "He didn't think it was necessary. Has lived with two women for a total of fifteen years since the divorce. I think he's skeptical of legal commitment." "He still loved my mother and was hurt by other women." "I think he was afraid a stepmother wouldn't treat us fairly." "He did remarry after I was an adult and I am relatively certain it was because of his responsibility to me."

"He didn't want to get hurt again." "Because he felt we should be grown first and on our own." "Relatively little time for social life like dating, was raising family, farming, etc." "Fear of failed second marriage." "He did. His second wife died, leaving him with three more small children." "He idolized my mother." "He was too bitter and thought we kids wouldn't have liked it. However, I think it would have been a good thing." "I wish my father had remarried, but it was my sister that felt threatened and begged him not to." "I remember my father asking me if I wanted a new mother. My reply was, 'No.' Years later I learned that he almost got married again because people were telling him that a man in his 50's couldn't possibly care for small girls. It would have been a marriage of convenience. He didn't love the woman so when I said 'No,' he decided not to get married."

Single Mother Families

For the single mothers who did not remarry, family responsibility was listed as the primary reason. A higher percentage of single mothers were

THE TWO-PARENT FAMILY IS NOT THE BEST

said to be "angry at men," compared with single fathers who were said to be "*angry at women.*" A lesser percentage idolized their husbands as compared with single fathers who idolized their wives. For single mothers, religious reasons interfered with a possible marriage more so than for single fathers.

Comments from the single mother group included, "*She didn't find someone she could love until 20 years later and he's worse than my father was.*" "*She enjoyed her independence.*" "*She was just 'not interested.'*" "*She remarried after I grew up. The rules of the Catholic Church prevented it sooner.*" "*She blamed it on us but I believe she was simply not inclined to do so.*" "*Fear of men.*" "*She fears/dislikes intimacy.*" "*Strict Catholicism, fear of child abuse/molestation by prospective step father. Fear of being hurt, 'burnt' again.*" "*Not willing to sacrifice for another man simply because he was a man -- expected more understanding on their part.*" "*She was too rejecting to everyone. Saw all their faults.*" "*Mainly I could never accept anyone else as a father figure.*" "*She is very afraid of men.*" "*She had been hurt too many times before.*" "*No one to live up to her standards.*" "*Because she is strong minded.*" "*We, her children, and our welfare, were her top priority.*" "*Too angry at men.*" "*Would not permit anyone to exercise authority over us but herself in our home.*" "*Didn't want to deal with the demands of another person.*" "*She was afraid for my brother and me. She thought people (step parent or strangers) would try to take advantage of us - especially sexually.*" "*She doesn't see the marriage ritual as a meaningful institution.*" "*She loved my father very much. She suffered an emotional breakdown when he died and she never got better." "Poor self image and her Catholic Church did not recognize that she was not married." "She wanted to be free, and she wanted to keep my father's memories."*

WHY PARENT DID NOT REMARRY							
	1	2	3	4	5	6	7
Sing. F.	28%	17%	11%	7%	6%	1%	18%
Sing. M.	19%	11%	14%	3%	11%	6%	35%

1. Family responsibility
2. Idolized former spouse
3. Angry at opposite sex
4. Children didn't want it
5. Enjoyed non-marriage
6. Religious beliefs
7. Other

In the single mother group there were many whose answers fell into the category of "other." These included comments such as, "*She was a rejecting person.*" "*No one asked her.*" "*She was bitter.*" "*She didn't want to get hurt again.*" "*Too self-centered.*" "*Low self-esteem.*" "*Too strong-willed.*" "*She was afraid.*"

Conclusion

There are patterns running through the reasons why the women in this research believed their parents did not remarry, whether the parents were single fathers or single mothers. Most of the parents, men or women, who did not remarry, who were left to care for their children without a spouse, took their responsibilities seriously and put their children's needs first. Not every parent had the opportunity to remarry, but it seems that most did, and many rejected the idea for the reasons mentioned. Most remarriages which did occur, took place after the children had been raised by their single parent for many years, and some did not occur until the child had grown and was out of the house.

It is very likely that single fathers were more inclined to find a mother for their children than single mothers were inclined to find a father for their children. The idea of a child growing up without a mother is, to many, unnatural. The idea of a child growing up without a father is more acceptable.

Fathers are often commended for remarrying and providing a mother for their children, but the mother who remarries is apt to be criticized as having secured a meal ticket for herself. The economics are different between these two groups. The single father who remarries usually takes on the support of a woman and this may also include her children. The single mother with children who remarries is sometimes seen as a burden to be supported.

In the step parent families, it must be remembered, these children did not have two sets of parents, as is the case when both parties in a divorce remarry. In this study, for the most part, one of the biological parents had died when the children were about five years old.

Whatever the reason for not remarrying, more children seemed to benefit by their parents' singlehood, than by their parents' remarriage. In the step parent group a few women appreciated their step parents, but they were the exception. The single parent who stays single may have periods of loneliness. He or she may feel like the *"fifth wheel,"* at social gatherings. But those negatives can be offset by the likelihood of raising a happier child, at least when considering the comments from step children.

ALCOHOLISM

"I was afraid to bring my friends home. I never knew when my mother would be drunk."

Over half of women in all groups said there was alcohol in their home, and in most of these homes, alcohol was used moderately. The questions asked were, *"Was there alcohol in your home? Did your mother/father drink moderately or often to excess?"* Whether these parents who often drank to excess could be considered alcoholics is questionable, but, according to their daughters, the parent's excessive drinking was a family problem. That is one of the criteria for alcoholism.

Of those who said there was alcohol in the home, about one-third of these women in the biological parents group reported that their fathers often used it excessively as did about one-fifth of their mothers. .

DID YOUR FATHER DRINK EXCESSIVELY?	
	Yes
Bio.	31%
Sing. F.	21%
Step F.	15%
Bio. F. Stp. Grp.	20%

One woman in the biological parents group whose parents were both alcoholic wrote, *"during my pre-teen and teen years I usually took care of them and babysat them instead of the other way around."*

One woman who had a biological mother and step father wrote, "*Probably the essence of my poor relationship with my dad (step father) was his alcoholism. He had been a bachelor until he married my mom, and he had a drinking problem when she married him. When he drank, he'd be good humored in phase 1, then always 'snap' and lay into one of the kids or my mom. As the oldest child, I would be terrified when things got out of control. I can remember his being drunk and shoving my mom around. She'd always ask for help and I was trembling with fear, afraid to interfere, afraid to call a relative for help, afraid to call the police, afraid when things got quiet again that he had killed her. I never ever brought a friend home in junior high, high school or college because I never knew when my dad would be drinking.*"

DID YOUR MOTHER DRINK EXCESSIVELY?

	Yes
Bio.	19%
Sing. M.	16%
Step M	12%
Bio. M. Stp. Grp	4%

Conclusion

Excessive drinking can destroy families, or at the very least, it can contribute to disharmony among

THE TWO-PARENT FAMILY IS NOT THE BEST

family members. No group in this study was without excessive drinking. Within the four major groups which had fathers, the fathers in the biological parents group had the highest percentage of excessive drinkers.

Within the four major groups which had *mothers*, the mothers in the biological parents group had the highest percentage of excessive alcohol consumption. One woman in the biological parents group with two parents said her mother became alcoholic as her marriage deteriorated. She stayed in the marriage, "largely because she was in no condition to support herself and had no inclination to be responsible for herself or her children."

Children are sensitive to the way alcohol excludes them. Or when the drinker does include them, children are sensitive to the ways in which this inclusion is manifested, sometimes with attention not otherwise given, or with emotional or physical pain, punches or sarcasm. It may be a pain inflicted by the offender who then forgets the moment. But the pain inflicted on the women years ago by alcoholic parents still persists. The pain surfaces in the comments which reveal a smoldering resentment against adults who were compulsive drinkers and did nothing about it.

Alcoholism today is a growing phenomenon. Excessive drinking kills people on highways, in bar fights, in domestic violence and it serves to emotionally cripple children. The child is more than twice-hurt. She herself may be physically or emotionally abused and in addition she carries with her the stigma of an alcoholic parent, hiding her mother's or father's drinking from her friends. Or in the case of some families, hiding both parents' drinking.

Why the biological parents group had more excessive drinking than other groups would be difficult to determine. One could guess that the social drinking between two people became such a regular pattern that it took over. Possibly single parents had less time, or as in the case of single mothers, less money. That would not explain why the step parent group had the lowest percentages, since they could be involved in social drinking between the two of them that could get out of hand.

The percentage differences of excessive drinking among groups are not great, but what is noticeable is that whether biological father or biological mother, parents in biological families engaged engaged in more drinking than the other groups. What is the particular family dynamic involved here?

There is praise given to people who have been married many yeras, but this says nothing about the quality of the marriage. Some long-term marriages may be marathons with the partners escaping into their own individual alcoholic haze, ignoring or abusing their children.

PHYSICAL ABUSE

"She had a round stick and used it weekly. Usually on her day off."

To determine if there had been physical abuse from parents, several questions were asked. *"Did your father/mother use ordinary spanking as disciplinary measure? Did your father/mother beat you? If your father/mother beat you, was it seldom or frequently?"*

Parents have the right to correct and guide their children appropriately, but physical abuse is not appropriate behavior for raising children. For the purposes of this question, the emphasis is on whether or not a girl was beaten, and if so, if she was beaten frequently. It was arbitrarily assumed that if one answered she had been beaten frequently, that would have been once a month and that would constitute physical abuse. If these women had been physically abused, it would be of importance to learn if there were a difference in this kind of parental behavior from group to group.

FATHERS BEAT DAUGHTERS	
	Yes
Bio.	12%
Sing. F.	6%
Step	16%

The answers revealed that more fathers in the biological parents group than in the single father group beat their daughters, but fewer in the biological parents group beat them frequently than did the single fathers.

OF FATHERS WHO BEAT, PERCENTAGE WHO BEAT FREQUENTLY	
Bio.	38%
Sing. F.	66%

Of the *mothers* who beat their daughters, fewer in the biological parents group beat them than did those in the single mother or step parent group. But of those in the biological parents group who beat their daughter, the same percentage beat them frequently as those in the single mother group.

MOTHERS BEAT DAUGHTERS

	Yes
Bio.	13%
Sing. M.	21%
Step	20%

OF MOTHERS WHO BEAT DAUGHTERS, PERCENTAGE WHO BEAT FREQUENTLY

Bio.	27%
Sing. M.	27%

When the mothers in the step parent group are separated as to step mother or biological mother, this reveals that of the 12% of the *biological* mothers who beat their daughters, 33% did so frequently. Of the 28% of *step* mothers who beat their daughters 86% of these beat their step daughters, frequently.

STEP PARENT GROUP WHO BEAT

Step M.	28%
Step F.	8%
Bio. M.	12%
Bio. F.	16%

OF STEP PARENT GROUP WHO BEAT, PERCENTAGE WHO BEAT FREQUENTLY	
Step M.	86%
Step F.	100%
Bio. M.	33%
Bio. F.	50%

Of the step mothers and step fathers who beat their daughters, almost all beat them frequently. In this step parent group the biological parents who beat their daughters did not do so with such regularity as did the step parents.

There were almost no comments from the women following the answers on the questionnaire, except from the step parent group. One woman whose biological mother beat her frequently said she resented her step father because, "*He let my mother beat me.*" Another wrote of her biological mother, "*It was pure hell everyday with my mother. She would beat me and then two days later ask me where I got the bruises. I tried running away but she always found me and brought me back and beat me some more.* " A mother with a biological mother wrote, "*I was beaten every night before going to bed.*"

All of the other comments were from women who had step mothers. One woman who reported that her step mother beat her, though seldom, said, "*I was careful to avoid beatings.*" Others wrote, "*She was afraid my grandmother would find out.*" "*She used a wooden spoon -- it wasn't severe beating, but we were always black and blue.*" "*It was worse when she was

THE TWO-PARENT FAMILY IS NOT THE BEST

drunk which was most of the time. It didn't make any difference if I had done anything wrong or not. When I think of it now, the beatings seemed almost like a hobby."

Conclusions

The girl most likely to be beaten by her *father* was the girl in the step parent group who was beaten by her biological father. The girl most likely to be beaten by her *mother* was the girl with a *step* mother. Almost a third of the girls growing up with a step mother were beaten frequently. More single mothers beat their daughters than did mothers in the biological parents group.

Women in all groups suffered physical abuse. As destructive as this was, the women in this research who were beaten frequently do not appear to project the subliminal anger and resentment about physical abuse that surfaces in the comments of women whose parents abused alcohol and whose daughters were victims of neglect, and mean sarcasm.

Yet beating, as separated from spanking, and specifically frequent beating, is nothing less than physical abuse. Though there is great anger, either repressed or manifest by those who have been physically abused, often the abused tends to forgive the physical abuser more so than she tends to forgive the alcoholic or the sexual abuser. They recognize that their parent has the right to discipline them and often do not see the difference between spanking and frequent beatings. Unlike sexual abuse, with physical abuse from a parent, the child ma[y feel] she deserved the beating.

The profile of the physical abuser is one w[ho] is isolated, whose spouse is somehow collusive, who was deprived of basic mothering, who has no sense of the pain of others, and who denies that she or he has a problem. Often the physical abuser punishes the child in public, causing the child greater shame.

There is a long history of physical abuse of children in this country. As parents assume a right to spank their children, this sometimes translates into the right to beat their children. It is only in recent history that there are such agencies as Child Protective Services where the rights of the child to remain unmolested are looked after.

Many women in this research grew up in a period when children were meant to be seen and not heard. And many, if they even cried, were spanked again for crying. There was no relief from a violent parent. One simply learned to adapt.

There is public recognition that abusing parents need help and agencies such as Child Protective Services are available to offer this help. Parents can learn to control their excessive anger vented on someone smaller and dependent on them. And if they cannot control themselves they can find help for doing so. It may save them from beating the life out of the child they love.

...Y IS NOT THE BEST

...ABUSE

*"...exually abused me was my
...ed me in at night while my
... the living room."*

...ccurred in all four groups, but most... parent group where girls were molested by their... fathers and by other relatives. In sexual abuse cases, single fathers raising daughters are often suspect. And they, too, molested their daughters. Biological fathers in the two-parent family, also molested their daughters. One might have thought, in the two-parent family, a woman's presence would have prevented a father from molesting his daughter. But of the women who were abused in that group, many were abused by their fathers. Mostly, however, other relatives were the principal abusers..

    Of those who answered that they had been sexually abused, many said they were revealing this, although anonymously, for the first time. While it is true that many allegations of sexual abuse have been questioned as unreliable because of the victim's young age or lack of evidence, the revelations of sexual abuse by the women in this research are no doubt valid. Several women wrote that they are now in counseling, some individually and some in groups, in their effort to face and live with the knowledge of the terrible injustice done to them as children.

SEXUALLY ABUSED?

	Yes
Bio.	17%
Sing. F.	24%
Sing. M.	19%
Step	27%

SEXUAL ABUSERS

	1	2	3	4	5
Bio.	11%	11%	66%	0%	11%
Sing. F.	19%	16%	35%	0	23%
Sing. M.	9%	18%	14%	18%	41%
Step	0%	15%	38%	31%	15%

1. Father
2. Neighbor
3. Relative
4. Step father
5. Other

Except for the single mother group, the highest percentage were abused by relatives. Most of the girls in the single mother group who had been abused referred to neighbors and step fathers equally, the step fathers coming into the household years after the single mother had been widowed or divorced.

Biological Parents Families

Women in the biological parents group who had been sexually abused, who referred to "*others*" included janitors, landlord, "*father's friend who tucked me in at night,*" "*my father's good friend,*" "*brother's friend,*" "*babysitter's son,*" "*the adult who most influenced me as a child, the one who listened and accepted and loved me, unfortunately seduced me when I matured.*"

Single Father Families

Almost one-quarter of the women in the single father group had been sexually abused, and many by their own fathers, though most were molested by other relatives, even grandfathers.

Single Mother Families

Of the women in the single mother group who had been sexually abused, many said they had been abused by their own fathers before the divorce or separation, or on visitations, many more by their neighbors, by their relatives, many by step fathers when their mother remarried. Most referred to "*others.*" One woman in this group wrote, "*I was an incest child...I am very confused by men since they lump together with my father. A 'good' father would have protected me, not raped me, and a 'good' mother would have stayed sober and been available.*"

Step Parent Families

About one-third of the women in the step parent group had been abused and those mostly by their step fathers or other relatives. One in the step mother group wrote that her brother had regularly sexually abused her since she was eight and that her step mother was also involved. She wrote, "*I honestly believe my father knew what was going on. This abuse continued until I left home at 16, worked full time, graduated from high school with honors, was the best musician in the state as a junior and being the first female to receive a letter for sports in the history of the high school with no parental support. This was embarrassing and degrading beyond belief.*"

Another woman described her experience. "*When my stepfather came to my bed I was about eleven and it lasted about a year until I started having periods. He never 'went all the way,' I guess because he was afraid of getting caught. He may have thought that I'd stayed asleep because I would lie very still and keep my eyes closed -- just waiting for him to go away. I never understood what he was doing or why.*"

Conclusion

Incestuous families tend to be highly controlled, outwardly very religious, and workaholics. They appear to the outside world as examples of the good family. The victim knows better and must hold that a secret.

THE TWO-PARENT FAMILY IS NOT THE BEST

It is estimated that currently there are approximately thirty-four million women in this country who were sexually abused as children. As children, they believed they were bad and they carried this shame for years. The abused child was alone in her family and alone in herself. Then there was the problem of trying to separate from the abuser who was often a nurturing parent, and whom the child was expected to love. Abused children learn to hide their feelings, often in addictions to food, or work, or drugs, or sex. Anything, to not have to deal with their awful feelings. The one hope was that someone would eventually convince her that it was not she who was bad, but the "*other.*"

Glamour magazine in 1989 surveyed American women and revealed that of those who said they had been sexually abused, 29% said they were first abused by their biological father and 31% by another relative, 13% by their step fathers. The article pointed out that there are estimates that about 30% of adult women and about 70% of adult men were abused before they were 18 years old. These, the magazine said, are conservative estimates. Nevertheless, the article continued, in spite of solid evidence, people don't want to believe widespread abuse happens.

Parents of either sex need to be watchful of signs of possible sexual abuse of their children, boys and girls. They may become withdrawn, appear to feel bad about themselves, spend too much time alone, not relate well to friends, have a changed relationship with an older adult family member or friend. This is truly a case where "*an ounce of preven-*

tion is worth a pound of cure." Sexually abused children carry that shadow with them forever. Parents can prevent this abuse, unless they are the perpetrators.

In a five year study released by the University of California, researchers learned that, though molestation is traumatic, most children do recover, with the right kind of help. The report indicated that those children who had an easier recovery were those whose mothers were supportive and spent time with their children and whose families sought professional help. The children who had the most difficulty were in families which avoided dealing with the subject and refused to talk about the incidents.

PARENTAL PRIDE IN DAUGHTERS

"My father was proud of me when I did things that took courage."

"My mother was proud of me when I went to college early, fixed the plumbing, sewed my first garment, or did anything that needed creativity and commitment to get done."

When the most important people in a child's world are proud of her, her confidence soars. When she has met or exceeded someone else's expectations and they let her know, then she can go on to the next attempt. Maybe she will fail at that attempt, but she will no doubt have the courage to try again, or to try something else. This compares with the child who is constantly *"put down,"* and is never permitted to please her mother or her father. Or the child whose parent always finishes the task because *"Mommy can do it better."* When this happens she is discouraged from venturing or from doing much of anything because she has been taught that she can't do it right anyway. Parents who show their children they are proud of them, give them an irreplaceable gift. They strengthen their child's resolve to do things well.

Two fill-in questions were asked, *"Your father was proud of you when?" "Your mother was proud of you when?"*

Most women indicated that their parents, mothers and fathers, were proud of them when they did well in school, performed at some function,

GROWING UP

received awards, did well in sports, or later, attained job success.

FATHER PROUD OF YOU?		
	1	2
Bio.	96%	3%
Sing. F.	96%	3%

1. Yes
2. Never

Single Father Families

In addition to being proud when their daughters were good persons, were obedient, conformed, did what was wanted, were honest and persevered at tasks, there were also miscellaneous responses from the single father group which included, *"Had the house cleaned and all kids dressed and fed," "Out-talked him," "Became political," "Got married." "He was proud of me most of the time as any normal father would." "Made good grades. Actually my dad frequently told me he was proud of me for many reasons." "Took care of a dying friend of his." "A long time ago I was dedicated to making this family work without Mom. And he was proud of me for taking on all of the responsibilities." "He was proud of me when I accompanied him on a trip to the funeral of his brother." "Was always proud of me and very supportive." "When I showed strength and independence." "When I did not make waves."*

THE TWO-PARENT FAMILY IS NOT THE BEST

The n*egative* responses included, *"Proud? Was he? He was always pushing me. If I had a report card with 3 A's, 2 B's, and 1 C, he saw the C and wanted to know why?" "I have no way of knowing if my father was ever proud of me. He never spoke or acknowledged my existence." "I don't know that he was ever proud of me. He only criticized me always and felt that because I was the oldest girl I must be the one who did wrong so I took the blame for everything and my sister was much more aggressive and would tell him off or defend herself against him." "My father was proud of me when I was most like him, a hard-nosed S.O.B., but he never expressed his pride to me. I tried hard to win his approval."*

Biological Parents Group

Women in the biological parents group indicated their *fathers* made them proud for specific reasons. A few of those occasions, other than those of success at school or various accomplishments included, *"When I reflected glory on him." "Was complimented by his friends." "Stayed in the limelight and flattered his ego." "Solved problems, showed initiative." "Made him look good." "He was proud of me all the time." "He was proud when I was artistic, independent, took risks and 'went on adventures.'" "Stood up to him with solid reasoning or sincere beliefs." "Did well in science and fishing." "Kept peace in the family," "Stayed at my grandmother's death bed for two days because he was unable to handle it." "When other people complimented him on his daughter." "Displayed masculine accomplishments." "He always gave me the feeling he was proud of me." "Did as I was told."*

MOTHER PROUD OF YOU?		
	1	2
Bio.	91%	8%
Sing. M.	92%	1%

1. Yes
2. Never

A few more fathers expressed pride in their daughters than did mothers. Comments from women whose mothers were proud of them included, *"When I wore a bra and looked pretty." "When I looked pretty, got good grades, made her laugh." "My mother was always proud of me." "When I outdid my peers. When I was the center of attention." "Lived up to my Catholic upbringing which was seldom." "Did something that she wouldn't have to do." "Made excellent grades, dressed well, and behaved in a Victorian manner." "Made good grades and didn't do anything to upset anyone." "Conformed with her ideas and beliefs." "Conformed to the domestic responsibilities of a female."*

Women in the biological parents group who wrote their mothers were *never* proud of them, said such things as, *"I'm not sure she was ever proud." "She was never proud of me." "Never!" "I could never do anything to please my mother." "I always felt she was never proud of me in any way."*

THE TWO-PARENT FAMILY IS NOT THE BEST

Step Parent Families

Those who answered in the group with a step mother said their biological fathers were proud of them when they did well in school or achieved some other success. Other comments of when their biological fathers were proud of them, included, "*When I conformed.*" "*Helped him around the farm and especially when he was doing any mechanical work, he always asked me to lend a hand, and I loved it.*" "*Was sick one day but went to school anyway.*" "*I think he's proud of me all the time.*" "*When I quit drugs.*"

Of this same group, that is, women with biological fathers/step mothers, about one-fourth said their fathers were never proud of them. "*He was proud of me when I was seen and not heard.*" Many wrote, "*I don't ever remember him being proud of me.*" "*He did not believe in praising a child -- he only criticized.*"

In the step parent group with biological mothers, most indicated their biological mothers were proud of them, primarily when they did well in school. However, one-fifth said their own biological mothers were *never* proud of them. Their comments included, "*I can never recall or know if she was proud of me.*" Many wrote, "*My mother was never proud of anything I did,*" or, "*She was never proud of me.*"

In this same group, in answering the question about when their *father*, that is, their *step* father, was proud of them, about three-quarters answered that they were proud of their step daughters, most often mentioning when they did well in school, though some mentioned other times as for instance,. *"When I played a good game of pool..."*

About one-fifth of the step fathers were never proud of their step daughters.

Of the step *mother* group, many did not answer this question. Of those who did, about the same number of step mothers were proud of their step daughters as were never proud. The following comments are in addition to the many comments about being proud when they did well in school. *"Made good grades." "Conformed." "Did my chores without being reminded." "Acted like a lady." "Cleaned the house well." "Reflected credit on her -- when I did something she could show off." "Did her housework though nothing was said that she was proud of me for it."*

This same group, with step mothers, wrote comments about their step mothers not being proud of them. *"My mother was never proud of me. She kept me in my room and I was not allowed to come out except to eat and go to school." "My mother was proud of me when I wasn't around, if at all." "I don't think I ever meant that much to her to make her proud." "I don't recall that she was ever proud of me." "The more I tried to please her, the more she hated me -- jealousy." "She was proud of me when I f......up." "Never!" "I have never received any hint of pride as far as I was concerned." "Hard to say. Nothing I did was ever quite right, meaning done the way she would have done it. She was very critical but would never come out and say it."*

THE TWO-PARENT FAMILY IS NOT THE BEST

	STEP PARENT GROUP PROUD?	
	1	2
Step F.	77%	23%
Bio. F. Stp.Grp.	68%	24%
Step M.	46%	42%
Bio. M. Stp.Grp.	81%	19%

1. Yes
2. Never

Single Mother Families

Most mothers in the single mother group were proud of their daughters, particularly when they did well in school. There were miscellaneous reason for pride as well. "*Cleaned my room, cut lawn, hedges.*" Other miscellaneous remarks from the single mother group included, "*When I grew up I think she was proud of my doing things she considered 'manly,' driving a car, moving, attempting to stick up for my rights with anyone other than her.*" "*She was proud when I did almost anything. Even when I skipped school to see Tommy Dorsey. Very understanding and not judgmental. It was a shock that the outside world did not have the "high' regard for me that my family had.*" "*When I did anything or nothing. She was proud of me all the time. Telling me to stand up for what I believed in and to believe in myself.*"

Only one percent of the women in the single mother group wrote that their mothers were never proud of them "*Do not remember pride being expressed.*" "*The only time I remember was when she told someone I did my own washing. There was never praise -- only criticism.*"

Conclusion

In the families with two biological parents a higher percentage of fathers than mothers let their daughters know they were proud of them. Most single parents, fathers and mothers, let their daughters know they were proud of them.

In the step parent group most let their daughters know they were proud of them except for step mothers.

Knowing that parents are proud of them tells children they are accepted, approved of, doing well, validated as developing human beings. The child who does not know that her mother or father are proud of her, may have difficulty accepting herself, may have diminished self-confidence, lowered self-esteem, and a generally depressive outlook on life. Someone important to her must tell her she is okay, at least while she is growing up. Later in life she can learn to rely on her own inner value of herself and not on outside approval. But it is too much to ask of a child to believe that she is doing all right if she is never allowed to please the people who are most important to her. Children have a basic need to matter, and the parents are the first people to let them know that they do.

THE TWO-PARENT FAMILY IS NOT THE BEST

In the above percentages it appears that most of the women in this research grew up with acceptance, and learned to take pride in their accomplishments. An exception to this is women raised by a step mother/biological father. Those with biological mothers in this step parent group were aware of their mother's pride in them. But less than half of the *step* mothers indicated maternal pride in their step daughters.

What of father pride in daughters who lived with their *biological fathers*/step mothers - did their own fathers indicate pride in their daughters? It is interesting to learn that a lesser percentage of biological fathers in the step parent group expressed pride in their own daughters, than did the girls' *step* fathers. Their biological fathers in the step parent group did not do as well for their daughters as step fathers or fathers in the other group. One could imagine biological fathers might fear making a stepmother jealous of her step daughter.

WHAT ADMIRE/DISLIKE ABOUT FATHER?

"He was always caring, sharing whatever he had and gave good solid advice while we were growing up. Said he'd never give up my brother or me to anyone else for raising. He was an inspiration to me."

ADMIRE ABOUT FATHER

Of all the characteristics for which women admired their fathers, the traits were overwhelmingly those of *responsibility and caring*. Fifty-four percent of the women in the single father group, 32% in the biological parents group, and 27% in the step parent group admired their fathers for these traits.

THE TWO-PARENT FAMILY IS NOT THE BEST

WHAT ADMIRE ABOUT FATHER?							
	1	2	3	4	5	6	7
Bio.	32%	16%	9%	13%	27%	1%	1%
Sing. F.	54%	15%	1%	7%	18%	1%	1%
Step	27%	16%	10%	10%	18%	14%	0%

1. Responsible and caring
2. Good character
3. Positive behavior
4. Good looks
5. Other
6. Nothing
7. Everything

Good character values such as *integrity, strength of purpose, providing security, idealism, honesty, wisdom, stability,* were also reasons for their admiring their fathers in all groups where there were fathers.

Single Father Families

Many in the single father families spoke of how their father kept the family together at a time in history when fathers did not raise children. Comments include: "*I admired his intelligence, his dedication and drive.*" "*He was very hardworking and brought all his money home. He took custody of two young daughters with little or no assistance.*" "*When he was not drinking I admired his sense of humor.*" "*The way *he was able to provide a good loving home for my three brothers and me." "You knew what was expected of you without a harsh word. There was love and understanding."*

"He kept his family together even though my mother died during the depression." "He spent all his free time with us, and was very understanding. He felt that no problem was too big to deal with." "That he gave up so much of his personal life in order to bring up five children on his own." "He kept us together. I had cousins on Mom's side of the family that were put in an orphanage until their dad found a new wife."

"I think at that stage one always feels their father is a rock of security, love, and has all the answers. I wasn't any different." "He took care of me as well as my younger brother and sister rather than giving us to someone else." "His not dividing up us kids among relatives, keeping us all together when it would have been easier for him to separate us." "No matter what happened to him, he got up and tried again." "He didn't know the first thing about kids and he survived. He fought for us and always tried to teach us about love and communication and honesty." "Intellectual gifts and his encouraging us toward education and the world beyond the end of our noses." "I am aware that my father was a very special person. While he taught us survival skills at an early age, he also stressed compassion for others." "I was never made to feel that, in order to attract and keep male attention, I had to play dumb."

"He had a hard time but he kept us together." "Flexible, kind, easy-going and treated me as an intelligent adult long before I was one." "Kind of strict.

THE TWO-PARENT FAMILY IS NOT THE BEST

Never made me feel like he didn't love me." "Caring. He worked very hard to raise his four kids." "His knowledge and self control. Felt that swearing and drinking were a sign of ignorance." "Perseverance, hard worker, healthy appetite, quit smoking, taught me to survive." "His wisdom, the pride he gave me for being me and he always kept a roof over our heads, food on the table, and clothes on our backs." "Good businessman, smart, cool sense of humor, loved his children, missed my mother, provided good lives for us." "Independence and stability. Ability to raise four kids alone." "He kept our family together in a time when single fathers were unheard of." "I deified my father because he did bring us up and did not desert us when our mother left." "I feel my father was very rare since he took the divorce so hard and yet could go the rest of his life without saying anything bad about my mother." "My father was a man of integrity and of innate kindness who taught by example more than by words. He brought me up to be honest and open in my dealings with others. He showed me that all individuals have worth and that kindness and courtesy are important. He taught me that no honest work is demeaning and that there is no disgrace in failing as long as you keep on trying." "My father certainly made me feel I could do anything I wanted and also that I should have a challenging career. He is the reason I have had a successful career." "My father taught his children there was no such thing as 'can't be done,' at least until you'd given it a try. He felt women and men were equal in intelligence and ability." "Dad tried to teach us to think 'Globally.'" "He taught us to deal with death."

One wrote of her father's preparing her as he would prepare her brother. "*Along with my driver's license and first car came a set of basic hand tools: screw drivers, pliers, wrenches, and sockets. All three of us kids were expected to be able to do our own basic maintenance and repairs. When my car ate the engine I was up to my elbows in oil and engine parts along with my dad.*" And another wrote what was said often, "*Growing up with my father working and no one at home, I became self-sufficient, self-reliant and very independent. These are traits which I have never outgrown.*"

There is an unmistakable gratefulness expressed by women in single father families that their fathers did not pass on the responsibility of raising their children to someone else. Also, because many women in the single father group mention their fathers' loving and caring, it might be that as men assume the child raising, this act may permit their feminine side to function openly. They may therefore express their loving and caring as a single father when, if they had wives, they might have felt their wives were providing that for the children and therefore not shown that side of themselves.

While it has been said that men who take on the role of a single parent may be more nurturing types to begin with, that does not seem borne out by the remarks of some women in these single father families who resented their father's coldness and lack of caring.

THE TWO-PARENT FAMILY IS NOT THE BEST

Biological Parents Families

Empty father-daughter relationships were reflected in a small percentage of the biological parents and single father groups who said they admired "*nothing*" about their fathers.

Positive comments from women in the biological parents group who admired their fathers wrote, "*Steadfastness and stability.*" "*His righteousness and intelligence.*" "*He would catch ill birds and animals, nurse them back to health, put a splint on a wing, etc.. When they were well he would set them free.*" "*His main goal in life seemed to be in providing for his family.*" "*Commitment to his career and civil rights.*" "*Very quiet, caring.*" "*Good storyteller.*" "*Brains, power.*" "*Everything.*"

"*His brains and logic. His dependability.*" "*Hard working and loving.*" "*He was lively, handsome, and he worked diligently when he had work.*" "*His gentleness.*" "*His sense of humor.*" "*His quiet ways. His honesty.*" "*How he excelled in his work.*" "*My father came from a family where all the kids lived in tar paper houses without plumbing and with cars up in blocks in the front yard. They all had more kids than they could afford to raise, and the husbands never held steady jobs. My father had no education and no particular skills, yet he was a responsible, hard-working man whose family always came first.*"

While a few women in the other groups admired *everything* about their fathers, no one in the step parent group did. Similarly, in answer to the question of what they admired about their fathers, *more* in the step parent group than in others admired *"nothing."*

Step Parent Families

No one in the step parent group admired *"everything"* about their father.

STEP PARENT GROUP, ADMIRED NOTHING IN FATHER

Bio. F.	9%
Step F.	19%

Of those in the step parent group with biological fathers, comments included, *"I don't know how he put up with my step mother and still loved her, cared for her." "I admired him because of the way he tolerated my step mother." "I don't know how he lived with my step mother."*

Positive comments from step parent group with biological fathers included, *"His gentleness, love of children, wide range of interest." "Boundless energy." "Sense of humor, non-violent discipline. His fairness." "His unselfishness, his true desire to provide a home for his children, his love of life, strength of character, generosity." How hard he tried to provide for his family." "His ability to forgive, love without conditions."*

THE TWO-PARENT FAMILY IS NOT THE BEST

WHAT DISLIKE ABOUT FATHER

"*Unreasonable, bad temper, yelled a lot, could never talk to him, judgmental, never complimented.*"

Though many women said there was "*nothing*" they disliked about their father, there were many who wrote of things they did dislike. The highest percentage of women in each group with fathers, said that what they disliked in their father was his being *uncommunicative* and *unaffectionate*.

Almost to the same degree for all groups, their fathers' bad moods and nagging were the traits listed *second* as those which bothered women in each group, as did their fathers' drinking and rigidity. Women in the biological group listed many complaints about their fathers and sometimes more complaints than women in the other groups. It might be expected that fathers in the biological group would be under less stress than single fathers or fathers in step parent families, and therefore more congenial, or at least not so unpleasant, but that was not so.

WHAT DISLIKE ABOUT FATHER							
	1	2	3	4	5	6	7
Bio.	21%	19%	9%	12%	5%	6%	22%
Sing. F.	22%	13%	13%	10%	14%	11%	16%
Step	14%	18%	4%	10%	6%	10%	29%

1. *Uncommunicative and unloving*
2. *Moods and nagging*
3. *Drinking*
4. *Rigid*
5. *Bigot, and bad behavior*
6. *Nothing*
7. *Miscellaneous*

Single Father Families

In answer to the question, "*What did you dislike about your father?*" in addition to the 11% in the single father group who said they disliked nothing, about one-fourth complained about the lack of communication and love. Others complained about bad moods and nagging, and still others about drinking, bigotry, physical and sexual abuse, and the rest for miscellaneous reasons.

Negative comments from the single father group included, "*Bad moods, impatience.*" "*His closed mindedness, his attitude, his temper.*" "*Unable to communicate with me as I got older. He was overprotective and rigid.*" "*Temper and sexual abuse.*" "*His remoteness, unbreakable rules, stubbornness, inability to show love.*" "*His drinking. He was drunk by 4:30 each*

THE TWO-PARENT FAMILY IS NOT THE BEST

evening. He spent most weekends hunting and leaving me alone." "My father has a narrow view of the world. He judges and dislikes groups because of the actions of a few." "Drinking and subsequent mean behavior." "His temper, inability to apologize or admit he was wrong."

"His inability to display loving emotions. He was bought up in the old style when emotions were a sign of weakness. Also he was never satisfied with my accomplishments." "He sometimes drank too much. Changed personality then to a bickering man." "Erratic and dogmatic." "Coldness and detachment." "He never told me he loved me." "Getting money from him was difficult even for basics like bras." "Overprotective. I didn't start to grow up until he died." "His pomposity. He wouldn't listen to anyone he didn't agree with."

"He had no affection or compassion, no understanding or caring and was a perfectionist in everything." "Can't argue with him successfully -- he was always right." "He was chauvinistic, didn't give praise. We were not to express our feelings or attitudes especially if they differed from his. As we grew up it seemed that he thought we owed him us. He didn't like it when I got married as he lost my help and attention and I was forty years old." "Mixed in with tooth pullings, and bedtime stories, was the rage and violence that erupted and was aimed at me when Dad would drink. Broken promises and drunken rages have left me with very mixed feelings about my father."

It is important to remember that, while these comments are negative, many women wrote that they disliked "*nothing*" about their fathers. Also, of the women who wrote of traits which they disliked, these same women in all groups wrote of traits which they did like.

Biological Parents Group

Again, women complained about their fathers' *uncommunicative* and *unaffectionate* behavior. Others disliked the nagging and bad moods, others the drinking, rigidity, bad behavior including being a bigot. Aside from 6% disliking "*nothing*," Miscellaneous reasons, were, "*Overeating.*" "*The way he treats my mother.*" "*Short temper on family trips.*" "*Goes out of his way for strangers, but treats my mother like a maid.*" "*He was oblivious to my pain when I would be upset.*" "*Insensitivity and lack of appreciation.*" "*Too much of a perfectionist.*" "*His conviction that he knows everything and is always right.*" "*His impatience.*" "*Criticism, sharp tongue, restrictiveness.*"
"*His arrogance, his contemptuous ridicule, the way he treated my mother.*" "*His womanizing.*" "*He didn't treat my mother very well.*" "*Always preferred my sister instead of me. She was sexually abused by him.*" "*Chauvinistic attitude about women.*" "*Overbearing.*" "*I never knew him well enough to like or dislike anything about him.*" "*He punished us when we cried.*" "*Always thinks he is right. Believes women are inferior. My father was head of the house and never let anyone forget it.*" "*He favored his sons over his daughters.*" "*Belittle's my mother's and his children's abilities.*" "*Tried to make me feel guilty about things.*" "*He never had time for me. He seemed to favor my younger sister. She, by the way, was sexually abused by him.*"

THE TWO-PARENT FAMILY IS NOT THE BEST

"My father used ridicule and contempt to keep others in their place, namely, beneath him. A pompous man, he expected to be looked up to. He treated my mother patronizingly and was openly contemptuous of her abilities, her ideas, her actions. Their relationship was apparently based on sex; he was constantly patting her on the butt and acting amorous toward her in front of us kids. That upset me a lot. The two of them seemed to have no real communication; they'd complain about each other to me, get in scraps where my mother would pout and my father would bombast. I suppose they're actually quite average people, but I felt wounded and harassed by both and sought any sort of escape. The only thing that prevented me from getting married to escape was the sure knowledge that if they were an example of what married life was like, I wanted nothing to do with it."

Step Parent Families

In the step parent group where one-fifth with *step* fathers admired "*nothing*," there were various comments."*He let my mother beat me and didn't say anything.*" "*He seems to be more willing to go out of his way for strangers then he is for us. Treats my mother like a maid, not a wife.*" "*His inflexibility, and the way he treats my mother.*" "*He is narrow minded and suspicious.*" *He believed praise was not good for kids.*" "*His apparent lack of compassion.*" "*Self-centered, childish, inconsiderate, lies, petty, racist, unfair, didn't do housework, screwed any woman who'd have him.*" "*He'd get angry over small things.*" "*Domineering --

fought with my brother." "Loud mouth, nagging, always having to have the last word and being right." "The way he interfered with my relation with my Mom." "Belligerent, verbally abusive, overly strict."

Of the women in the step parent group who had *biological* fathers, one-tenth wrote they admired "*nothing.*" about their fathers. The remaining 90% wrote comments and a few of those are included here. "*Uncommunicative.*" "*Not home enough.*" "*His temper. He could be violent when angry and I was afraid of him.*" "*His right-wing biases and prejudices.*" "*His self-centeredness.*" "*His never being there when I needed him and he always took my step mother's side.*" "*His ignoring how my stepmother treated me.*" "*He was rigid, angry and not emotionally approachable.*" "*He never spoke to me and did not allow us to speak.*" "*He cared for himself primarily. His children were a very low priority.*" "*Being drunk whenever I saw him. Being able to beat his kids.*"

FATHERS WHO DON'T COMMUNICATE

Many women in all groups were hurt by their fathers' lack of communication which is often interpreted as lack of affection and lack of caring. Though the fathers were said to not communicate, the women would then explain how the fathers *yelled at them,* or *read the riot act to them.* So it is not that the fathers were not communicating, but rather that they were not communicating what the daughters wanted to hear. Often the words, *"uncommunicative"* were followed by *"unaffectionate," "cold." "Uncommunicative"* is interpreted as uncaring. And in many cases that was true.

That men don't communicate is a common complaint, not only from the women in this research but also in the mass media. Magazines and talk show programs provide a platform for women to speak of this disappointment. It is almost a lament. Women, who like to talk about their feelings, and often do so with their women friends, want men to talk about *their* feelings. But men have been taught to *repress* their feelings, and therefore not to think about them let alone talk about them.

In her book, *Intimate Strangers,* Lillian Rubin explains this lack of ability to communicate as a result of the difficult process of a boy's growing up. She writes that the father as an infant was most likely nurtured by his mother or other women. Then in his young boyhood he had to disengage himself from her in order to begin to become a man. A *Mama's Boy* is ridiculed so he must be spared from acquiring that label. *His* father's role is to start the process of making a man of his son. The boy begins to see that he is physically different from his mother and in order to establish *his* gender he must now begin to identify with his father, and to reject and denigrade his mother's gender. As Nancy Chodorow explains in her book, *The Reproduction of Mothering,* the boys' identification is not so much with their fathers, as it is a denial of their mothers.

Because infant boys are surrounded by female images they must be <u>taught</u> to be masculine. Girls do not need to be taught to be feminine. At the age when boys are in the primary grades they withdraw from their young female playmates, and in groups, the boys make fun of girls, call them "cooties," and other belittling names. The boys learn at an early age that in order to become masculine they must value their gender as superior to their mother's and sister's. When the young boy awakens to this need to separate himself from the feminine side of his family and the feminine side of himself, he tells his sister, literally, "You can't play in my club house." For an explanation to the sister who has always played in his club house, he tells her scornfully, "You're a <u>girl</u>!"

Now it's time for his father to take his little boy fishing and to the ball games and to other stereotypically male activities. Gradually, his mother withdraws as primary parent and there is more shared parenthood with the son. She gently pushes him away from her, praising him for *masculine* things he does, and discouraging his emotional dependency. He learns not to cry so easily, not to be so physically affectionate with her as he had been in earlier years. In order for the boy to make a satisfactory transition to boyhood, his mother must reject his dependent babyhood, and he must repress his emotional need for what had been her continuing abundant affection. He must reject the feminine in himself and what the psychiatrist Jung calls *the all-powerful mother* to achieve his separation.

Because he is not permitted to love his mother physically as his father can, he is injured. The first love of his life loves someone else more. Women are therefore forever untrustworthy. He must disconnect himself from his mother and renounce those warm intimate moments with her. As Rubin says, he renounces that part of himself which allowed vulnerability. He must steel himself to become a man. He is also being prepared for decreased emotional participation in any relationship, including his own future family. He eventually accepts this somewhat emotionally sterile trait as his own true nature, when in fact it is the product of indoctrination.

In all of this, the young boy experiences a sense of betrayal by his mother which can lead to anger and rage, and a contempt for women which many women in all groups in this research mentioned in describing their fathers. Because of this growing-up process for boys, it is easier for them to act out their anger than it is for them to express all those emotions they had to repress when they separated from their mothers, that is, sadness, fear, and dependency. They had to deny attachment, not only to the feminine person in his family, but to the feminine part of himself. This wrenching from his mother in childhood and the consequent denial of his feelings may be the reason why men have few close friends male or female, compared to the many close friends which women have.

That, generally, men are uncommunicative, seems to be part of their nature, but actually it is a developed trait with negative results. But Rubin suggests it need not be so negative if fathers would have more to do with raising their children. As long as mothers or other women are the principal caregivers in the children's early years, the boys will have this separation problem from women, one that girls do not have because they don't have to become *different* than their mothers. But if fathers have more intimacy with their infant sons, the sons will not have to separate from their nurturers in order to begin the process of becoming men. There will not be that sense of betrayal and there could, then, possibly be a lessening of contempt for women. But another big advantage of that change could be that boys and men would be more communicative, not so afraid of their emotions, their fears, or their dependency.

One of the conclusions of this research is that there is, generally, no loss to girls (and in fact there are some gains) in being raised by fathers. Rubin suggests that there will be gains also to boys, and to their future families, if fathers participate more in early childhood nurturing. For one thing, there should be less anger at women, and more acceptance by men of their own vulnerable weaknesses which they often camouflage with rigid self-righteousness. The country would also benefit, as government and other established institutions, would eventually be at least partly comprised of men who do not devalue women and do not exclude them from full participation in society. The feminine principle of caring for all people would have a better chance to share equal billing with *machismo*.

WHAT ADMIRE/DISLIKE ABOUT MOTHER?

ADMIRE ABOUT MOTHER

"*Although she was riddled with fears, she remained resilient and courageous. She was deeply touching.*"

Again, mothers as well as fathers were admired for their *responsibility and caring* and for their *good character traits*. In the question about fathers, only one woman mentioned her father's good looks. But being "*attractive*," was mentioned by many women in all groups in answer to the question, "*What did you admire about your mother?*"

THE TWO-PARENT FAMILY IS NOT THE BEST

WHAT ADMIRE ABOUT MOTHER?

	1	2	3	4	5	6	7
Bio.	24%	25%	10%	8%	19%	6%	2%
Sing. M.	23%	36%	8%	15%	14%	3%	1%
Step	14%	27%	10%	10%	22%	20%	4%

1. Responsible and caring
2. Good character
3. Good looks
4. Worked hard
5. Other
6. Nothing
7. Everything

Single Mother Families

Many mentioned their mother's strength, their courage in the face of adversity, and their independence, the admirable qualities of being responsible and of caring for the family. Many mentioned they admired their mothers for working hard to keep the family going. "*She managed the welfare money well. Made sure we had clothes to wear.*" "*Her strength and courage.*" "*She stands up for what she believes in. Will not allow anybody to put her 'in her place.'*" "*Her ability to make deals on cars, houses. Her lack of prejudice against race, religion, or sexual preference.*" "*She was beautiful and very much a lady until she was crossed. Then she defended herself like a Sherman Tank.*" "*Her strong sense of love and caring for us.*" "*She showed off her children's talents and inspired imagina-*

tion." "Strong and protective, always putting her children's interests above her own." "Always interested in what I was doing." "She never complained about feeling ill." "She had the strength to withstand a divorce when her pregnancy was almost full term." "Her ability to rise above her situation. She kept busy which was probably her way of tolerating her grief." "I was impressed when she could fix something around the house, i.e.the toilet, electric cords." "She kept her family together and never complained about her fate." "She enjoyed activities that my sister and I enjoyed -- skiing, hiking, travel, swimming; she never left us so she could do her thing." "Her ability to 'stand up for herself.'" "She was not self-sacrificing." "Her fighting spirit, independence, ability to cope with whatever came along." "She always seemed happy though life was pretty hard on her." "She was a survivor."

Biological Parents Group

Women in the biological parents group also admired their mothers for *"responsibility and caring,"* and for *"good character traits."* Some of those traits included, "*Her ability to quietly rule the home. Her ability to work and keep a good, clean home.*" "*Her ability to cope with boredom.*" "*Her gregarious nature.*" "*Her openness and friendliness.*" "*Her sense of humor and style. Her ability to make friends.*" "*Her skills at mother-type behavior. Her devotion to taking physical care of herself, her intelligence, her making sure I got exposed to culture.*" "*She was smart.*" "*Her organization, attractive appearance, and outgoing personality.*"

THE TWO-PARENT FAMILY IS NOT THE BEST

"Cooking and housecleaning abilities, very elegant and mannered." "She was generous." "Her total loyalty and devotion to her family." "Her assertiveness, her sense of independence."

Step Parent Families

Subdividing the step parent group into those with *step* mothers and those with *biological* mothers, the following comments are from women who had *step* mothers. *"I admired her because she was willing to raise her own 3 sons and take on my 4 brothers and I also." "Her ability to make people feel wanted; she was a very warm person." "Very loving and expressive." "She could work all day and still cook dinner for everyone." "I think she tried to be fair with her children and me. I think she tried to normalize my life." "She raised three kids who were not hers with no favoritism -- much love and patience and she tempered our father's anger." "Her willingness to marry a man with four small children and raise them as her own." "She taught me how to keep myself clean as well as how to clean house." "She was young and pretty." "She tried to do what she thought was right." "Her quiet faith."*

Thirty-six percent of the women with *step* mothers admired *"nothing"* about them. Many were adamant. *"I grew to hate her more and more as I got to know her, even now I only tolerate her since it is the only way I can get to see my father." "I hate her. I still hate her and it's been years since I've lived at home." "There is virtually no quality I admire about my step* mother." "What do I admire about her? Not a single thing except that she can live with herself."

The women in the step parent group with *biological* mothers wrote of admiring "*Positive attitude.*" "*Ability to organize.*" "*Independence. Knows how to manage money.*" "*Could pull it together with seven kids and keep her marriage healthy.*" "*Always seemed in control, was well dressed and knew how to do everything.*" "*She had three children she took very good care of, raised all our food, went to college, taught school, was always fair and enjoyed good music, books. She was funny. Taught us all very good values. She was very poor for many years. After my father died she managed all on her own until she remarried.*" "*Her independence -- before she married my step father.*" "*Hard working, took risks.*" "*Strong, non traditional woman, usually assertive, good sense of humor, good mind, interested in others.*" "*With all her own problems she let us know we were loved and to be proud of ourselves.*" "*She was extremely strong when our father died. She thought of us first no matter what she did. She was extremely loving and caring, always encouraged us to do our best.*" "*She stood up for my half sister and myself even if she got blamed.*"

The big difference in groups here is in the numbers in the step parent group who admired "*nothing*" in their mothers. A few women in the biological parents group and fewer yet in the single mother group admired "*nothing,*" in their mothers. But in the step parent group one-fifth admired "*nothing.*" Of those, more than one-third had step mothers.

THE TWO-PARENT FAMILY IS NOT THE BEST

STEP PARENT GROUP, ADMIRED NOTHING IN MOTHER	
Bio. M.	15%
Step M.	36%

DISLIKE ABOUT MOTHER

"When mad or angry she would not talk about it -- would give me the 'silent treatment.'"

The answers to the question, *"What did you dislike about your mother?"* had many more different answers than the answers to what was disliked about fathers.

	DISLIKE ABOUT MOTHER						
	1	2	3	4	5	6	7
Bio.	22%	18%	5%	2%	30%	4%	1%
Sing. M.	18%	22%	10%	4%	30%	14%	1%
Step	14%	12%	14%	8%	29%	4%	6%

1. Rigid, nags, bad moods, controlling
2. Demanding
3. Cold
4. Never went to school functions
5. Miscellaneous
6. Nothing
7. Everything

Single Mother Families

"I disliked her intrusiveness into my life, her manipulations, use of guilt to control me." "Her overprotectiveness of her children." "Didn't give rational reasons for her demands." "Too dominating, yelled at me, called me names." "She nags." "Violent rages, sud-

THE TWO-PARENT FAMILY IS NOT THE BEST

den mood swings, viciousness toward my divorced father, closed-mindedness, martyr." "Her desire to control. The way she beat my sister...it made me very submissive." "She would get upset very easy and holler and argue over nothing. Sometimes we were afraid of her. She never showed us any love or affection." "Her temper."

In addition to those who disliked their mothers for their domineering or nagging, many of the women in this group disliked their mothers because of their coldness. For instance, *"She was friendly but distant and dealt with me in a negatively reinforcing way which I rebelled against." "I disliked her coldness. Her needing to ask other people in decisions regarding me." "She never smiled." "Not demonstrative or affectionate." "She would punish me by not speaking to me for two or three days -- just ignoring me." "Her coldness and lack of trust."*

Biological Parents Families

Women in the biological parents group disliked their mothers' rigid and controlling characteristics as well as their demanding, intrusive traits, and their nagging. *"Pried into my diary and made false accusations." "I resented her pushing me to be successful whether with boys or school or career." "Violent temper, non affectionate." "Always bothering (nagging) me about my appearance and posture." "Her nagging and yelling." "Her alcoholism and tendency to blame others for her failures." "Her violent, childish temper. She'd ignore me and 'pout' for days!" "Her yell-*

ing." "Her anger and her temper." "I hated how she could drink and not get any help and not care how I felt about it."

Miscellaneous comments included, "*She was very difficult to please and she was always right.*" "*She was too much of a slave to my father.*" "*She didn't stand up to my father who was always picking on my older brother.*" "*She was fat, disorganized, too opinionated, closed minded, self-centered.*" "*Her frequent statement that life would not be so hard if she had not had us children.*" "*Her drinking.*" "*Her need for praise and recognition and she competed with my friends.*" "*She ridiculed me. She was so embittered and dissatisfied with her own life that she kept up a constant stream of complaints, usually muttered but with an undercurrent of violent emotion to which she expected me to react. She used violent emotion and vague threats to control me. She often threatened to break my neck or throw me out or leave me somewhere. Her emotions were like a physical force to me - they hurt.*"

Step Parent Families

Most women in this subdivision of the step parent group indicated they disliked their mothers for the same reasons as the other groups, that is, "*bad moods,*" "*rigid and controlling,*" "*demanding,*" "*cold.*"

A few comments from these women in the step parent group with *biological* mothers follow: "*She yelled and used put downs. Also slapped us when she was angry.*" "*She's very selfish and she is jealous of my accomplishments.*" "*She always knew 'best' and*

THE TWO-PARENT FAMILY IS NOT THE BEST

was so conservative -- had little humor about small things." "Unable to express feelings. Seemed cold." "Lazy dependency - always depressed and tired." "She felt sorry for herself but wouldn't do anything to solve her unhappy situation. She acted the martyr." "She married my step father." "She had a short temper." "That she could nag and use guilt feelings to control me." And one more from a women who had a biological mother,"*I couldn't understand why she hated me.*"

The women in the subdivision in the step parent group with *step* mothers indicated by their comments the lack of affection from their mothers."*She didn't know who I was. She was horribly critical, she humiliated me, she was disinterested in me.*" "Her inability to show love to me or my sisters... Her concern about what other people think in all matters." "Her rejection of me." "Her neglect of her own children, her nasty temper, her negative references to my mother. She always put me in the middle of her and Dad's fights." "Her hatred of me. Her lack of interest. Her abuses." "She is dishonest, immoral, cruel, vicious, violent, greedy, selfish, unreasonably jealous, deceitful, cunning." "A hypocrite, constantly bad-mouthing my dad (her husband) and the rest of my family behind their backs." "The drinking, the beatings, the sexual abuse. Having no childhood." "No love." "Allowed my dad to discriminate against me and continues to defend him today." "She favored her children over my sister and me." "The way she treated me and my siblings." "High but unexpressed expectations. I had to guess what she expected and felt punished if I guessed wrong." "She took over the entire household and everything had to be her way."

One described her step mother as, "*an opportunist. My step mother had three children when she married my father. He raised them as his own including helping them buy cars and go to college. When the last one finished college she left. My dad had no other warning.*" Another describes a change in her step mother. "*This woman (I never referred to her as my step mother, always my father's wife) and I were very good friends before they got married. I never have figured out why she changed so drastically so fast, except that she was 'in love' with my father's security.*"

THE TWO-PARENT FAMILY IS NOT THE BEST

WHAT WAS MISSED NOT HAVING A MOTHER

"Physical comfort, being cuddled. I felt I missed out on being a kid and the comforts a mother traditionally provides."

Women in single father families were asked to complete the sentence, "*The thing I missed most about not having a mother was* ..." Separating the completions of these sentences into what would be termed "*superficial feminine qualities,*" and "*deep feminine qualities,*" most women yearned for the *superficial feminine qualities.*

Superficial feminine qualities are such things as providing creature comforts, clothes, shopping, food on the table, how to apply makeup. Deep feminine qualities are such things as love, caring about the person, and understanding.

Most of the women raised by single fathers had a great need for the superficial feminine qualities. These included "*Not being able to talk about boys, not having someone to help me learn how to dress, wear makeup, etc.*" "*I can't cook, sew, or get a date.*" "*Shopping, tea parties.*" "*Personal attention to grooming.*" "*Having someone to talk to about being feminine, someone to shop with.*" "*Someone to ease the burdens of work.*" "*Companion for 'girl stuff,' someone soft to cuddle.*" "*Not having a mother to hug.*" "*Learning how to act and be feminine.*" "*The smell of pot roast cooking when I came home from school. What did that mean to me? Someone else in my life to love and care for me." "Physical hugs." "The social life women seem to be responsible for." "Housework done by someone other than me." "A strong female role model, the traditional stable home." "Someone to take care of me." "Touching --how mothers do." "Affection." "Learning how to be feminine." "Receiving unconditional mother's love." "Having her at home after school to go places with." "A home prepared for friends upon arrival home after school." "Learning more about men." "A mother's approval of how you looked, what new dress she would sew for you, to curl your hair."*

One-third of the women said they missed *deep feminine qualities* which included, *"Deep emotional closeness." "Her loving care and concern for us." "Acceptance and validation and feeling of being an okay person." "My girlfriends seemed to have a 'friend' in their mother." "Feeling loved." "Close understanding and protection I believed would be there for me." "Someone to share my feelings with." "Friendship, companionship and knowledge we could have shared." "Sharing intimate feelings." "Understanding during my adolescence." "Advice and guidance." "Concern and loyalty." "Friendship with a mother, as many daughters seem to have." "Companionship."*

Whether the women expressed the need for *superficial* or *deep feminine qualities*, there is a yearning for girls in single father homes to have someone to talk to. For single fathers who are today raising their daughters this would point to the need for having an understanding and communicative woman in the neighborhood or in his circle of friends or relatives available for their daughter. Women talking

THE TWO-PARENT FAMILY IS NOT THE BEST

together is important. It has been said that though men talk together, it is through "the game." They talk about football or the stock market or cars, and those are the metaphors for the desire for intimate personal male talk.

One can hear from these women, also, a concern for themselves that they want to discuss. If a girl has menstrual cramps, for instance, she knows that her mother probably had them too, would understand and would help. Fathers might be more apt to dismiss the subject, or girls with single fathers might be too embarrassed to bring it up.

"*If I had a mother,*" one woman wrote, "*I might have developed more traditional feminine traits and not developed masculine traits. I was lucky to have a father who treated me as a person.*"

WHAT MISSED NOT HAVING A MOTHER				
	1	2	3	4
Sing. F.	53%	33%	3%	7%

1. Superficial feminine needs
2. Deep feminine needs
3. Nothing
4. Miscellaneous

The three percent of the women who said they did not miss anything in not having a mother wrote,"*You don't know what you've missed if you've never had.*" "*I wasn't aware of missing a mother because I didn't know the difference.*" "*At the time I really didn't miss having a mother.*" "*I missed nothing.*

Mother represents pain. My father took me away because she was extremely physically and mentally abusive to me. He divorced her shortly after and even though he said she could see me when he was around, we didn't have contact ...She chose not to see me." "*I don't think at the time I missed a lot. But when I talk to friends now I feel I missed a certain bond moms and daughters have.*"

Another woman in the single father group wrote, "*What comes to mind when I think about growing up without a mother is that I feel cheated. My father didn't know, didn't have time to learn, didn't have enough money, didn't know how to be 'female.' I remember calling him at work to tell him that I finally got my period -- a major milestone for most women. I don't remember what he said, or his reaction, but I remember crying in the locker room at school. I remember growing out of bras, and not wanting to have to ask for money for new ones, and having the mother of one of my friends read him the riot act because they were so small and I wasn't.*"

But another woman in the single father group writes of a different reaction. "*I remember calling my father at work when I started my period. He was so excited but also concerned. He didn't know what to do so he offered to buy every product on the market associated with periods and when he picked me up at school at those times he always had the seat of the car covered with a blanket.*"

It was always the *ideal mother* who is missed. She is, as one woman said when referring to a fantasy mother, "*almost like a fairy godmother*". One woman reminded herself, "*I would have preferred to

THE TWO-PARENT FAMILY IS NOT THE BEST

have a mother -- to be more like a 'normal' family, but I had to keep reminding myself I could have had a rotten mother."

One woman whose parents were divorced when she was nine years old, simply wrote, "*Growing up without a mother was a very painful experience. It took me a long time to get over the hurt. I can't think of any real advantages to it.*" Yet another says, "*I don't think being motherless really harmed me. My dad says I might have done the same dumb things anyway. Rather I learned to cope with adversity at an early age, and there's nothing wrong with that.*" As another said, "*I had no Mama to model myself after, but also, no Mama to fall short of in comparison. Of course there are drawbacks. I felt keenly that I alone was responsible for my well-being. I am today afraid of betrayal. As a child, I felt my mother's death was a kind of betrayal of our love and our need for her.*"

Another from the single father group wrote, "*I missed my mother very much and 'spoke' to her when in bed at night. There was little loving support from a distant father. I felt very alone. Later I looked to boys for the love I didn't feel at home and became sexually promiscuous as a teenager.*" Another, "*To me, without a mother, all the warmth, beauty, comfort that one could find in a family situation was absent in mine. There was no 'home base' to return to. I have throughout my life, looked for a 'mother replacement.*" I have never found one. Maybe I have idealized my mother into something she never would have been.*"

Many women said they might have learned the following from their mothers: *How to be attractive, how to defer to men, how to be socially correct, how to put themselves last, and how to accommodate others.*

From most, one can hear the sincere longing for a loving, caring, nurturing, communicative, non-critical adult, and often one who also takes on the responsibility of the typically feminine tasks such as housecleaning, shopping, cooking, sewing, family grooming and social engagements. Is it any wonder mothers are so important?

WHAT WAS MISSED NOT HAVING A FATHER

"As a child I always wished I had a family like everyone else."

The categories for the answers to this open-ended question are many because the answers did not easily fall into just a few. The categories and the percentages of the women without fathers who wrote what was missed are these: *Protection, financial security, 19%;* "*Nuclear,*" "*balanced,*" "*normal,*" *family, 19%; Nothing, 14%; Male role model, male point of view,* 12%; *Male affection, love,* 6%; *Father/daughter relationship,* 6%; Combined together under *Miscellaneous* includes, *Time lost from my mother because she had to work,* 4%; *The opportunity to have one,* 4%; *No answer,* 4%; *Learn male/female relationships* 3%; *Guidance and his teaching me specifics,* 3%; *More limits placed on me,* 2%; *A second opinion,* 3%; Miscellaneous, 2%.

Most women without fathers missed having *financial security*, and they missed "*being like other normal families.*" The next highest percentage indicated that many women *did not miss* having a father (14%) This compares with 3% of the women in the single *father* families who said they did not miss having a *mother*.

Many women in this single *mother* group said they missed knowing what the male role was all about.

NO WOMEN IN THE SINGLE FATHER GROUP MISSED KNOWING WHAT THE FEMALE ROLE WAS ALL ABOUT.

In their housework and child caring responsibilities when they were growing up, women in single father families were living the female role. Also women in the single father group probably had women in their extended family, or in their neighborhood, who helped these single father families from time to time. It is more likely that single fathers have help from women outside their home, than that single mothers have help from men outside their home.

WHAT MISSED NOT HAVING A FATHER

	1	2	3	4	5	6	7
Sing. M.	19%	19%	14%	12%	6%	6%	23%

1. Protection, financial security
2. "Normal" family
3. Nothing
4. Male role and point of view
5. Male guidance, love
6. Father/daughter relationship
7. Miscellaneous

People are apt to feel sorry for a man raising a family by himself, and nurturing-type women in the neighborhood often lend a hand when they can. These women then act as role models and their presence teaches the girls more about what a woman's role is. This experience of learning the role

THE TWO-PARENT FAMILY IS NOT THE BEST

of the absent parent is not likely to be replicated for girls with single mothers. Though there are many more single mothers now, in the years when the women in this research were growing up, single motherhood was not only not accepted in many communities, it was often looked down upon. The community would not as readily come to the aid of a single mother as it did for a single father. And that is apt to be true today.

What help there was for single mothers probably did not come from men in the community, but from *women* who helped out in babysitting from time to time. Therefore, male role models were not as available for girls as were female role models.

Since so many women from single mother families mentioned that they missed having a male role model, or at least missed knowing what the male function in a family was, it seems important that single mothers today, if they can, should enlist the support of brothers, or other male relatives, or reliable male friends to help with this part of child raising. There are organizations like Big Brothers whose members make friends with fatherless boys and provide a male role model. The organization of Big Brothers has a sister organization known as Big Sisters. Members of Big Sisters are women who are female role models for girls in their communities. It would be good if there were a cross-over, where male role models could help fatherless girls understand and respect males.

Many fatherless girls have been deserted by their fathers and have been conditioned by their mothers to view men suspiciously since these mothers were injured and many were left relatively destitute. Not only do fatherless girls have few, if any, male role models, they also absorb their mother's negative opinions of men. This affects their male/female relationships throughout their lives. It would be good if as much effort which is expended to provide male role models for boys growing up could be provided for their sisters. As one woman wrote, "*When I was growing up there were no men. I didn't know any men and didn't understand them -- a true mystery to me.*" As for the male role model, many said they had no idea what it was.

The women in the single mother group who missed financial security, wrote they would have liked to have, "*A better house and a better economic situation,*" or would have liked to "*Live in a house instead of a housing project.*" Another said if she had had a father, her mother would not have been on welfare.

Of those missed having a "*normal family*," one comment stands out. "*Not having a father, I felt very anxious about anything happening to my mother. I grew up very independent and resourceful and I have strong survival skills and instincts, but financially it was very hard when I was a child because of no stability, no security for mother and myself. I also felt like an outcast, like I was different -- all the time. I was different.*"

Under miscellaneous reasons about what was missed in not having a father, "*A father would probably have moderated or dispelled my mother's wrath.*" "*The STATUS a father would have provided, as in 'My Daddy won't let me,' being too precious to be*

THE TWO-PARENT FAMILY IS NOT THE BEST

allowed the freedom I had." "Knowing what it felt like to have a masculine person hug or kiss me." "I missed someone else taking responsibility. YET now I feel good about the consequences of that! I could, and can, choose my own way."

Several women in the single mother group said they missed learning about the male/female interaction.

LEARNING ABOUT MALE/FEMALE INTERACTION WAS NOT SIGNIFICANT WITH THE GIRLS IN THE SINGLE FATHER GROUP WHO HAD NO MOTHERS

"I missed seeing my mother having a man in her life like other mothers." "Seeing a married couple interact with each other." "Not seeing a close relationship between man-woman. I don't really know what that is." "Seeing an at-home love relationship to use as a model in my own marriage."

Fourteen percent of the women without fathers said they missed "*nothing,*" in not having a father. This compares with 3% of women without mothers who said they missed "*nothing,*" in not having a mother. In answer to this question of what was missed, fatherless daughters answered "*Absolutely nothing!*" "*What you never had you never miss.*" "*I did not really miss not having one because I have no real perception of that relationship.*" "*I missed nothing. My life was rich with only my Mom. She is my best friend and my confidant, my mentor and my Mom. Life without a father wasn't empty. My Mom filled it up with love!*" "*I didn't miss a father. Because I went to a private girls' high school, I grew up believing that there was nothing a woman could not do, if she worked at it."*

It was more likely that women without mothers missed having a mother, than for women without fathers wishing they had a father.

To summarize some comparisons between girls growing up without a father and girls growing up without a mother, those without a mother knew what a woman's role was, but many without a father said they didn't know what a father's role was. Those without a mother did not miss seeing the male/female interaction in their family, possibly because they were part of that interaction. Girls growing up without a father said they missed the male/female interaction and they missed the male point of view. But girls growing up without a mother did not miss the female point of view.

WITH A MOTHER - HOW LIFE WOULD HAVE BEEN DIFFERENT

"Maybe I'd be less adventuresome."
The question asked was, *"If you had a mother, how would your life be different?"*

	WITH A MOTHER, HOW WOULD LIFE HAVE BEEN DIFFERENT?						
	1	2	3	4	5	6	7
Sing. F.	18%	18%	13%	5%	8%	3%	34%

1. Would have more superficial feminine skills
2. Would not be as strong
3. Would be stronger
4. Would have deep feminine skills
5. Would have had happier family
6. Would have male/female role models
7. Miscellaneous

With the same definition for *"superficial feminine qualities,"* the highest percentage of women in the single father group said that they would have had more of these skills. An equal percentage said they would not be as strong. For instance, those who said they would have more superficial feminine skills wrote of such things as, "*I would have been more poised.*" "*I might be more feminine in appearance and style.*" "*I might have learned to cook or sew.*" "*I would have had more social interaction.*" "*More gracious manners, more social know-how.*" "*I would have had* more clothes from her, sewing for me." "I'm sure I would have gone to the 'right' schools, met the 'right' people, have had a nicer life socially." "She would have sewn lots of clothes for me."

Those who wrote that they would *not be as strong*, were referring to *stereotypically masculine* skills that they now have. For instance, "*I wouldn't have been as responsible so early.*" "*Maybe less adventuresome.*" "*I would be less independent.*" "*I would not have had as much confidence.*" "*I would have been happier, more relaxed but probably would not have advanced as far professionally.*" "*My girl friends were more controlled than I was.*"

A high percentage of women wrote that they would be stronger than they are now. These were references, also, to *stereotypically masculine* skills, such as have more confidence, being more secure, having better self-esteem, and being more disciplined. "*I would have been more confident and have more confidence.*" "*I think I would have had more specific goals which would have influenced my schooling.*" "*I would have been more concerned with my career.*" "*I probably wouldn't have quit school.*" "*I would have more self confidence.*" "*I wouldn't be as independent as I am today.*" "*I would be afraid to experiment in life.*" "*I wouldn't have been so responsible so early.*"

Several comments reflect ambivalence. "*I think I would have been totally different. I would have had the self confidence to do what I wanted. My education and religious beliefs would have been strengthened. Unfortunately, I probably would have been taught that women are somewhat inferior to men,*

THE TWO-PARENT FAMILY IS NOT THE BEST

to marry early, and have a bunch of kids (barefoot and pregnant). My father would have treated me differently because my mother would have never let him be the way he is now." "I would be different but not necessarily better. I might have learned to cook or sew and be more feminine." "I think I would have developed more of the social graces, but on the other hand I feel I grew up less penned in by ideas about what little and older girls should be like."

Some women felt they would have had to trade their masculine skills for the feminine ones. "I wouldn't be as strong. I would be superficialy feminine with social graces, pretty." "I would have been less independent, have a more traditionally feminine, needy personality." Several refer to characteristics in themselves which they don't like which they believe would not exist if they had had a mother. "I wouldn't have been overweight since I wouldn't have had control of the food." "I would have been thinner." "I wouldn't be so shy."

Some women were skeptical. "I'm not sure it would have been any different." "I've never thought about it." "It's just idle speculation."

Longings for what might have been a better life for some are expressed. "I would have been a child and grown up at a slower pace, had fun, gone to college and married at an older age." "I would have been a better student, been better disciplined." "I wouldn't be as hard as I am today. I would have had someone to share my ups and downs with. Someone would have cared. I would have been loved."

Some were happy they did not have to grow up with the mother they had. "Life with my mother *would have made me an emotional wreck. My parents definitely needed to divorce." "I would have probably killed myself."* Another wrote, *"If my mother had lived my college would have been paid for, I would have had much less responsibility at an early age, and life would have been more 'normal' for me. But I am sure I would have lived at home much longer, probably had less freedom and I would have been a nurse by now (her choice). Instead I am going into business -- like my father."*

One of the three percent who said they would have had male/female role models wrote, *"I would have been exposed to a couple and how a couple interacts. I have had trouble in my own male/female relationships.""*

Others had a different concern. *"I don't know what my life would have been like if my mom was around. I never knew the experience to miss or compare -- this saddens and frustrates me."*

A few miscellaneous remarks include, *"I would have been more hostile toward men." "If my mother had stayed around I would have had very materialistic values." "I may have been more outwardly affectionate with my husband." "Dad probably wouldn't have drunk so much." "I probably wouldn't have quit school." "A mother would have had more rules." "There would have been arguing and more siblings." "I would have been home more." "My life would have been conventional...it wasn't until after my father died that I knew what regular bathing was, or daily schedules, or discipline, or restraint, or manners." "I think I would have married a man. I would be divorced eventually because I am gay. I believe my*

THE TWO-PARENT FAMILY IS NOT THE BEST

homosexuality would have surfaced sooner or later." "I might have spent less time being angry at men." "My dad would have been happy." "I wouldn't feel so close to my father as I do " "I would have learned to play the piano." "My father would have been nicer to his children." "My grandmother wouldn't have been so important." "Wouldn't have felt so alone raising my children." "I would not have been so compassionate for people who have had bad times." "My father's girl friends came and went and contributed to my lack of trust in people staying in my life." "I would not have had to 'mother' my father. There would have been time for me to be a child."

WITH A FATHER, HOW LIFE WOULD HAVE BEEN DIFFERENT

"We probably would not have had so many hardships."

WITH A FATHER, HOW WOULD LIFE HAVE BEEN DIFFERENT?							
	1	2	3	4	5	6	7
Sing. M.	17%	16%	15%	9%	6%	4%	30%

1. Would have more financial security
2. Would relate better with men
3. Would be stronger
4. Would not be as strong
5. Would have had unhappy family life
6. Would have had happier family life
7. Miscellaneous

The women who believed their financial situation would have been easier if they had had a father wrote, *"My mother would not have had to work." "There would have been more money." "We would have had more of the necessities of life. I would not have had to work at such an early age and perhaps had the opportunity for more education." "More money, more stability." "I can speculate only on the financial aspect of the question of how my life would have been different with a father: possibly better. Maybe not. Imponderable." "My mother would not*

THE TWO-PARENT FAMILY IS NOT THE BEST

have had to work and I would not have had as much responsibility for the house and my sibling." "It would have been financially easier. Also I would have grown up with an ally; I could have grown up to be 'me.'" "I would have had more money and I probably would have stayed in high school."

"Financially better and maybe not so many fights in our household." "I think I would have finished school and made a good career." "Simple. Less poverty!" "Because my mother had to work, I was cheated of having a mother. I would have had a mother." "I would have had more things." "No money for vacations. Holidays would have been better too." "We would have lived like an Upper Class like my dad did." "We would have had a higher standard of living, more socializing, more traveling." "Maybe I would have had a chance at college." "I would have had less struggle to buy basic needs" "I'm almost positive we would have had a higher standard of living." "Money would not have been such a constant struggle."

Many believed their relationships with men would be better, or they would respect men more, if they had had a father. "*I would have a more positive image of men.*" "*My relationship with men would have been better.*" "*I might have been able to show affection, to be more at ease as an adolescent with males.*" "*I wouldn't be so angry at weak females and afraid to trust men.*" "*I'd feel more secure about myself while having contact with men.*" "*My sexuality in relation to men would probably be clearer.*" "*I think my perception of relationships with men would not have been so negative.*" "*I'd be less awkward around men and more confident in myself." "My ideas and assumptions about men would probably be different if I was raised with a father in the house." "I would be able to be more intimate with men, less estranged from them."*

"I'd have more realistic expectations of marriage, less need to have the attention of a man." "I do not think I would feel such a need to be accepted by men." "I'd have had to share my mother. I'd have learned how men and women relate intimately, day by day, share responsibilities." "I feel I might have been more able to have a 'normal' (platonic?) relationship as opposed to a 'sexual' relationship with men." "Perhaps I wouldn't be so angry at men." "I would not have relied so heavily on 'sexuality' in relating to men." "I would not have had so many problems in my love life. I always felt desperate if a relationship was ending, even if I knew the relationship was no good. I would feel abandoned..."

Fifteen percent of the women in this single mother group wrote that if they had had a father they would have been stronger. *"I would feel confident and like the way I look." "I would have been better 'adjusted' at an early age." "I possibly would not have been afraid of taking risks and would not need constant approval." "My self image was very poor. I would have been able to 'compare' myself better -- not so self-critical." "I would have had more confidence, more self-respect, fewer financial problems growing up, and I wouldn't have been so desperate for male attention." "I would have had more self-esteem -- I think." "I would have felt less insecure, not felt abandoned."*

Then there is the 9% who felt if they had had a father they would *not* be as strong. *"I would have*

THE TWO-PARENT FAMILY IS NOT THE BEST

had more restrictions growing up resulting in less independence now." "Perhaps I would not have been such a strong, independent woman." "Because he was protective of 'his girls,' I think I'd be less independent." "There would have been more rigidity in rules, less freedom, less responsibility and less independence." "I would either have been bullied into nothingness or forced to learn to conform, adapt, and discipline myself as I did not under the influence of a too trusting and admiring mother." "Probably wouldn't be as career oriented." "I would be less independent." "I would perhaps have been more traditional and I would probably be less independent."

Of those who said their family life would have been *unhappy* if they had had a father, their comments included, "*I think with my parents together it would have been hell. Our life was pretty serene." "It would have been worse with original father. Mean and stupid." "If my mother and father had stayed together, with the friction I understood took place, I probably would have been affected by that." "It would have been hell! I was always passively resisting my father and I was never good enough." "It would have been more difficult because there would have been two disciplinarians." "If my parents had remained married I think my home life would have been very unhappy.*"

A few comments from the 4% who believed their family would have been happier if there had been a father at home follow: "*We would have been a 'closer' family." "Had he not had a dependence on alcohol, I'm sure that our lives would have been secure and happy. He had a great personality and was well liked when sober." "Mother would have been happy.*"

Miscellaneous comments included, ""*I felt that all the bad things that happened to me were because I didn't have a father.*" "*I would not have been abandoned so often.*" "*I might have had male, paternal affection instead of being an object of anger.*"

THE TWO-PARENT FAMILY IS NOT THE BEST

FATHER/MOTHER HAVE TWO PARENTS?

The question asked was, "*When your mother/father was growing up, did he/she have two parents?*" At least about one-quarter of the single parents in this research were conditioned to living in homes with a single parent. They had prior knowledge of the problems and particular difficulties of single parent homes and also had the assurance from their own experience that the task could be done.

FATHER HAVE TWO PARENTS WHEN HE WAS GROWING UP?	
	Yes
Sing. F.	74%

MOTHER HAVE TWO PARENTS WHEN SHE WAS GROWING UP?	
	Yes
Sing. M.	77%

EVALUATING FATHERS

"He accepted the responsibility of raising six children as if we were each precious and special."

The questions asked were, "*Do you consider your father an exceptional man, an average type, other. Please explain,*" and "*Do you consider your mother an exceptional woman, an average type, other. Please explain.*"

EVALUATING YOUR FATHER			
	1	2	3
Bio.	59%	32%	9%
Sing. F.	60%	21%	18%
Step F.	31	42	27
Bio. F. Stp. Gp.	40	28	32%

1. Exceptional
2. Average
3. Other

Single Father Group

Most women in the single father group considered their fathers to be exceptional men. Those who said their fathers were exceptional wrote such comments as, "*Very loving, caring, FUN to be with.*" "*A brilliant but unhappy man.*" "*He raised two children alone.*" "*An exceptional man for raising a child and he* had only a third grade education." "He succeeded in overcoming obstacles some people never could." "He never deserted us and he continued to provide for my grandmother until her death, even after we all grew up and left. She was his former mother-in-law." "He is a very fair man." "His ability to stick it out when times were hard." "I think most women who have a good relationship with their father feel their father is an exceptional man." "My father excels in everything he attempts." "Kind of a mother and father." "He had a very high I.Q. and was exceptionally good with people, except his family." "He was 49 when I was born and he devoted his life to raising two girls." "He instilled good morals in us." "My father was a better nurturer than my mother ever was. Also he made current events 'real' for me." "At age 55 he was raising two young children. This was more typical, even expected of females, but not males at that time." "I have more admiration for him than I can tell you because of all he sacrificed for us kids." "He was a college grad in 1906 [which was unusual then] and built our house. Then he wired it for electricity and the nearest electricity was twenty miles away."

Women in the single father group who said their fathers were *average*, wrote, "*An average man who did an exceptional job with the task laid before him.*" "*For a man of his generation he did the best he could. It just wasn't enough.*" "*He was there to provide, but emotionally distant.*" "*Easily influenced by others and relied on them to help him make decisions.*" "*He's an average guy who did an exceptional job.*" "*He had no friends and was not close to his family. But he was caring during holidays with seeing that cousins who had lost their father were included in our family gatherings." "Average with an exceptional commitment to family. Ability to show caring. Also he is exceptionally honest." "I think he is an average guy who did a few exceptional things." "An average man with an above average pain." "Although he was basically an 'average' type of person, he was more involved with his children than men usually were at that time. He played with us, took us places, etc."*

Women in the single father group who wrote that their fathers did not fit the *'exceptional'* or *'average'* category, checked the answer, "*other.*" Some of the comments in this category included, "*He lacked self-esteem and had an image of failure.*" "*Someone who gave up somewhere along the line. He could have done more with his life.*" "*He was brought up in an orphanage and emotionally damaged by it.*" "*He is a sad, angry man who doesn't know how to be happy.*" "*He was a man with a lot of psychological problems.*" "*He was a good man, an incompetent father.*" "*A totally ECCENTRIC man!*" "*An ordinary man who did things society considers extraordinary in men simply because he was in a position where he HAD to -- just like the majority of single mothers.*" "*Schizoid personality.*" "*He is somewhere between 'exceptional' and 'average.'*" "*He is a great man. He did a lot for his children -- more than a lot of fathers I've seen in my dad's age bracket.*" "*Playboy.*"

THE TWO-PARENT FAMILY IS NOT THE BEST

Biological Parents Group

Almost as many women in the biological parents group as in the single father group considered their fathers to be exceptional, though fewer wrote comments. *"My father is hugely creative! He has made a career which has allowed him to use that creativity." "Cultured, artistic, understanding." "He was always embarrassingly wonderful with my friends." "He never made a lot of money but he was the only one of 13 children to complete college."* "Exceptional especially in comparison with my husband's and child's father from the men of this 'new age.'" "Charming, devoted husband. Above average provider. Not a good father." "Exceptional for having the guts to run his own business; average for playing 'the man of the house,' though it was clear mom wore the pants, i.e. she controlled the finances." "My father came from a cold and unloving family. He spent the first 10 years of marriage (my growing up years) learning to show affection. By the time I was 20 years old I finally got to know my dad. He has learned to show affection and overcome other childhood maladjustments." "He is a brilliant and fine mechanic who can build a house, wire it and plumb it, repair almost anything. He is a community leader." "Moved up from poor background to successful career." "Exceptional in salesmanship -- average as a person."

Of those who checked that they considered their fathers to be an average type, there were no written comments.

Of the women in the biological parents group who checked the category, "*other*," their comments included, "*A man who was less than he should have been.*" "*How can I really respect someone who's so weak.*" "*A narcissistic jerk.*" "*Exceptional in his 'ideals' but not necessarily in their practice.*" "*Average type with exceptional qualities.*" "*He's got a lot of emotional problems.*"

Step Parent Group

More *biological* fathers in this group were considered exceptional than were *step* fathers. Of those who considered their step fathers exceptional, only one woman wrote a comment. "*So strong and caring.*" Of the women who considered their step fathers average, no women wrote comments. And of those who considered them "other" than exceptional or average, the few comments included, "*Never could tell what would get him angry.*" "*He's extremely talented at carpentry and can talk to others casually, but he's so analytical he puts people off.*" "*Perverted.*" "*Unhappy with himself.*" "*A nobody.*"

Of those who considered their *biological* fathers exceptional, comments were, "*He was totally devoted to his family.*" "*Completely self-educated and socially and politically committed to a better world.*" "*He worked very hard to provide for his family financially.*" "*Gentle, non-violent, nurturing, intelligent and well-informed.*"

Of the women who considered their fathers average, only one wrote a comment. "*Average, but he is an exceptionally 'responsible' person.*" The women who said their fathers were neither exceptional nor

THE TWO-PARENT FAMILY IS NOT THE BEST

average wrote, "*He is basically a very self-centered individual, not capable of perceiving or anticipating other's needs.*" "*Very liberal. I don't think most dad's are.*" "*He was emotionally weak.*" "*He is a mean drunk.*"

EVALUATING MOTHERS

"She raised a child alone on very little money and never made me feel poor."

EVALUATING YOUR MOTHER			
	1	2	3
Bio.	57%	22%	21%
Sing. M.	72%	17%	11%
Step M.	24%	20%	48%
Bio. M. St. Grp.	50%	27%	23%

1. Exceptional
2. Average
3. Other

Single Mother Group

Some of the comments from the single mother group who considered their mothers exceptional included, *"Exceptional with limitations re alcohol."* *"She was always there for us no matter what our need."* *"She was not of her time."* *"She maintained a home and supported two children long before it was fashionable."* *"Even though she complained constantly, she endured much."* *"Because she is my mother I hold her in highest regard."* *"She raised children all by herself, sending them both to college."* *"She did more than most mothers."* *"She tested gifted I.Q. She per-

THE TWO-PARENT FAMILY IS NOT THE BEST

severed in seeing her daughters college-educated; she coped with failing health with courage." "As a result of having endured single motherhood." "She fought like crazy for me and herself under very difficult circumstances." "She raised three 'bratty' girls by herself." "My mother went through Hell as a child. Her life was as good as she could make it." "She raised 4 girls in inner city Detroit to all be professionals, by herself." "Exceptionally dear and exceptionally exasperating."

There were only two comments from the 17% of the women in the single mother group who considered their mothers average, and both said the same thing. "When I was growing up I thought she was average. Now, on reflection, I consider her exceptional." "I know now she was more than average."

Twelve percent of the women in the single mother group considered their mothers to be "other" than exceptional or average. Asked to explain, they wrote, "My emotional involvement is too close to simply characterize her." "She has serious problems." "She is weak and self-centered." "She's different. She's always done what she wanted. She never followed the crowd." "A pathetic child." "Not like other mothers." "Can't explain my feelings." "I consider her a very poor mother." "She wants her way."

Biological Parents Group

Though not as many as in the single mother group, most women in the biological parents group considered their mothers to be exceptional. "She is always supportive and cheerful. Everyone loves my mother." "I was always glad she was my mother and not one of my friend's mothers." "She overcame a lot of obstacles, i.e. raising an only child and working in a very competitive occupation." "When my mother died people came to the funeral who hadn't seen her in 40 years." "Loving and determined. Very liberal in politics." "She was a leader with extreme courage. A 'Rock of Gibralter.'" "Top achiever at anything she put her hand to." "She was bright and imaginative and loving. All three gifts crippled by her own fear of success and commitment." "Ahead of her time." "Could have been anything she chose to be." "My mother could do everything well. Even play piano and accordian. She had many lady friends and relatives who loved her a lot."

Of the women in the biological parents group who considered their mothers average, no woman wrote comments. Of the women who wrote that their mothers were "other" than exceptional or average, some wrote, "Well read -- resourceful." "She was no mother material. Below average. My mother always made us feel that we were burdens to her." "Very closed minded." "Cultured, elegant and very artistic in terms of fashion and interior design." "Insecure." "Not happy with self or anyone else." "A woman with emotional problems never treated." "She's got a lot of emotional problems." "She could be exceptional but instead she is less than average." "She wanted the best for me but not for her." "Borderline psychotic." "A conniving, manipulative juveniled disturbed alcoholic." "Tried to accept herself despite limitations." "Overly rigid." "Struggling to be a human." "Sheltered middle class product."

THE TWO-PARENT FAMILY IS NOT THE BEST

Step Parent Group

In the step parent group, one half of the women with *biological* mothers considered their mothers exceptional, but only one-quarter of those with *step* mothers considered their mothers exceptional.

Comments from those who considered their *step* mothers to be exceptional, "*She was a professional who married my father when she was 50. She'd never been married before. She kept her career AND raised us! This in 1959.*" "*Exceptional but not necessarily in a positive way.*" "*Didn't have much intellectual capacity but was her own person and creatively resourceful.*" "*My step mother loved me the same as her own children.*"

The following comments are from the 48% of the step parent group who considered their step mothers to be "other" than exceptional or average. "*She is a very confused person who does not like herself.*" "*I consider her extremely complacent in her role.*" "*She is a 'good' woman who has had a rather hard life and remained gentle and kind.*" "*She was poorly prepared for the role of my father's wife.*" "*An opportunist.*" "*Very different, had few friends.*" "*She was too dependent.*" "*Emotionally unbalanced. Sometimes she could be nice and sometimes mean.*" "*I consider her a sick woman.*" "*Many people in the community thought her wonderful and giving. In a way she was much nicer to strangers because she didn't have to share any of herself.*" "*A hateful woman.*" "*A drunk and crazy lady.*"

Of the 50% of the women in the step parent group with *biological* mothers who considered them to be "*exceptional,*" two comments included "*She was extremely strong when father died. She thought of us first no matter what she did. She was extremely loving and caring and told us often how much we meant to her. Always encouraged us to do our best.*" "*Any woman who could raise four of her own and five step children and still be going strong at 87 is wonderful.*"

THE TWO-PARENT FAMILY IS NOT THE BEST

WAS YOUR CHILDHOOD HAPPY OR UNHAPPY?

"*As children we received no love and that has left scars.*"

To the question of whether or not their childhood had been happy or unhappy, the responses indicate that those raised by both biological parents had a higher percentage of women who considered their childhood happy than the other groups.

In the step parent group there is a significant difference between women raised by *step* mother or *biological* mother. Of those raised by with a biological mother almost twice as many indicated a happy childhood as compared with those raised with a step mother Many with step mothers wrote that their childhood was happy until their father remarried. One in that group wrote, "*The majority of my childhood is just too painful to write about.*"

Another writes, "*Growing up in my house when I was between 7 and 17 was probably the worst time of my life. All I could ever think about was leaving...the situation might not have been so bad if my step mother had not had a child of her own. But with her doing that I was able to see the difference of how she treated my step brother and saw that there was a big difference. My father through all of this was basically unaware of the actual dynamics of the situation, either that, or knew what was happening but just not what to* do about it...This entire situation has made me a very strong individual. My only regret is that my childhood had to end at age 6...."

Was Your Childhood Happy or Unhappy?		
	1	2
Bio.	74%	25%
Sing. F.	64%	36%
Sing. M.	62%	38%
St. M.	37%	63%
St. F.	63%	37%

1. Happy
1. Unhappy

Tolstoy wrote in "*Anna Karenina,*" "*Happy families are all alike; every unhappy family is unhappy in its own way.*"

MISCELLANEOUS COMMENTS

The following letters are printed in their entirety because they present a more complete picture of a variety of childhoods.

Letter Number One - Single Father Group

"*My earliest recollections of being raised by just my father were resentful ones, full of hurt and disbelief. I and my two brothers, one a year older and one a year younger, were being brought up by my mother and grandmother in Southern California. Around my 4th birthday my mother became ill and died. My father, who I did not remember seeing, appeared in our sheltered lives.*

"*I'll never forget the first time I saw him. I was playing jacks on the sidewalk in front of our house and I saw a man carrying a guitar, turn up the walk to our door. He looked angry, his eyes were chips of blue ice. 'That's my house,' I volunteered. He turned to me with the oddest look, 'I know.' I was shocked when my grandmother called me in to tell me that this was my father.*

"*He took us kids and a few household belongings and packed them into a small car and drove us to Alaska. The first few years all run together as a blur. The culture and climate shock were incredible. I remember staying in several different homes for awhile, then my father bought a two room trailer and 2 1/2 acres of property where I lived until I left home* at 17.

GROWING UP

The biggest change that I had trouble adjusting to was the abject poverty. We had no electricity, no running water, no telephone. Our first Christmas was traumatic. My dad simply told us, 'There is no Santa Claus.' We didn't believe him. Until Christmas morning came and there was nothing.

"*Survival was the name of the game. I, being the only female member of the family, cooked and cleaned. My brothers and father chopped wood and shoveled snow. The climate was harsh and my father was a hard and angry man. He showed us no affection at all and drove us to do our chores with curt commands and severe physical punishment.*

"*The positive things that I remember were that the wild woods of Alaska were our playground. When our chores were done we were free to climb trees, build forts, hunt and build snow caves. My father is a very intelligent man and taught us all to read before the 1st grade. All three of us children graduated with honors and have a love of learning that continues on in our lives. We all have successful careers. I am a teacher.*

"*I have always felt different than most women that had mothers. For one thing I am self-sufficient and very independent. I cannot imagine being totally dependent upon a man economically or otherwise. I am 30 years old and have never been married. Introspective thought leads me to believe that this is due to the relationship problems that arise from conflicting sex-role expectations. I EXPECT to be treated equally and find it impossible to defer to men. I have been told that I am too blunt and direct, as one friends put it, 'a pushy broad.'*

THE TWO-PARENT FAMILY IS NOT THE BEST

"When I stop to think of the research you are doing, the questions that come into my head are ones like, Are all women who were raised by just fathers assertive like me? Do they have relationship problems that they feel are directly related to how they were raised? How old were they when they left home? and How affectionate are they with their own children?

"My father never remarried and never dated so I had a very difficult time with boys during adolescence. I had no idea how to behave. I learned 'girl stuff' from my friends at school. I remember for the longest time I thought that I was just the same as my brothers. Sure, we were physically different and did different chores, but I could run as fast, punch as hard and climb higher trees than my brothers. Until puberty we even dressed pretty much the same.

"I believe that how my life is currently has a lot to do with my upbringing. I am a single mother raising a son. I have high aspirations of bringing up the totally non-sexist man. The differences between men and women are to be acknowledged and accounted for but not used as a basis for judgment of worth."

Letter Number Two - Biological Parents Group

"Both of my parents were college graduates but the Great Depression changed their lives and plans. My father was a civil engineer and my mother was a teacher of science in a hospital. Since the economy came to a screeching halt under the Hoover administration, both lost their positions and remained unemployed during my teenage years. The banks

GROWING UP

closed with all of the accumulated wealth of these two professionals. Poverty and poor living conditions left its mark on my parents, my brother and me. Having been raised by land owners of some prestige, my family were proud and resented being discriminated against because we were so lacking in material advantages. Too proud to accept welfare we lived on the edge of disaster. It ruined my mother's health and turned my father into a bitter, problem drinker. This of course affected all of the family in too many ways to describe here.

"*During the Roosevelt presidency my father returned to work but never regained the affluence which he formerly had. The damage to his ego was permanent and his health deteriorated under the stress associated with the "jobs" assigned to him. I carry with me an inferiority complex which was always a handicap in anything I attempted. Poverty and intelligence were not considered possible combinations so my teachers, professors, acquaintances and friends(?) ignored and ridiculed me and all awards, grants, and recognitions which I received. My brother received the same treatment though both of us graduated in the top ten of our classes. Outside the so-called social circles, unable to associate with our intellectual equals, we more or less walked alone, ostracized by our financial equals because we were well-read and spoke correct English. It is difficult to recall all of the insults leveled in our direction. We were all good looking and that was also a disadvantage. Here I interpose a fact of great importance - we were a close family, very supportive of each other. But the scars of our poverty-stricken years are with me yet. In actuality none of us ever recovered*

THE TWO-PARENT FAMILY IS NOT THE BEST

from bankruptcy of the banks which swallowed all of our worldly wealth.

"I went to college on scholarships and loans with moral support from my mother primarily. I did not want to be a teacher but few other opportunities were open to women in 1936. My parents were unable to give me anything but love and encouragement. My mother's health was poor. She had lived under stress for so many years. She had intestinal cancer. All of this affected me to the extent that I was under continual nervous strains, very insecure, and as a result often made premature and disastrous decisions. I absorbed the values of my parents -- hard work, unselfish devotion to duty, to God, country, and family. I am still wary of the growth of the Welfare System.

"Since you are primarily interested in parent-offspring relationships I may have gone off the subject.

"Mine was not a happy or congenial family due to a lack of the necessities of life. We had been wealthy and we did not descend to poverty gracefully -- especially my father. He took his frustrations out on his wife and children. We suffered under his criticisms and impossible demands until he ceased to be a father-figure and became instead a persecutor. By the time I finished college I felt only fear in his presence. Not until he became ill with an incurable malignancy did my fear turn to pity. Never love as it could have been. My mother returned to teaching science in a hospital some years before my father's death and my brother and I continued to support and love her although she never regained her lively, happy disposition. She became a complaining critical person with a pessimistic view of

life. We understood the reason and tried our best to make her happier.

"I believe my relationship with my father was part of the reasons my marriage was not happy. My husband was as domineering and demanding as my father was. Although I like men as friends, the personality of my father interferes with a lasting, peaceful relationship. After my husband's death I remarried another man exactly like my father and my first husband. But for my Lutheran indoctrination I would be better in a relationship not bound by a piece of paper. Early religious dogma rears up and makes that impossible.

"I m rearing a granddaughter whose mother is deceased. My son lives in another town. I am attempting not to lay heavy burdens on her as were laid on me, but my early training often pops up and I fear she will be filled with the same anxieties and hang-ups that I have carried with me all my life. Poverty still dogs the South and I am faced with a one-parent situation. She's an academically gifted student. Her mother died when she was five.

"Your research is of great interest to me."

Letter Number Three - Step Parent Group

"I had a very happy childhood. My step mother has always been very warm and loving. The only difficulties I had as a step child was once a year when I went to stay with my grandmother, my real mother's mother, in a other state. She and my maiden aunt lived together and they constantly talked about 'my mother.'

To me, as a child, this was my step mother that I considered 'my mother.' However they were talking about my real mother. I found that very confusing.

"They also made a lot of negative comments about my step mother when they thought I was sleeping or out of ear-shot. This really bothered me, but I never mentioned this to anyone until years later. I told my father and step mother why I was never happy when I had to visit my grandmother because of these remarks. Other than this, I think that my step mother was a very positive influence in my life and I'm glad my father had the good sense to marry her so soon after my real mother's death."

Letter Number Four - Biological Parents Group

"*I was born on September 21, 1911, literally in a tent, on a little ranch four miles from Rapid City, South Dakota. The reason for the tent birth was that my mother was recovering from tuberculosis, a fairly common disease in those days. There were no T.B. sanatoriums in this part of the country, so she had been 'taking the cure' on her own. She had intended to come to town for my birth, but when the time came, she was afraid to try to climb up into the buggy. My uncle, who had a car, had started from town to meet them, and as he left his office he met the doctor on the stairs and asked if he wanted to ride along. So my mother was attended by her doctor, and he always called me his 'tent baby.'*

"My parents had been married for seven years when I came along. I know I was supposed to be a boy, because they had no girls' names in mind, and I went unnamed for six weeks.

"My parents had met when both were attending the South Dakota School of Mines. My father also taught engineering there for several years. My mother was studying mathematics and drafting, so that she could help her building contractor father with his work. When they were married, she was almost certainly the first married co-ed on campus. In the summers, my father would take summer surveying jobs which would be camping trips. Mother went along, and of course she got to do the cooking for a crew of four or five men. This would have been campfire cooking. She told of one time when one of the 'boys' held an umbrella over her and the griddle while she fried pancakes.

"Probably it was on these summer survey trips that she began to become interested in the field work of the engineering business. Since both she and my father were ahead of their times, she began working with him in the engineering work, and became his chief assistant. She worked as rodman on the surveys, did the courthouse research, and drew the final maps from my father's preliminary maps.

"After my birth, and the bout with T.B. they decided that in order for her to continue the outdoor living that was supposed to be the thing for T.B., they would get into the cattle ranching business. They bought a small ranch in eastern Montana, and when I was two years old they made the trip by wagon and buggy, 250 miles west, where we lived for the next ten years, until I was twelve, when we returned to Rapid City.

THE TWO-PARENT FAMILY IS NOT THE BEST

"During those years on the ranch, there was no school available. I studied at home, my mother doing most of the teaching, although my father took some part in it, especially in math and science. There was no formal school program. I would do my studies while mother did the morning chores, dishes, etc., and directed me. I could easily do a day's school work in an hour, and the rest of the day was free. Sometimes, if it was spring and the weather was nice, we would skip the school work and plant the garden or do other outside work. It was easy to catch upon on the next rainy day.

"We subscribed to many magazines, and our English rancher neighbors passed on the English magazines such as 'Punch,' 'The Tattler,' and 'The Passing Show.' I read a great deal of material that most girls my age would never have looked at, and enjoyed it.

"I had horses, dogs, cats, and all the farm animals, but no playmates since I was an only child and the nearest neighbors with children my age were four miles away, and the only way to get there was by horse and buggy or horseback.

"My parents leaned over backwards to make it possible for me to have playmates, but still, we could not visit the neighbors very often. Four miles is quite a distance by horse, and a visit would take all day. Many times the time could not be spared from the ranch work. We always tried to visit them, usually for overnight on Thanksgiving and Christmas. The neighborhood always had a big picnic on the Fourth of July, often at our place.

"By the time we children were older, like nine or ten, we would ride back and forth on our horses. Without telephones, this must have been very worrisome for our mothers who had no way of knowing if the child had arrived safely or been thrown from the horse and injured. Of course these visits could only be made in good weather, and if there was time to spare from the farm chores.

"I was raised with a combination of a great deal of freedom and a great deal of responsibility.

"I remember, when I was eight, my parents had gone some place for the whole day, taking a lunch. They must have been riding after cattle or building fence, or something of the kind, and figured it would be too tiring a day for me, so I was left alone. About noon two or three cowboys rode in. Cowboys never carried any lunches, so it was accepted custom that you offered a meal to anyone who was at your place near a meal time. I invited them to stay for 'dinner' as the noon meal was called. Of course the boys helped me, but I furnished them a passable meal and was very proud of myself that I had upheld the family honor. At the same time, I had the feeling that after all, I had only done what was expected.

"Sometimes I would be very unhappy when my parents had to leave me alone for most of a day. But I don't think they ever knew it. I realized that sometimes that was just the way it had to be and it would only make things worse if I 'fussed.' But my imagination did conjure up some pretty frightening perils before they would get home. The worst was the fear that something would happen to them and they would never come home.

THE TWO-PARENT FAMILY IS NOT THE BEST

"*Altogether, between the ages of six and twelve, I attended about a total of seven months of school. When we moved back to Rapid City in April of 1924, the school principal didn't really know what to do about me. I was put in a class with my age group, with the idea that if I couldn't keep up, they would keep me in the sixth grade with the class next fall. I went on all the way through high school with that same class, graduating fifth in the class of 100. But it took until about the eleventh grade before I really felt I 'belonged,' because I was so much younger in some ways and so much older in others.*

"*So far as I know, my parents never quarreled. They would argue spiritedly about politics or business or whatever, or debate most any subject, but they did not quarrel. My own marriage was quite similar.*

"*That sounds wonderful, but sometimes now I have a few doubts. My daughters have all been through some stormy marriages, and they tell me that part of their troubles, they think, were due to expecting all marriages to be like what they had seen with their grandparents and parents. But I thought that was the real world. I was just lucky myself and really was never close to any really 'bad' marriages, so how was I supposed to teach my girls to cope?*

"*Probably because my parents had been married for seven years before I was born, they were so closely bonded that I sometimes felt a bit left out, or like a third wheel on their bicycle. None of this was intentional on their part, but they just sort of thought and moved in unison. I was sort of separate from them, and always felt it a little.*

> "*An only child often has the full burden of elderly parents. My father lived to be 86. My mother lived to age 101. Her last few years we lived together.*"

Letter Number Five - Single Mother Group

The following is a letter from a single mother to her daughter who is a respondent in this research:

"*All the little things you do to brighten my days now and then, definitely do not go unnoticed.*

"*I hope you don't think, by my silence, that I am not grateful for your thoughtfulness. I am always so touched by it, that I sometimes don't know how to respond, so I do and say nothing. However, my thoughts are always with you, and with all my children for that matter, at so many different times of the day and in so many different ways. Each of you are special to me, because in my heart you are all special children. You have had to endure with me, through me, and because of me, in so many situations through the years, that I can hardly believe sometimes how great you all turned out. But understand one thing; everything I have ever done or tried to do, no matter how critical, (and I am critical) has been done because I love you all so much and wanted to bring out the best in all of you, the best that I know is there. I haven't always gone about things in the right manner, this I am aware of. I am too critical, harsh and overbearing at times and I always realize it afterwards. But I've gotten a little better over the years and now I think it's time to cut the cord and let you all be the adults I know you are. Although I always want to be here, if needed for all of you.*

THE TWO-PARENT FAMILY IS NOT THE BEST

"*Just know that I love you, care what happens to you, and there isn't a day that goes by that I don't think of you and your family. My children will always be with me. You always have been and you always will be. Love, Mom.*"

Letter Number Six Step Parent Group

"My Norwegian immigrant father, ten years older than mother was killed by a train while driving to town to get gas. I was only one year old then and started to walk the day of the accident. Though we found in recnt years that he was born out of wedlock so I've wondered how my life would have been different had he lived. He was more educated than my mother, attending boarding schools, etc. Came to start a new life in America. He was a city boy, but was pushed into farming as that's what everyone else did in the host family. He was an avid reader and traveled the United States before settling down.
"I was the third child which made me more contented. My older sister had a lot of hang-ups, was sickly with bronchitis all her life, never married, but is still living and enjoying what she can with her breathing problems. I never envied her in any way except she received better grades and appeared smarter. I was never an intellectual even though I graduated from college. We were five years apart, but outside of paper dolls from the Sears catalog, we did little together.

"I played mostly with my younger brother, but I don't remember much of what we did but swing from a big tree and wander around our property.

"I never felt my step father was a real father, as we seldom talked. He did not give any opinions or discipline me. Mother had complete control of what we did or didn't do. He must have given us demonstrative love as preschoolers or early grades as he loved children, but I never remember him putting his arms around me. I don't remember doing that either.

"School was always a pleasant experience except in third grade when I couldn't see the blackboard and cried when I was called on. Never received glasses until college. I did not do much reading through the years until college.

"I don't remember any hunger, unhappiness or desperation except the one episode of this old neighbor grandpa who took me to his house and exposed himself to me. I told my husband about it before we were married and I think I cried.

"My step father was always supportive to my mother and all of us children. I do remember several times when he was depressed on pay day. The pay check was so small, but so were our expenses. He did have a car which helped his ego. He was very quiet, got up every morning and made himself a hearty breakfast which he still does at 93. He never allowed things to bother him which I feel is why he has lived so long. My mother, step father and younger brother moved to California after my college graduation. My step father worked in a paper mill and my mother in garment factories. They always rented until the last 15 years before she died at 83."

THE TWO-PARENT FAMILY IS NOT THE BEST

Letter Number Seven - Single Mother Group

"My mother, who is dead now, told me a few things about raising two daughters alone. The strongest thing I remember her saying is, 'I always tried to appear STRONG.' And she was, but I sense now it was a cover-up for her being scared and often depressed. Getting money was hard for her as she had no help from our father. It was for her a mixed bag of fear, insecurity and depression, and joy over our growing up and our accomplishments. She said to me in regards to raising us, once when she was old, 'I did all right, didn't I?' I said, 'You sure did.' I miss her a lot."

Letter Number Eight - Single Mother Group

The following is a letter from a single mother of one of the respondents in this research:

"Having been a single parent for twenty years (widowed) has not been easy. I think the hardest part was the total and immense responsibilities, once being shared by two people, were now having to be handled by one. It was a heavy job for a 27 year old with a 4 year old child. All decisions, responsibilities, emotional stability (for both me and my child) financial concerns, and taking on the role of mother and father were now up to me. Devastating, to say the least!

"My great fortune, as I look back, was my child. She made most of the above an easy chore. She was good in school (both grade school and college), never boy-crazy, never insisted on having what everyone else had, never got into the drug or alcohol scene, learned *how to make decisions concerning her life, and since college has done extremely well in her profession.*

"How did I/she survive? We loved, respected and supported each other!"

Letter Number Eight - Single Mother Group

The following is a letter from a single mother of one of the respondents in this research:

"About raising a child alone. I never gave it a thought. It was my responsibility. It never occurred to me that I was doing anything unusual. There was one other woman I worked with who had children she was raising alone. I never had to worry about you because I had such faith and trust in you. I can never remember worrying about what you were doing. There was less danger in those days in the 1930's. I knew all your friends (good Catholic girls). Financially we got along because our food was taken care of (she worked as a waitress in the city's best 'tearoom'). Our apartment cost $25.00 a month."

Letter Number Ten - Biological Parents Group

"My childhood was definitely one of keeping quiet and trying to stay out of trouble. And I largely succeeded at that.

"My father was a very troubled man. I believe he was both physically and mentally ill. He was the ultimate in changeable. One moment he could be laughing and joking with you, the next screaming and striking out. More than once, I experienced the 'unexpected

THE TWO-PARENT FAMILY IS NOT THE BEST

slap.' You are sitting calmly, say something that in no way can be construed as anything other than childish babble, and from nowhere this hand slaps you across the face. It was truly the most disconcerting thing I've ever experienced.

"My brother was beaten over the head with my favorite doll one evening because he was too noisy. I was forced to sit at the breakfast table with a bowl of cereal turned over on my head, the milk and corn flakes pouring down my body because of some minor misdemeanor. Once, while crying over some punishment, my father took me into the bathroom and washed my face with a cloth, told me to stop crying and that everything was all right; when I continued long-drawn out sobs that I couldn't prevent, he slapped me across the face, telling me to stop. I'd sob, he'd slap -- and I really couldn't control myself, even by holding my breath. It was horrible.

"And, somehow, my father was always able to make his anger your fault. If you were just better, you see -- Daddy doesn't like to get mad at you but when you do this, he just has no choice. Do you promise to be better? Now stop that crying, now stop it, DO YOU HEAR ME -- stop it!

"At times, he was the most pleasant of men. He'd tell stories, buy you a surprise, joke. But you never knew when these things would happen -- or how long they would last. And that engendered deep feelings of suspicion; you absolutely couldn't trust him.

"We had a modest income, but instead of new school shoes, etc., etc., my father indulged himself with expensive toys -- photo processing equipment, jewelry-making sets, stamp collections, coin collections, rock *polishing equipment -- and lost interest in them within a week or two and left them sitting there collecting dust. Meanwhile our furniture was dilapidated and we wore hand-me-downs. Occasionally, my father got so furious that he tore up all the furniture in the living room. He broke the coffee table in two once, oddly enough using a crutch that he was forced to walk with after his leg was amputated. I know his physical problems were frustrating but to break an entire room of furniture always seemed to me a stupid solution.*

"*I always felt much older than my parents; my father was a baby and my mother seemed willing to put up with it, afraid to strike out on her own. And that used to infuriate me. But I hated the idea of anger so much -- and besides would have been punished by my parents for displaying any of it -- that I secretly tried to hurt myself, twisting my ankles in the hope of breaking them.*

"*My father forced my mother to work, and she was made to turn over her entire pay check to him. Occasionally, he gave her $5.00 and she'd walk with us down to the dime store and use it to buy coloring books for us and something pretty -- usually some shiny piece of blown glass -- for herself. It hurts me to think that a $1.98 piece of purple glass was the only pretty thing in her life.*

"*Oddly enough, I still consider my father the weak parent in my family and my mother the strong one. He was the child; she was the forgiving adult. She was strong to put up with all that without killing him. My mother is the most incredibly loving person I've ever met -- optimistic, cheerful, willing to do absolutely horrible jobs and still keep a sense of humor.*

THE TWO-PARENT FAMILY IS NOT THE BEST

"Because she was crippled, no one would hire her for the office work she was trained to do because 'it didn't look nice' to have a person on crutches in your office where everyone could see. So she was forced to do what was really manual labor, lifting huge pots of potatoes, standing in a hot kitchen, picking up loads of dishes in her work as a cook. My father's jobs were easy, involving checking on machinery and occasionally helping supervise a load of ice going onto a train's vegetable car. So he was soft and flabby; my mother was hard and muscular, strong. Daddy got sick, Mama never did.

"I told her when I was a teenager I wished she'd leave him; she told me that he would reveal to a court certain secrets that would mean she'd never have custody of us kids. And she said she loved him and he really wasn't that bad. I made her cry and she said he was a good man, he really was. I just didn't understand. She was right; I didn't. I knew that if any man ever tired to hurt me when I was grown up, he'd regret it. And no man ever has. I don't know if I became strong and honest because of my childhood -- or whether I've just become a good judge of men. But most of my experiences with men have been happy ones, especially my marrige which is more truly an equal relationship than any I've ever seen.

"I loved my father and I knew that he died at a time when I was really rebelling and finally getting away. His plans were for me to get a teaching degree -- 'you'll never make it in journalism because you're too shy' -- and then come home and live with him. I could save all my money and every summer take them on *wonderful vacations. My entire being rebelled at that one.*

"*Odd, but when I left home, I was frightened that my father would eventually kill my mother because I wouldn't be there to prevent it. (I'd become adept at having hysterics just when he was about to REALLY hurt her -- knife at throat, etc -- in time to stop whatever horror was going on. I really thought they relied on me to keep them from going any further into violence. They survived. So did I.*

"*But I feel scared by my childhood, afraid of too much. I feel I've made progress in dealing with my fear, but it has been a hard thing to handle. I sometimes wonder what my relationship with my father would be if he'd lived. He died when I was 22, just graduated from college and on my first job as a reporter, doing quite well, despite his attempts to destroy my confidence and make me come home.*

"*Would we have worked some sort of relationship out? Would I understand him better? Would I have ever had a conversation with him in which I wasn't afraid to say anything? I liked to think so. I've grown up and I can only wish that he would have too.*"

Letter Number Eleven - Single Mother Group

"*My mother is unable to write but I spoke with her about your project and what, in her view, it was like bringing up children alone.*

"*She said 'it was hard, so hard,' and that she doesn't know how she did it. She spoke mostly of the work, the pure physical drudgery, the never having*

THE TWO-PARENT FAMILY IS NOT THE BEST

enough and how it limited her life and profited ours. She believes that it was all for us, so that we could have a 'better life' than hers. And she takes what is in part a justifiable pride in the fact that we are 'better off' than she was. This pride obscures the fact that we grew up in a time of greater social and economic opportunity than she did though.

"She remembers small things she did - a certain dress she bought me, a particular shirt for my brother and how we were clothed 'as nice as anybody.' And since all memory is selective, I never discourage these fictions. But I sometimes listen in astonishment at how our memories conflict. And yet both versions contain truths. Yes, she bought us dresses and shirts, never failing to remind us how unworthy we were of such strenuous efforts on her part.

"So on another track, I asked her if she ever had any fun. 'If I did, I don't remember it,' she said. And I'm sorry she doesn't remember it, because it cost my brother and me so much emotionally when she left us alone and afraid at night while she went out with her friends. I'm sorry that neither she nor we profited from those excursions.

"Perhaps for her the comfort comes in this benign 'forgetting' of what would otherwise be unendurable. For me it comes in forgiving. I don't know how it comes for my brother.

"Last year my mother was very ill, seemingly near death, so I called my brother. He said he wouldn't come, not then nor whenever she does die. 'I got out of all that years ago,' he told me -- whatever that means.

"After hanging up, I remembered once when we were talking about our mother and I mentioned that *one of the few truly warm memories I have of her was that of watching her daily ritual of tossing her scraps to the birds. And I was dumbfounded by the torrent of abuse this unleashed in him. He too remembered it vividly. He saw her lavishing concern on something he considered insignificant while denying her children the same. Funny how differently two people can interpret an event. I later wrote the following poem.*

> *Each morning*
> *my mother, who hoarded*
> *her emotions like rare coins,*
> *tossed the scraps*
> *of her meager breakfast*
> *to the waiting birds.*
> *As a child, I spied upon this*
> *unsuspected tenderness,*
> *hoping to tap*
> *its congealing vein.*
>
> *Each day*
> *my mother struggled with*
> *the chronic ills of a world*
> *gone out of control, her*
> *terrible grief welling up*
> *to daunt our relentless needs.*
> *And yet she kept her shoulder*
> *to that awful wheel*
> *when others failed.*
>
> *Each year*
> *my mother grows more remote,*
> *a large drowsing child,*

THE TWO-PARENT FAMILY IS NOT THE BEST

*the best and worst that she can imagine
being past. And still I want
to cup within my hands this little
that is left, a small candle
against the wind.*

PART II

THE PRESENT

How have the women in this research fared in their adult lives? What was their educational achievement, what are their occupations, their marital or live-in status, their physical condition, their relationships with other women, and with men, their assessment of their personality, attitudes about equality, and about mothering and fathering? Is there a difference among groups? But first, a few demographics.

When the participants volunteered for this research they ranged in age from 18 to 88. The median age was 35 and the average age was 39. Most are caucasian with Western European nationalities though there also are blacks, Asians, Native Americans, and Hispanics.

Half have children and half do not. Approximately one-fourth of women in all groups have

THE TWO-PARENT FAMILY IS NOT THE BEST

grandchildren. Most grew up in the eastern part of the United States. The second largest group grew up in the midwest. The fewest number grew up on the western part of the United States. Several women grew up in Canada and several outside the United States.

One third of the single father group and the step parent group grew up in towns with a population of under 10,000. The situations, opinions and feelings of the respondents from all four groups follow in more detail.

EDUCATION

Most women in this research are well educated. Over seventy percent of all women in the study attended college, if only for one year. About one-fifth of women in all groups have graduate degrees, with little difference in percentages among the four groups.

It could be that people who are motivated to volunteer in a research project such as this, have a better than average education, or that magazines in which the advertisements for volunteers for this research were placed, appeal to women with higher education. The magazines which brought the highest percentage of respondents were *Ms.*, *Psychology Today*, and *Mother Jones*, which carry thought-provoking social or scientific articles. Though advertisements were placed in *The National Enquirer, True Story, Modern Romance* and others, to achieve a balance in the sample, not as many women responded from those advertisements as they did from the magazines first mentioned.

Because the highest percentages of women *who graduated from college* are in the single father group and the step parent group, it could be conjectured that when children grow up in a situation where they are expected to "*go bad*," as many women mentioned, such as the girl growing up without a mother, or with a step parent, these girls might accept the negative remarks about them as challenges and proceed to excell as a way of "*showing them.*" Then again, this is simply conjecture.

THE TWO-PARENT FAMILY IS NOT THE BEST

Education

	1	2	3	4	5	6	7
Bio	6%	20%	16%	9%	22%	7%	20%
Sing F	6%	18%	13%	13%	27%	3%	21%
Sing M	7%	22%	11%	14%	22%	5%	18%
Step	0%	14%	12%	14%	33%	4%	22%

1. Less than 12th grade
2. 12th grade
3. One year college
4. Two years college
5. Four years college
6. Graduate work
7. Graduate degree

Subject Major in College

	1	2	3	4	5	6	7
Bio	45%	13%	10%	19%	10%	1%	0
Sing F	49%	1%	10%	25%	11%	4%	0
Sing M	48%	22%	15%	1%	10%	1%	1%
Step	44%	8%	11%	8%	17%	5%	4%

1. Social Science
2. Liberal Arts
3. Business, Law
4. Education
5. Health
6. Science
7. Other

OCCUPATION

Most women in this research are employed in the trades, such as sales clerk, office worker, beautician. Many are in managerial positions, several are students, housewives, retired, or unemployed. The highest percentage of women in professional positions are in the single father group and the step parent group.

Occupation							
	1	2	3	4	5	6	7
Bio	16%	16%	37%	4%	4%	12%	12%
Sing F	29%	13%	28%	2%	9%	14%	5%
Sing M	18%	18%	37%	1%	10%	10%	7%
Step	29%	24%	14%	2%	2%	14%	14

1. Professional
2. Managerial
3. Trades
4. Laborer
5. Housewife
6. Student
7. Other

THE TWO-PARENT FAMILY IS NOT THE BEST

	Yearly Income				
	1	2	3	4	5
Bio	29%	27%	25%	16%	1%
Sing.F	39%	29%	17%	10%	4%
Sing M	35%	34%	20%	7%	4%
Step	35%	18%	18%	22%	2%

1. 0 - $9000.
2. $10,000.- $19,000.
3. $20,000. - $29,000.
4. $30,000. - $49,000.
5. $50,000. - $100,000.

THE PRESENT

MARITAL STATUS

The marital status of the women in this research follows in the chart below.

Marital Status	1	2	3	4	5	6
Bio	36%	38%	7%	17%	2%	1%
Sing F	39%	36%	8%	13%	2%	1%
Sing M	37%	36%	6%	16%	4%	1%
Step	41%	22%	6%	27%	2%	2%

1. Married
2. Single
3. Widowed
4. Divorced
5. Separated
6. Co-habiting

PHYSICAL CONDITION

The Dept. of Health & Human Services Scale for Acceptable Weight Range for women was used to classify respondents as to whether or not they were overweight or underweight. If the respondent was more than ten pounds over the top weight related to a specific height, she was classified as overweight. Women were considered underweight if they were ten pounds or more under the lowest weight in a specific height category.

Physical Condition			
	1	2	3
Bio	3%	62%	32%
Sing F	1%	76%	21%
Sing M	1%	79%	18%
Step	0%	67%	31%

1. Underweight
2. Average weight
3. Overweight

One woman in the single father group wrote that when she saw a therapist she was told her eating disorder was the result of having grown up too fast and being a *'mini'* wife who could never do anything good enough to suit Dad, and that she had been abandoned three times, once when her mother died, once when her Dad couldn't cope with her, and the third time when, 14 years after her mother's death, her father remarried.

If this research were to be repeated with other groups, questions about childhood illnesses should be asked.

ORGANIZATIONS

Categorizing organizations as *social, political, women's, peace and environment, homosexual, educational, religious, union or work*, most women belonged to union or work related, women's or social organizations, though many belonged to the other organizations as well. Many women belonged to more than one organization, indicating that the respondents were active, interested women.

Organizations							
	1	2	3	4	5	6	7
Bio	13%	8%	11%	5%	13%	23%	27%
Sing F	10%	8%	13%	2%	24%	16%	27%
Sing M	7%	12%	16%	6%	7%	21%	31%
Step	14%	4%	18%	4%	18%	18%	24%

1. *Social*
2. *Political*
3. *Women's*
4. *Peace and Environment*
5. *Work and Union*
6. *Misc., education, gay, religious*
7. *None*

POLITICAL PARTY

When asked about their political party, most indicated they are democrats. The number of women who pointed out they don't vote, was highest among women in the single mother group. This is interesting in that it is the single mother group which has the highest percentage of women involved in political organizations.

Women who said they didn't vote wrote, "*I choose not to vote.*" "*Not politically involved.*" "*I vote for NO MEN!*" "*I do not wish to participate in politics. I'm unhappy with a democratic system of government.*" "*Politics don't make a difference.*" "*I do not vote. I will when I see someone worth voting for.*" "*I believe in anarchy which in its pure form is a system of government in which all members of society are equally and immediately responsible for all aspects of society's functioning.*" "*I don't like politics so I've never voted. It doesn't interest me at all.*"

Many women in all groups grew up being treated equally in their homes, only to find that educational, governmental, religious and business instiutions do not treat women equally with men. They are then left with several choices. Women can learn to accommodate the prejudice, they can try to work to eliminate the prejudice, or they can revolt against it in their own way. For more women in the single mother group than in other groups, it appears that they might be revolting against *the system* in the one way open to them at this time.

THE TWO-PARENT FAMILY IS NOT THE BEST

	Political Party			
	1	2	3	4
Bio	12%	59%	22%	4%
Sing F	15%	58%	22%	2%
Sing M	17%	54%	17%	9%
Step	16%	61%	14%	2%

1. Republican
2. Democrat
3. Other
4. Don't vote

THE PRESENT

RELATIONSHIPS WITH MEN

"How has being brought up by a single father/mother/biological parents/step parents affected your relationships with men?"

More women in the single father group have good relationships with men than the others groups, followed by women in the biological parents group. Most women in the single mother group have negative reltionships with men. Almost half of the women in the step parent group have poor relationships with men.

One woman in the single mother group wrote that she had no positive relationships with men while growing up. *"Saw mother's boyfriends as sexual threat and feared physical harm."* One in the single father group wrote, *"I get along well with both men and women. I don't gossip, compete, and don't use 'feminine wiles.'"*

THE TWO-PARENT FAMILY IS NOT THE BEST

	Relationships with Men			
	1	2	3	4
Bio	0%	29%	29%	42%
Sing F.	6%	20%	23%	51%
Sing M.	2%	68%	22%	8%
Step	11%	46%	18%	21%

1. Hostile
2. Negative
3. Difficult
4. Positive

When 68% of the women raised by a single mother have negative relationships with men, compared with the considerably lower percentages of the other three groups, it would seem there are some problems in raising girls who have little or no experience with men. Not only does the girl have few opportunities to associate with men, but often her mother has had bitter experiences of desertion and non-payment of child support. *Her* negative attitude about men is apt to affect her daughter's attitude and subsequent relationship with men.

Women in the single mother group wrote as, "*I seriously feel that if I had had a father, my relationships with men would have been better. My mother taught me how to be independent, self-supporting, strong-willed and how to be dominant. I have an emptiness inside and I really don't know how to get rid of it. I feel cheated and lost.*" "Men have always been

THE PRESENT

somewhat of a mystery to me. I tend to put them on a pedastal. I believe I am looking for my father."

RELATIONSHIPS WITH WOMEN

"How has being brought up by a single father/mother/biological parents/step parents affected your relationships with women?"

While most women growing up without a father have negative relationships with men, most women growing up without a mother have good reltionships with women.

It is possible that the girl without a mother has more opportunity to be associated with women as she is growing up. Most elementary teachers are women. Mothers in the neighborhoods often fill in for absent mothers. The girl who grows up without a father, however, has fewer opportunities to associate with men. There are few male elementary teachers, and men in the neighborhoods do not generally take on a fatherly manner for fatherless children.

More women in the step parent group than in the other groups said their relationships with women were hostile.

	Relationship With Women				
	1	2	3	4	5
Bio	2%	7%	19%	72%	0%
Sing F.	2%	16%	26%	56%	0%
Sing M.	2%	20%	9%	73%	2%
Step	6%	24%	29%	29%	7%

1. Hostile
2. Negative
3. Difficult
4. Positive
5. Benign

Relationships in The Workplace

"Has being brought up by a father/mother/biological parents/step parent made it easier or more difficult in your interaction in the work place?"

All groups wrote that how they were brought up had made it easier in their place of employment.

However, one woman in the single father group wrote about the difficult. *"I feel that being raised by my father has made it more difficult for me in the work place in that there are stereotypical roles for young women in office situations which is where I supported myself through school. Most men (and*

THE TWO-PARENT FAMILY IS NOT THE BEST

women too) expect a woman in my situation to play the 'cutsey little floosy,' the exact kind of woman I abhor and certainly have no desire to behave like. Many men are threatened by women who don't buy this set of rules. My father had no respect for the office 'Baby Doll,' and did not raise me to behave that way."

SEXUAL PR[EFERENCE]

"If you are hetero[sexual, to what do you at]tribute this?" "If you are ho[mosexual, to what do you at]tribute this?"

Most women in [all groups attributed their] heterosexual sexual preference to [...] *"genes."* The category with the next highest percentages was in the category of *"I like men."* Several women in all groups said their preference was based on Biblical teaching, or *"Don't know,"* or *"Never knew there were other choices," "Societal," "Good male/female relationship at home," "Women do not appeal to me as sexual partners." "Seeking a father in lover," "No mother at home," "T.V. and romance novels."* Some said their sexual preference was *"not attributable."*

In response to the question, *"If you are homosexual, to what do you attribute this?"* Many women answered, *"Natural," "Genes," "Don't know," "Sexism," "Fear abuse of men's power," "Need a nurturing, gentle woman," "Freedom of choice," "Sexual abuse as child," "Genetic. Strong female role model," "Nurturing relationships with women all my life and awesome women role models," "I am a lesbian and prefer women but I don't hate men!" "I don't know. Men are too distant and bossy." "How I processed men and their actions as a child." "I believe it is attributable to some not yet identified biological/chemical/genetic factor." "An overwhelming need for 'gentleness.'" "I seek someone who can truly identify with me as a*

*a patriarchal society. Sexual, physical, emo-
...buse of my father. Seeking love of my mother."*

A few women in the single father group thought their homosexuality was the result of seeking love from the mother they didn't have, but just as many said they did not believe it had anything to do with whether or not they didn't have a mother. As one wrote, "*I don't agree at all that parental influence is responsible for a person's sexual preference or identity. I don't feel I 'turned to a woman' as a sub-conscious way to replace the woman I lost early in life (mother)*". And another, "*I used to think it was because I was raised by a man, but now I think it is biological.*"

One woman from the biological parents group wrote, "*I live as a heterosexual but I have bisexual leanings which I think everybody has to varying degrees. I admit it more than other people because I am a feminist because my conscience and common sense tell me feminism is right and because boys were very mean to me when I was growing up. Also, when I was growing up, maleness was considered the norm. Therefore, movies and TV shows operated as if all their viewers were male. When it came to sexual things, I was confused when I was young and many of my girlfriends were too. We thought that we were supposed to be thrilled and excited when we would see a naked or half-naked woman, or a woman as a sex symbol. We never thought of men sexually because they were never shown as sexual to females. This confused thinking has continued somewhat into my adult life.*"

SEXUAL PREFERENCE

	1	2	3
Bio	89%	9%	2%
Sing F.	83%	13%	4%
Sing M.	92%	4%	4%
Step	92%	6%	2%

1. Heterosexual
2. Lesbian
3. Bisexual

BECAUSE OF PARENTAL SITUATION, ARE YOU DIFFERENT?

"I grew up believing my step mother was my mother. When she left I felt abandoned for the second time. It took many years to be comfortable with other women and often I am still uneasy."

Though it seems apparent that the women from the single parent group and the step parent group did not *appear* to be different to their friends and others when they were growing up, they did have strong *feelings* about being different. The questions were asked, *"Do you feel because you were raised by a single mother/single father/step parent that you are different?"* If so, *"Different in what way?"*

Three-fourths of the women from the single father group, and over half of the single mother and step parent group said they felt different.

THE PRESENT

BECAUSE OF FAMILY SITUATION, ARE YOU DIFFERENT?	
	Yes
Sing.F.	76%
Sing.M.	65%
Step	53%

DIFFERENT IN WHAT WAY?"				
	1	2	3	4
Sing.F.	47%	12%	14%	26%
Sing.M.	30%	25%	10%	35%
Step	14%	19%	24%	43%

1. Masculine Traits
2. Feminine Traits
3. Can't Tell
4. Sense of Loss or lack of something.

Single Father Families

Comments included, *"Orientation toward a career may be the result of having been brought up by a father." "Not as apt to fall into a female role." "More efficient -- independent." "More matter-of-fact, clearer thinking." "Not as concerned with sexual boundaries. If I had a mother I might have developed more traditional feminine traits and not developed the masculine traits." "More independent, creative, interested in*

THE TWO-PARENT FAMILY IS NOT THE BEST

people than in family. Have more platonic friends among men." "More sensitive to what my daughter needs in a mother." "Very self-reliant. I can be aggressive and opinionated, sexually free. No double standard." "I would have learned more feminine skills." "I find it difficult to be close to women." "I tend to be a mother to the world and try to help everyone I can." "Less able to share and express feelings." "Have both masculine and feminine traits which are sometimes advantageous but also can be conflicting."

"Learned to be independent and self-sufficient in my young years because we didn't have a mother to run and cry to. My brother and I were very close because of this." "I think I understand men better than the average woman does." "Self-reliant, enjoy company of men, confident of my femininity." "Independent and self-confident. Had opportunity, incentive and encouragement. Would attempt almost any task. I was often my own teacher." "I don't fit in with the average woman." "Allowed me to build self-confidence and try for the top." "Perhaps I am happier." "I'm more direct. Frills are not necessary. Socially inept." "I have had special problems with men and intimacy." "Bolder, not easily intimidated, love sports and rugged outdoors activities." "Have a more masculine than feminine attitude." "Never experienced female 'ritual' experience -- like putting on eye make-up." "Shy in other people's family situations. I lack a certain confidence. Hard to explain." "Can't explain. I feel different but can't explain it." "More aggressive and head-strong." "Can't stand 'helpless' little women." "More self-reliant, independent because I was mostly left alone to handle my upbringing myself." "Never learned to be what society

THE PRESENT

considers feminine. Have masculine traits and gestures. Need to be accepted and have to prove myself." "Probably would not be homosexual." "Learned to rely on myself and know myself very well."
"I'm a fighter. Possess masculine skills." "Probably have male 'imprinting,' acting like a man." "Independent, strong, more so than people raised in two parent families." " More forthright and less saddled with how a woman ought to be." "I don't like the housework roles I have to do." "Don't have a real understanding of the 'traditional' family." "Content to be on my own. Don't need a man as much as other women." "Independent. Protect myself emotionally." "Independent, not easily put down by a male dominated society." "More independent, but don't tolerate women very well." "Stronger bond with father than other women have with theirs." "Not feminine enough. Hate housework." "Don't feel feminine, don't gossip, not emotional or don't show it." "Concerned with money and the future too much." "Relate easier to men, competitive with women." "Identify less with traditional sex roles." "I have a different outlook on life."

Single Mother Families

Comments include: *"My entire perspective is different than people who weren't raised by a [single] woman." "I have more understanding of children. I'm quite independent. Also a man completes my life. He does not make my life." "I would probably have more masculine traits and I would not be as sensitive as I*

THE TWO-PARENT FAMILY IS NOT THE BEST

am. I might have learned how to be stronger emotionally." "Forced me to realize life isn't a fairy tale. But it helped me grow." "I was never told to ask a man for permission so I grew up not realizing men had as much power as they do." "I'm the only woman I've met who doesn't want to marry. In some ways I am very masculine." "I'm not balanced in knowledge of men and women's attitudes. Men seem like another species. Women' don't seem to need men for much and can get along fine without them."

"I feel that I can juggle family and career." "I am different but not in a negative way. True, I have problems, but I'm also a strong person and have grown toward being a better person through my experiences." "A greater sense of independence." "Sad, regretful, empty, missing an essential experience, more difficulty in getting along with others, especially women." "Different perspective. Less reliance on males." "I seek approval of men and need them to need me." "I'm independent. My mother is sort of both mom and dad so I've probably both roles in me. I don't know which role is which or which made me stronger." "I don't accept sexism." "Simply. I am more independent." "I was assertive long before I knew what that word meant! For me it was survival." "My family relationships were closer than in two parent families." "Half the intended equation is missing. I appreciate value of FAMILY." "I am more independent. With two parents I may have been spoiled more." "I don't know how to have any kind of relationship with a man other than sexual." "I am self-sufficient." "I've only had one viewpoint about things. I sometimes feel I do not know exactly what a father does." "I'm more self-reliant and more able to

THE PRESENT

take on responsibility." "I felt like an outcast because I had to grow up very quickly." "I think I've done things to get male attention/affection that I wouldn't have done had I had a father." "I think we are much more dependent on ourselves. Some men dislike this." "I am not opportunistic, have no idea what it is like to exert 'feminine wiles.' I am very emotional and very intuitive. I have a highly developed sensitivity. Artistic."

"My view of the world and my place in it is more defined, clearer, I know myself better." "I hurt in different ways." "I feel that I have been deprived of something important in life." "I've missed half the world -- fathers and brothers." "We seem to be more mature." "In spite of brothers, countless boyfriends, fiances, husbands and cousins and two sons, men are mysterious to me. I think males and females learn about each other in their parents' home and their inter-relationships." "Even after raising a son I don't have an understanding about men." "Less confident than most. Needed a male figure to identify with for security, love, etc." "More ability to cope with stress. I am a survivor." "I didn't have a male role model so I didn't have positive expectations toward men." "I don't feel 'well-rounded.' No role model for being part of a 'couple.'" "I have no role model as a father to base my relationships with men in my home."

Step Parent Families

Comments from the women in the step parent group who were raised with a *step* mother and *biological* father include:"*I'm not sure if it was just that*

THE TWO-PARENT FAMILY IS NOT THE BEST

I was raised and abused by a step mother that made me different." "More adaptable to situations." "I feel that I grew up faster than my peers. I was forced to reevaluate my relationship with my family at an early age." "I am different than I would have been if I had stayed in my Grandmother's home." "Difficult to establish friendships, inferiority, poor self-esteem." "The different standard in our family for my sister and me led me to feel that we were different. There was a strong underlying message that we were inferior." "I am more aware of how important love given to children is. I am able to better see the type of mother/person I don't want to be. I have more empathy for one-parented children." "No real love in growing up." "Less secure than people with both parents."

Comments from women in the step parent group raised with their *biological* mother and *step* father include: *"I never got the emotional foundation I needed." "My independence. I'm more careful in my choice of male companions, friends as well as lovers." "I felt left out. My step father constantly told me, 'You got those ideas from your side of the family.'" "Less intimidated by men than I would have been only exposed to my family." "I might have been different had I known my father's family and felt that I had an identity with them." "I have a difficult time with male relationships." "We were never really a family." "I know that it's not blood that creates the bonds."*

Throughout this research, women in the single father group have written that they believed they had stronger masculine traits than other women. Yet a comparison of the four groups with the answers in the Gough Adjective Check List, Masculine Attributes Scale, does not indicate that many more women in the single father group scored higher in the Masculine Attributes Scale than women in other groups. In the single father group, 64% scored 50% or higher in the Masculine Attributes Scale, but this was closely followed by 61% of the women in the biological parents group scoring the same, and 52% for both the single mother group and the step parent group.

One has to remember that these are *stereotypical* concepts. While the word "*assertive*," for instance, can be used to describe many women, it is a word *stereotypically* applied to men. Stereotypes are gradually changing, but in the Gough Adjective Check List the words refer to those attributes which currently best describe *stereotypes* of an attribute. Some women may be offended by words ascribed to feminine and masculine attributes, feeling that these reflect sexist attitudes. It will be well to keep in mind that words in the descriptive scales refer to those which are accepted as the stereotypes. It is the stereotypes which feminists are attempting to change.

Stereotypes are gradually changing, but in the Gough Adjective Check List the references are to those attributes which the designers of the scale believed still currently, for the most part, describe the *stereotype* of an attribute.

The Description of the Scales of the Adjective Check List refers to the Masculine Attributes Scale as follows: "*The interpersonal and descriptive implications of the Masculine Attributes scale are quite clear for both sexes. High-scorers will be seen as ambitious and assertive, impatient when blocked or frustrated, quick to take the initiative and get things moving, and stubbornly insistent on attaining their goals. Low-scorers will be seen as kind, gentle, and considerate, fatalistic about personal misfortune or adversity, vulnerable to attack and aggression, and willing to substitute day dreams and fantasies for more direct or tangible experience. In their cathexes, high-scorers stress action, visible rewards, and vigorous assertion of self, whereas low-scorers value inner feelings and an intuitive evocation of identity.*"

When the women in this research checked the adjectives on the Adjective Check List they were not aware that these adjectives would then fall into certain groupings. That is, they were not aware that they were checking adjectives which would describe their masculine or feminine attributes, among other characteristics.

Women in the single father group indicated in the original Research Questionnaire they believe they have more masculine traits than other women and that was verified by 64% who were high scorers on the Adjective Check List. However, of the women in the biological parents group who did *not* believe they had more masculine traits than others, 61% were also high scorers on the masculine attributes scale in the Adjective Check List. It is possible that the women in the biological parents group who were raised with a mother, and therefore expected that they had taken on feminine traits, did not expect that they were also taking on masculine traits, when in fact they were.

But what of feminine attributes? It would seem that the women from two biological parents, or from the single mother families would have the highest percentage who were high-scorers in the Feminine Attributes category. But that is not what the figures indicated in the Adjective Check List. The group that had the highest percentage of women scoring 50% or higher in Feminine Attributes was surprisingly in the single father group with 49%. The two groups who had the *lowest* percentage of women scoring 50% or higher in Feminine Attributes was in the biological parents group and the single mother group, each with 38%. Of the step parent group 44% scored in the 50% or higher range.

The Description of the Scales for the Adjective Check List Feminine Attributes is as follows: *"The high-scorer on Fem prompts positive reactions from others and in turn treats them in a cooperative, considerate, and sympathetic manner. The low-scorer keeps others at a distance, is skeptical of their intentions, and rejects their overtures. Observers see the high-scorer as appreciative, cheerful, and warm, whereas the low-scorer is viewed as fault-finding, hardheaded, and opinionated. The high-scorer values intimacy and mutuality in relationships with others; the low-scorer prefers autonomy and detachment."*

THE TWO-PARENT FAMILY IS NOT THE BEST

The following chart indicates the percentages for each group as they scored on the Masculine Attributes Scale:

MASCULINE ATTRIBUTES		
	1	2
Bio	61%	39%
Sing F	64%	36%
Sing M	52%	48%
Step	52%	48%

1. Above 50%
2. Below 50%

The following chart indicates the percentages for each group as they scored on the Feminine Attributes Scale:

FEMININE ATTRIBUTES SCALE		
	1	2
Bio	38%	62%
Sing.F	49%	51%
Sing.M	38%	62%
Step	44%	56%

1. Above 50%
2. Below 50%

PERSONALITY TRAITS

To assess how the women in the research believed that their family situation had affected their personality, they were asked to complete this open-ended sentence, "*The three most important things about my personality due to having been raised by a father/mother/both biological parents/a step parent are . . . . .*"

Stereotypical *masculine* traits such as *independent, self-reliant, self-confident*, were listed as their first important characteristic for most women in each group, though more in the single father group than in the others.

For the second and third traits, stereotypical *masculine* traits were listed again as the most important characteristics for all groups *except* the biological parents group where most women listed stereotypical *feminine* characteristics such as *caring, being a good housekeeper, being attractive to her mate*, as the result of their parentage.

In the step parent group the highest percentage listed stereotypical *masculine* traits as their first and second characteristic, with their third most often stated characteristic as being stereotypically *feminine*.

In other words, most women raised either by a single father or a single mother listed *masculine* traits as their strongest characteristics. Given the option to list three traits, most women in single parent groups listed three masculine traits, the single father

THE TWO-PARENT FAMILY IS NOT THE BEST

group having the highest percentage in first, second, and third traits.

Once again, how do these self-analyses compare with the results of the Gough Adjective Check List, Masculine Attributes and Feminine Attributes Scales? As mentioned in the previous section and repeated here for emphasis, many women, especially in the single father group, said they believed they had more masculine traits. This is borne out in a comparison with the Gough Adjective Check List, wherein over two-thirds of the women in the single father group scored over 50% in the Masculine Attributes Scale. This was closely followed by women in the biological parents group where 61% scored in the 50% or higher category of Masculine Attributes.

As will be mentioned again, the single father group which has the highest percentage of women who scored 50% or higher in the Masculine Attributes Scale also had the highest percentage who scored over 50% in the *Feminine* Attributes Scale.

THE PRESENT

First Trait in Personality as Result of Family Situation

	1	2	3	4
Bio	46%	20%	21%	13%
Sing F	72%	13%	9%	6%
Sing M	58%	17%	18%	7%
Step	33%	29%	22%	16%

Second Trait in Personality as Result of Family Situation

	1	2	3	4
Bio	23%	39%	19%	19%
Sing F	61%	19%	9%	11%
Sing M	54%	20%	17%	9%
Step	31%	27%	22%	20%

Third Trait in Personality as Result of Family Situation

	1	2	3	4
Bio	20%	31%	22%	27%
Sing F	55%	15%	10%	20%
Sing M	33%	28%	21%	18%
Step	27%	31%	14%	28%

1. Stereotypical masculine
2. Stereotypical feminine
3. Androgenous
4. No Answer

THE TWO-PARENT FAMILY IS NOT THE BEST

PARENTS EMBODIED IN THEIR CHILDREN

Generally speaking, children first acquire their male and female personality traits from their parents. The girl acquires much of her femininity by interacting with her mother, and much of her masculinity by interacting with her father. The same process applies to boys. Some may feel that girls should not acquire masculinity or that boys should not acquire femininity. But the healthy personality is the androgenous one which has a balance of the stereotypical feminine qualities of caring and understanding, and the stereotypical masculine qualities of independence and self-confidence.

In order for children to develop androgenously, they need to have relationships with positive male and female qualities and to incorporate these qualities into their personalities as they develop. What then, of the child who is missing a parent, or of the child who has a bad example of either femaleness or maleness? Is the girl without a father unable to develop the masculine side of herself? Is the girl without a mother unable to develop the feminine side of herself? And what of the child who has parents, either single parents or both parents, who absent themselves either physically or emotionally, or who abuse their child or are otherwise unable to parent adequately? How does this child develop the *missing* parent or reform the inadequate parent in herself?

THE PRESENT

Linda Schierse Leonard in her book, *The Wounded Woman*, writes of women who have been wounded by their fathers. Some fathers have died with the daughters hating them. Leonard says, in this case the daughters need to establish a cordial relationship with the memory of their fathers. The suggestion seems to be that even if the father is dead or unapproachable, the daughter needs to understand and accept her wound and to "*appreciate what has been lacking so that it can be developed within.*" This would likely be a long counseling process but one which might reshape the woman's concept of her father as she embodies him.

For women, this wound may have been inflicted by her personal father, or by the patriarchal father of society "*which functions like a poor father, culturally devaluing the worth of women.*" How this would be resolved for women who have been wounded by society's sexist prejudice is not clear. It is women's persistent struggle to overcome this violence.

In later sections of this research it is recorded that women of single mothers, from the results of the Adjective Check List, were seen as those who would most profit from counseling. Most are also seen as having strong masculine traits. This might appear to be a contradiction since these women did not have fathers. But they were able to supply the missing parent in themselves by acquiring the masculine qualities which their mothers already had or which they developed in order to provide for their families.

THE TWO-PARENT FAMILY IS NOT THE BEST

Women in single father families acquired the feminine qualities of their fathers which they already had or which they developed in nurturing their families. The acceptance of these traits within themselves is true for most women in these single parent groups and is further explained in Part III.

Many women in the two-parent families, that is the two biological parents and the step parent groups, have also been wounded by either their fathers or their mothers, or both. Until these wounds are understood and healed the woman carries within her personality the imperfect parent who wounded her.

Sylvia Plath, the poet who ended her own life at 30, had suffered a major wound at eight years old when her father died. Later in life she refers to her father in her poetry as a Nazi storm trooper. He had come from Germany in 1900 so he couldn't have been a Nazi. Possibly she thought if he had stayed there he would have been a storm trooper who killed Jews. Her mother was probably part Jewish and Sylvia writes herself into her poetry as Jewish. She refers to the man who died too soon, "*You died before I had time,*" and of the man, who "*bit my pretty heart in two*." "*Daddy,*" she wrote, "*I have had to kill you.*" It is possible that in killing herself she was killing the Nazi storm trooper she had incorporated in herself.

It is hoped that the wounded women in this research and elsewhere can be helped to understand their injury and the perpetrator, and come to terms with the missing or abusive parent embodied in themselves.

DESIRED QUALITIES IN MATE

"What Do Women Really Want?"

Believe it or not, most women want men with stereotypical feminine qualities. Most women in all groups prefer mates who have stereotypical *feminine* qualities such as *communicative, caring, listening, being expressive, sensitive, understanding, being flexible, a good listener*. Or they prefer mates who have androgenous characteristics which include *having an open mind, a good sense of humor, a non-addictive personality, being non-judgmental and being honest*. Now that women generally can support themselves, they no longer feel they need the physically strong, protective bread-winner type of man to lean on. Being able to earn their own living, women seek companionship, warmth and love in their partners.

The *lowest* percentage of the desired qualities in a mate (except for the single mother group) are in the stereotypical masculine category, that is the least often preferred qualities are *financially supportive, independent, hard-working, reliable, responsible*. Because many women in the single mother group grew up with financial hardship, it is understandable that they desire mates who can make a good living and will be responsible for the family. Though 34% of the single mother group indicated a desire for mates with stereotypical masculine characteristics, and had the highest percentage of women who preferred these characteristics, even more of the single mother group, that is 46%, preferred mates with androgenous characteristics.

Desired Quality in Mate			
	1	2	3
Bio	18%	38%	44%
Sing F.	37%	62%	1%
Sing M.	34%	20%	46%
Step	31%	51%	17%

1. Stereotypical masculine
2. Stereotypical feminine
3. Androgenous

Freud asked the question, "*What do women want?*" But it was probably not a question. More likely it was a statement that said women don't know what they want. In this research there is no question what women want. Throughout the study there is a call for nurturing, desired from mothers, from fathers, from step parents and from mates. There is a call for the stereotypical feminine characteristics of understanding, listening, communicating and caring. Except for the desire for financial soundness,

THE PRESENT

there is not only a rejection, but almost an aversion to stereotypical masculine characteristics.

This corroborates the findings in Shere Hite's book, *Women and Love: A Cultural Revolution in Progress*. Hite's methodology has been criticized, but the popularity of the book attests to its *"hitting the mark."* Many bestsellers such as *Men Who Hate Women and the Women Who Love them, Women Who Love Too Much,* and *The Peter Pan Syndrome,* all speak of the men's distancing themselves in relationships with women and then ridiculing or humiliating women to the point where women are overburdened with the emotional weight of the relationship.

It is possible that with the increasing number of women raised by single parents -- women who can support themselves, who are independent and self-reliant -- the macho male may find himself *left out in the cold.* If women cannot find mates who have listening and understanding qualities, they may simply opt to raise their families by themselves, as their single parents did.

OPINIONS ON EQUALITY

Almost three quarters of all but the single mother group said there should be total equality between the sexes. The single mother group was divided about two-thirds saying there should be total equality and one third saying equality should be modified.

Modified Equality

"I don't sound like the feminist that I am, but I think mothers set the tone of the household and that they must be a little more willing to compromise."

Single Mother Families

The largest percentage of women who believed there should be modified equality is in the single mother group. Some comments include, *"I am opposed to women entering into strictly masculine fields, such as mining, highway work, telephone line work, etc." "I want separate restrooms and dressing rooms." "Modified to the extent that women are not able to do heavy physical work." "Maternity leave, alimony to make up for society's attitudes regarding salaries, etc." "It is important to realize that different is not bad. Men and women have different strengths and weaknesses. We should work together rather than trying to be everything to everybody. This is of course easy to say but difficult to accept on ourselves." "I've gone to both extremes but being pregnant and breastfeeding require special attention." "Equal pay for equal work. Biologically we are not able to do all things equally. Abilities are usually in different areas." "Differences between ALL humans is desirable. Gender is just one visible difference some people choose to focus upon at times." "I don't think either should be 'boss' but I think there are real differences which have to be dealt with, except for physical strength." "Modified to deal with the nurturing characteristic of women."*

One woman in the single mother group who believed there should be total equality wrote, *"WHAT IS EQUALITY? (Complex issue). Is paid maternity leave equality? Some think not. Misogynists think: 'You want equality, OK: No alimony, (women make far less than men), no support for daycare, pregnancy, maternity, etc.'"*

Single Father Families

The next highest percentage who believed there should be modified equality was the single father group. Of these who believed equality should be modified, most said their reasons were because *men are stronger*, some said men and women are different. Some of their comments follow: *"I believe there are some basic biological/instinctual differences; works to advantage of children and perhaps of society to acknowledge and make provision for." "Each parent should do what he or she excels at, not what is 'mas-*

THE TWO-PARENT FAMILY IS NOT THE BEST

culine,' or 'feminine.'" "In spite of my background, women are responsible for children and can never have complete equality." "One sex complements the other. It will balance out on its own without stressing equality." "Let the men rule the world and women rule the men with their hearts." "There will always be differences in men and women, even if its only physically. Men and women should be able to have the same jobs though. But there will always be some emotional differences in men and women." "I believe the husband/father should be looked up to as the prime provider for his family, and mom can go back to work when kids are in school." "A woman should have her own important place, but Dad should be family leader." "Economic, yes. But there are differences, biologically and physically. Women can't match men's strength, especially in upper body. Some double standards may be inevitable because of this."

Biological Parents Families

Of those in the biological parents group who said they believed equality should be modified, about one-third said their reasons were that *men and women are different.* Some comments include, *"Issues that involve physical strength and areas that make mothers absent from children." "The male is superior, the female is privileged." "Men and women are not the same at all, though both are valuable." "The buck has to stop somewhere when differences are not reconciled and a decision must be made." "Total equality for business and employment rights, credit, etc. But modified*

THE PRESENT

for child support issues especially since women usually are the custodial parent and make less than men." "*The only thing that would be limiting would be physical stature, but as a parent both women and men are equally qualified to do each others work, not only in the employment world but in 'home life'. Also some men that I know are more qualified to do the finer work as in home sewing repairs.*" "*I'm not into Women's lib and equal rights. I still think a man should be a man and a woman a woman.*" "*With women bearing the children, there will never be total equality, the two sexes are different and that's okay.*" "*I think that a woman who is bearing children should receive some special considerations from employer -- time off, daycare after birth of child, etc.*"

Step Parent Families

Twenty-two percent of the women in the step parent group said they believed there should be modified equality and of these, 100% said it was because men and women are different. Some of their comments follow: "*I am glad women are not asked to fight wars.*" "*Modified only to recognize the physical differences.*" "*I think there are certain things that men and women are better at so they could do that first and work at the other things.*" "*I love my feminine side and I have found men love it also. As far as jobs, etc. there should be total equality.*" "*I don't think 'equality' under present societal values is desirable.*" "*Women shouldn't be drafted until someone figures out how to prevent rape.*" "*Physical abilities can differ.*"

THE TWO-PARENT FAMILY IS NOT THE BEST

Opinions on Equality

	1	2
Bio	71%	22%
Sing F	70%	26%
Sing M	64%	34%
Step	76%	22%

1. Total equality
2. Modified equality

Explain Why Equality Should be Modified

	1	2	3	4	5	6
Bio	0%	38%	19%	14%	10%	19%
Sing F	36%	32%	0%	4%	4%	15%
Sing M	9%	41%	0%	5%	0%	45%
Step	0%	100%	0%	0%	0%	0%

1. Men are stronger
2. Men/women are different
3. Should be equal but can't be
4. Women should have special rights
5. Father should be family leader
6. Miscellaneous

When asked if men and women were equal or *basically different* in their *abilities*, over three quarters of all women said that men and women were of equal ability. But when asked if men and women were equal in their *feelings*, or *basically different*, only

330

THE PRESENT

about half of all of the women said that men and women were equal in their feelings.

Men and Women Different in Abilities?

	1	2
Bio	77%	22%
Sing F	77%	20%
Sing M	76%	20%
Step	78%	22%

1. The same
2. Basically different

Men and Women Different in Feelings?

	1	2
Bio	50%	48%
Sing F	52%	45%
Sing M	43%	54%
Step	53%	43%

1. The same
2. Basically different

THE TWO-PARENT FAMILY IS NOT THE BEST

IF NOT MARRIED, WHY NOT?

Of the biological parents group not married, most women said they like men but don't want to make the commitment. Of the other three groups, most women said they hoped to get married but the opportunity had not yet presented itself. Almost the same percentage of unmarried women in each group said they didn't care to get involved.

	\multicolumn{5}{c}{If Unmarried, Why?}
	1	2	3	4	5
Bio	28%	21%	16%	2%	33%
Sing F	15%	35%	15%	4%	31%
Sing M	10%	26%	19%	7%	34%
Step	5%	41%	14%	0%	40%

1. Don't want commitment
2. No opportunity yet
3. Don't care to get involved
4. Don't care much for men
5. Other

IF YOU DON'T HAVE CHILDREN, WOULD YOU LIKE TO?

Of the single mother group, about two thirds said they would like to have children. The other three groups were about evenly divided as to whether they wanted children or not. The only group with a higher percentage of women not wanting children than wanting them was in the step parent group.

Of those who said they didn't want children, when asked their reasons, most in the single mother group said they didn't like children, most in the biological group said they would not be good mothers. The single father group was evenly divided between,"*would not be a good mother*," and "*children would interfere.*" This was the same division in the step parent group.

If You Have No Children, Would you Like To?	
	Yes
Bio	56%
Sing F	55%
Sing M	67%
Step	48%

MOST IMPORTANT THING ABOUT MOTHERING

"*Nurturing*" was listed as the most important thing about mothering by all groups, and especially by the single father group, and the step parent group. The biological parent group had the lowest percentage, listing "*nurturing*" qualities.

Most Important Thing About Mothering					
	1	2	3	4	5
Bio	59%	3%	10%	9%	11%
Sing F	86%	7%	1%	0%	0%
Sing M	75%	3%	7%	3%	9%
Step	84%	4%	12%	0%	0%

1. Nurturing
2. Security
3. Communication
4. Be a role model
5. Miscellaneous

MOST IMPORTANT THING ABOUT FATHERING

Again, "*nurturing*" qualities are listed as *the most important quality of fathering, BY WOMEN IN ALL GROUPS.*

The highest percentage of women who listed "*security*" as the most important quality of fathering was in the single father group, a group which had had considerable financial security. One might have thought the single mother group would have had a higher percentage of women who felt "*security*" was most important because so many women in this group had suffered financial insecurity, but relatively few women mentioned this characteristic compared to the importance of nurturing.

One women in the step parent family wrote, "*Fatherhood involves a whole lot more than putting food on the table.*"

THE TWO-PARENT FAMILY IS NOT THE BEST

Most Important Thing About Fathering					
	1	2	3	4	5
Bio	57%	8%	8%	8%	11%
Sing F	71%	21%	1%	0%	1%
Sing M	54%	14%	4%	6%	7%
Step	76%	12%	10%	0%	0%

1. Nurturing
2. Security
3. Communication
4. Be a role model
5. Miscellaneous

WHAT THINGS

THAT A

Like most o
ended, with respon
The highest percen
in the single mothe
ing" a mother can d
highest percentage for all groups said *breast feed*, or "*have a baby.*" A few women mentioned "*teach social skills,*" and a few mentioned "*be confidential.*" Most women see mothers as being able to do it all, even those who had no mothers.

	Things a Mother Can Do That a Father Can't				
	1	2	3	4	5
Bio	33%	28%	10%	6%	23%
Sing F	25%	23%	13%	4%	35%
Sing M	40%	29%	21%	1%	9%
Step	30%	28%	17%	15%	10%

1. Nothing
2. Breastfeed or have a baby
3. Social skills
4. Be confidential
5. Other

...AMILY IS NOT THE BEST

...INGS CAN A FATHER DO THAT A MOTHER CAN'T?

There is "*nothing*" a father can do that a mother can't, according to most of the women in all groups except the single mother group where the women felt a man's point of view could not be communicated by a mother. Women in the single *mother* group, where male role models were scarce, where many women said they did not know what a father's role was, and where many indicted a father must be almost extraneous, still felt that a father was the person to transmit knowledge about maleness. For women in the single *father* group the opposite is not true. Women in the single father group did not indicate that they needed to know what the female point of view was or what a woman's role was.

THE PRESENT

| Things a Father Can Do That a Mother Can't |

	1	2	3	4	5	6
Bio	38%	28%	1%	0%	2%	31%
Sing F	51%	13%	3%	0%	3%	30%
Sing M	33%	37%	0%	1%	1%	31%
Step	41%	27%	0%	2%	0%	30%

1. Nothing
2. Give man's point of view or male role model
3. Be patient, understanding
4. Provide security
5. Grow a beard
6. Miscellaneous

THE TWO-PARENT FAMILY IS NOT THE BEST

KNOW ANYONE ELSE RAISED BY FATHER/MOTHER ONLY?

Two thirds of the women raised by single fathers do not know anyone else raised by their fathers only. This contributes to a sense of uniqueness for many of these women. When every friend or acquaintance has been raised by a mother, single or married, these women raised by single fathers felt that they were different.

Yet referring back to the percentages about whether or not the women in this research felt they had been *singled out as being different*, it is clear that women raised by single fathers were not noticeably "*different*" to others. Also, some women in *all* groups felt they had been singled out as being different.

About one quarter of the women in the single *mother* group said they have not known anyone else raised by a single mother. As the years pass, that figure would grow smaller with the increasing number of single mothers. But years ago single motherhood was rare, though not as rare as single fatherhood. These women who have not known anyone else raised by a single mother share some of the same feelings as the women raised by a single father who have not known anyone else so raised.

Whether or not the women with single parents knew of others who were raised as they were, appears irrelevant to their outward demeanor. Many women from the single parent group said they *felt*

THE PRESENT

different, but they were no more *singled out as being different* than children in other family situations.

Know Anyone Else Raised by Father/Mother Only?	
	No
Sing F	67%
Sing M	26%

CAN A FATHER BE A GOOD SUBSTITUTE FOR A MOTHER?

This question was not asked of the single mother gorup.

Overwhelmingly, the women in the single father family answered, "*Yes*," to this question. To a lesser degree, but still more than half of the other groups with fathers also answered, "*Yes*."

One in the single father group wrote, "*From experience I know men can do a good job of raising children by themselves and they shouldn't be let off the hook!*"

Can a Father Be a Good Substitute For a Mother?	
	Yes
Bio	57%
Sing F	70%
Step	59%

CAN A MOTHER BE A GOOD SUBSTITUTE FOR A FATHER?

One might have thought there would be a strong "*yes*," voice from the single mother group, but fewer in this group answered "*yes*," to this question than did women in the other groups.

More credit is given to men to handle the single parent situation than is given to women, yet there are many more single mothers than there are single fathers.

Women in the single mother and single father groups had different experiences with those who were parenting them of course, but have less confidence in a woman's ability to carry out a father's role than do women in the single father group have in a father's ability to carry out the woman's role.

Can a Mother Be a Good Substitute for a Father?	
	Yes
Bio	57%
Sing M	55%
Step	67%

HOW DO YOU EVALUATE YOURSELF AS A MOTHER?

The highest percentage of women who had children, who evaluated themselves as "*very good*" mothers is in the group of women who had no mothers.

The lowest percentage classifying themselves as "*very good*" mothers was in the group which had two biological parents.

Nevertheless, most women in all groups evaluated themselves as "*very good*," mothers. The women who evaluated themselves as *not* good mothers with the highest percentage was in the step parent group, but that was only 15% of those who had children. On the whole, all women in the research who had children see themselves as good mothers.

One of the goals of this research was to try to determine if women who had had no mothers when they grew up were handicapped by this lack of role model. It has been said that one learns mothering by learning how their own mother mothered. Apparently the women in the single father group, even though they had no mothers to teach them how to mother, feel they did very well as mothers. Their children also rate these women as "*very good*" mothers.

The highest percentage of women who rated themselves as "*average*" in their mothering was in the biological parent group. One might expect that this

THE PRESENT

group would have the highest evaluation of themselves and yet they had the lowest. It may be that they are comparing themselves to the mothering that they had and feel inadequate by comparison. Whereas the women in the other three groups had unusual mothering and may feel that by comparison they are doing better than what they had.

How Do You Evaluate Yourself as a Mother?				
	1	2	3
Bio	63%	33%	4%
Sing F	79%	21%	0%
Sing M	75%	20%	5%
Step	75%	10%	15%

1. Very good
2. Average
3. Poor

HOW WOMEN ARE EVALUATED BY
THEIR CHILDREN

Of the women who had children, most said their children rated them as "*very good*" mothers, the remainder were rated as "*average*," and a few women said their children rated them as "*poor*."

How Your Children Evaluate You as a Mother			
	1	*2*	*3*
Bio	87%	13%	0%
Sing F	87%	12%	2%
Sing M	82%	16%	2%
Step	85%	14%	1%

1. Very good
2. Average
3. Poor

HOW HAS UPBRINGING AFFECTED YOUR PARENTING?

The step parent group stands out as the group with the highest percentage saying as a result of their upbringing they are more affectionate with their children. This is interesting because it is in the step parent group where there was considerable emotional and physical abuse. Many women are giving their children the love that they missed when they were children.

How Upbringing Affected Your Child-raising						
	1	2	3	4	5	6
Bio	21%	11%	3%	3%	5%	57%
Sing F	17%	15%	7%	20%	5%	36%
Sing M	25%	13%	6%	22%	0%	34%
Step	48%	5%	0%	0%	0%	47%

1. I'm more affectionate
2. I help them be independent and responsible
3. I'm strict
4. I give time
5. I insist on equal treatment for all
6. Other

PART III

SUMMARY AND ANALYSIS

WHAT HAS BEEN LEARNED?

The results of this research represent the group of women who responded and the results *may* also represent most women in this country in each particular group. The results suggest a variety of indications about women who have been raised by both biological parents, or by single fathers, or single mothers, or by step parents. Five of the major indications are these:

The Two-Parent Family Is Not The Best

The most important ingredients for a happy, wholesome childhood are good relationships between the child and the adult or adults who are raising her, and good relationships *between* the adults themselves. Is the child listened to, cared about, supported and encouraged?. In some families *in all groups* in this study, girls were raised with the important ingredients for a happy childhood, and in some families *in all groups* girls were starved for affection and attention.

THERE IS NO ONE GROUP WHICH STANDS OUT AS BEING THE BEST FAMILY SITUATION FOR RAISING CHILDREN.

This research indicates that, contrary to a long-held belief, the two parent family is not the best family for children. Though a large percentage of this group responded that their childhood had been happy, followed closely by the two single parent groups, and though, on the Adjective Check List, the biological parent group had the highest percentage who scored above 51% on a number of positive traits, there are indications from the women's answers and written comments on the Research Questionnaire, that the family situation with two parents, while sometimes very good, was, also, just as often, not good at all. This does not say that the results concerning the biological parents group are wholly negative. But it does say that this group, which has always been thought to be the best family com-

SUMMARY AND ANALYSIS

bination for raising children, appears to provide no clear advantage.

For example, only slightly over half of the women responded that their fathers were "*there for them*" when needed. Most have negative relationships with men. There is a higher percentage of women among *single* parent families who felt their families were *close knit* than did women in two parent families. Where there were brothers in the family, fewer boys in this biological parents group shared in the household work than did brothers in the other three groups. This was also true of fathers sharing in household work. As a result, girls in the biological parents group did an unequal share of the housework. There was a general complaint among women in this group that their fathers spent much more time with their sons than with their daughters. Most wished their fathers had been at home more.

Girls in the biological parents group were least likely to be *on their own* and therefore least likely to have privacy. They were also least likely to have mothers who *permitted risks*. Though, as a group, they were high scorers on the Creative Personality Scale of the Adjective Check List, individually those who were not permitted risks scored lower on the Creative Personality Scale.

A higher percentage of fathers in two parent families used alcohol excessively than did fathers in any other group, and except for step mothers, the highest percentage of mothers who used alcohol excessively was also in this two biological parents group. A higher percentage of fathers in the two parent families beat their daughters than did fathers

THE TWO-PARENT FAMILY IS NOT THE BEST

in single father families and 17% of the girls in the biological parents group were sexually abused. Of those abused, 11% were abused by the girl's biological father. The highest percentage of women who are overweight is in the biological parents group.

Though the women in the biological parents group grew up with mothers, from whom it is said girls learn to "*mother,*" they have the lowest percentage who evaluate themselves as *very good* mothers. As high scorers on the Adjective Check List Nurturing Parent Scale, (see Appendix B)they view themselves as "*conservative, conventional, helpful, industrious, loyal, praising, and stable*". "*High scorers prefer continuity and the preservation of old values to rapid changes and shifts in convention....*" This corresponds with the many comments from this group responding to the Research Questionnaire who wrote of supporting *traditional family values.*

Even though women in this group were high scorers on the Nurturing Parent Scale, they had a slightly lower percentage of high scorers on the Nurturing Scale ("*providing material and emotional benefits to others*") than women in the single father group who had no mothers. Also, women in the biological parents group have the *lowest* percentage who said the most important thing about mothering is *nurturing*. It appears that *mothering* to women who have grown up with their two biological parents is not so much in *nurturing* as it is in providing stability and in conforming to convention. Or it could be that they took "*nurturing*" for granted because they were adequately nurtured.

SUMMARY AND ANALYSIS

In a recent conference of the 4400 member National Council on Family Relations, Graham Spanier spoke of an assessment of various family structures. He referred specifically to a report which pulled together the results of more than 100 studies of different family situations and their effect on children. The report was written by David Demo of Virginia Polytechnic Institute and Alan Acock of Louisiana State University. What they found was that there was no definite evidence that the family structure *per se* was crucial to the children's psychological and social well-being. What was important was the quality of the *relationship* between parent and child and, if there were two parents, the quality of the *relationship* between parents.

Negative impact on children's self-esteem was affected by parents not spending much time with their children, and greatly affected by persistent family discord. Spanier also referred to a study by Paul Amato, University of Nebraska, who found that adults who had experienced their parents divorce or a parent's death when they were young were no different in self esteem than those raised in a family that had not experienced such disruption.

This appears to be contrary to the results written in a book by Judith Wallerstein, "*Second Chances.*" In her book, Wallerstein tracks 60 families who had experienced divorce and concludes that "*almost half the children entered adulthood as worried, underachieving, self-deprecating and sometimes angry young men and women.*" Wallerstein's methodology is criticized by other researchers because she used no control group for comparison. It is possible she

THE TWO-PARENT FAMILY IS NOT THE BEST

could have tracked 60 families which had remained intact and found the same results with the children. There is no definitive study on the long-term effects of divorce. Wallerstein's results are criticized by Mel Krantzler, author of "*Creative Divorce,*" who says "*Any book that gives the impression to people that divorce is such a traumatizing experience that kids are permanently damaged for the rest of their lives is destructive. A child can understand that life has adversities...children can learn that they have the capacity to overcome a difficulty rather than wallow in it.*"

A 1991 article in the journal, *Science,* reported that 18,700 families were studied over a period of years in England and in the United States. What was learned was that the children of divorced parents had behavioral problems long before the actual divorce. This, the article stated, should cause people to question the blame they put on divorce for the children's problems. If Wallerstein had studied the children in her research before their parent's divorced, she may have found they had the same problems then as they had after the divorce.

Dr. Lindsay Chase-Lansdale, one of the study's psychologists at the University of Chicago said the findings indicate, "*if a marriage is in trouble, there are effects on the children whether or not the parents divorce.*" The co-author, Dr. Andrew Cherlin, a sociologist at Johns Hopkins University added, "*More attention needs to be paid to the children when there is marital conflict. Conflict hurts children, regardless of whether it leads to divorce or not. If there is conflict, the children need to be sheltered from it, not caught in the middle between warring parents.*" The

SUMMARY AND ANALYSIS

conclusion is that more of the problems which children had could be attributed to marital discord than to divorce. The study indicated that staying together for the sake of the children can be harmful to the children if the marriage is filled with conflict and discord. Difficult as it is, divorce is often a relief for many children.

There are also indications that children growing up in two parent families where the mother does not work outside the home, may develop excessive dependency. Because there is no particular prestige for women who are full-time homemakers, they are apt to overinvest in their children and to slow down their children's personal growth by not permitting adventuresome activities. Of the women who had working mothers in this research, 91% were in the single mother group and 49% were in the two biological parents group. Working mothers, single or married, require more responsibility from their children. Usually only women who have husbands who work full-time at good paying jobs can afford to not work outside their home. Because of the greater likelihood that mothers in the two biological parent families would not be working, it is these mothers who are most apt to overinvest in their children.

This research, based on a comparison of four groups of women raised in four different kinds of family situations is one in the over 100 already existing which says that whether a child has two biological parents or only one, or only one remaining step parent, or only one friend or grandmother or grandfather or whomever to raise her, she has a good chance of doing well if the personal relationships are

THE TWO-PARENT FAMILY IS NOT THE BEST

wholesome, caring and supportive. The myth that the two biological parents group is the best for children leaves people who were raised differently feeling at times like outsiders. And it leaves people who divorce, feeling guilty because they are led to believe that they are harming their children. That is not so, as long as the relationship between remaining parent and child is good.

Perpetuating the myth that the two parent family is the best, serves the *status quo.* It is politically and economically expedient to keep women in jobs which pay less than men, or to keep them in a position where they are in and out of the labor force depending on the needs to take care of their children which prevents them from building up job promotions, seniority or retirement benefits.

As long as society says that the mother is the best person to raise her children, then it is the women who will assume the major portion of this job. Not that the mothers are staying home. They are going to work in massive numbers and arranging for babysitters, but not without guilt. Also not without still accepting the major burden of childcare. This research, however, indicates that fathers can do as good a job as mothers in raising children.

2. Single Father Daughters Develop Strong

Feminine Traits.

Though most women in single father families felt *older than their years* and most said they had *lost*

SUMMARY AND ANALYSIS

their childhood because of their responsibilities as children, at least three-quarters had fathers who were *there for them* when they were needed. Also, more fathers were *helpful in their daughters' bereavement* when their mother died than were single mothers helpful when a child had lost a father. If there were brothers in the family, more were helpful with household chores than were brothers in the biological parents group

As might be expected in single father families where most fathers worked all day, most girls were *on their own* much of the time. Also within this group there was the highest percentage of fathers who *permitted risks.* Yet a higher percentage of women who reported being *permitted risks* scored over the 60th percentile range on the Adjective Check List Creative Personality Scale than did women who were not permitted risks.

Fewer fathers in the single father group than in the biological parents group had fathers who used alcohol excessively. Few single father, compared with fathers in other groups, beat their daughters.

The single father group is the group which grew up without mothers, yet apparently they feel comfortable in the role of mother, as most evaluated themselves as *very good* mothers. This group had the highest percentage who scored above 51% on the Nurturing Scale of the Adjective Check List which is described as "*To engage in behaviors that provide material or emotional benefits to others.*" Having a single father and no mother did not diminish the women's *mothering* or nurturing skills.

Also, the single father group had the highest percentage of women who said that *"nurturing"* was the most important quality for mothering and for fathering. The women in this group had the highest percentage who said that a father can be a good substitute for a mother.

Also 71% said that *"nurturing"* was the most important quality for *fathering* compared with 57% who said the same thing in the biological parents group. Fifty-one percent (compared with 42% in the biological parents group) have positive relationships with men. Having been brought up almost exclusively by a man, more girls in this group are comfortable with men than are those brought up by a man and a woman. However, not as many in the single father group (56%) have positive relationships with women as do the women (72%) in the biological parents group. When asked if their childhood had been happy, 64% reported that they had had a happy childhood.

Twenty-seven percent of the women raised by single fathers graduated from college, which is the second highest percentage, the highest being in the step parent group. Twenty-one percent have graduate degrees which is also second only to the step parent group. Both the single father group and the step parent group have 29% employed in professional positions, and both the single father group and the single mother group have the highest percentage earning $50,000. - $100,000. in 1987.

Though most said they felt *different*, and most of these because they believed they had more masculine traits than others, which correlates with their high percentage on the upper ranges of the Adjective Check List Masculine Attributes Scale, they also had the highest percentage who scored 51% - 100% on *Feminine* Attributes Scale. This group has the highest percentage which desires feminine characteristics of listening and caring in a mate. It would appear that the girl raised by her father has an excellent opportunity to develop an androgenous personality with both well developed masculine and feminine traits.

3. Single Mother Daughters Develop Strong

Masculine Traits

In addition to financial security, what the women in the single mother families missed most in not having a father in the home was an appearance of being "*normal*," or "*traditional*." Though three-quarters in the single father group said they had not known anyone else raised by a single *father*, and only one-quarter of the single mother group said they had not known anyone else raised by a single *mother*, that is, there are many more children who were raised and are now being raised by single mothers, it is the women in the single mother group who seemed to have suffered a stigma or a sense of shame for their family situation.

Most likely this feeling *different* or not *normal* was because when mothers, who traditionally earn less money than fathers, raise children by themselves, it causes financial hardship on children and they

THE TWO-PARENT FAMILY IS NOT THE BEST

compare themselves with their peers, who not only have two parents, but also have more *things*. One of the prerequisites for being "*normal*," may mean being able to be equal.

In their earliest years, life was lonely for many of these girls. Only slightly over half of their mothers were *there for them* when needed, and only one-quarter were helpful to their daughters when the girl's father died or left because of divorce or desertion. Nevertheless, women in the single mother group have the highest percentage who felt they had a *close knit* family, and the highest percentage where, if there were brothers, the boys shared equally in the housework. Sharing housework can contribute to a feeling of working together, being a team, and being *close knit*.

The women in this group also had the highest percentage who were *the little mothers*, taking care of younger siblings when their mother worked. Sixty-four percent said they felt *older than their years* though a lesser percentage said they had *lost their childhood* than women in the single father families. This group had the highest percentage who were *on their own*, slightly higher than the women in the single father families, and over half were *permitted risks* which were not permitted to other girls.

The negative result of being on their own was that many of these girls felt lonely. Yet others *on their own* explored and developed their creativity which was a positive result of being permitted risks. Being on their own, as with women in the single father family, these women were free to make many of their own decisions. About two-thirds described their childhood as *happy*.

Though many were plagued with financial insecurity, and 7% did not finish high school, 22% have college degrees and 18% have graduate degrees. Eighteen percent are employed in managerial positions and 18% in professional positions.

Fewer mothers in this single mother group used alcohol to excess than did mothers in the other three groups. Except for step mothers, women in the single mother group had the highest percentage of mothers who beat their daughters.

Women in this group have the highest percentage who have negative relationships with men. When answering the question of how life would have been different if they had had a father, the highest percentage said they would have had financial security, and the next highest percentage said they would have better relationships with men. This is the group which had the highest percentage of women who do not vote and who said they would not vote for any man. Their relationships with women are very good.

But with 68% having negative relationships with men, their distrust of men is high. Many are fearful that after they would become emotionally involved with a man, he might leave them as their father did. Since many have grown up without a man in the home and have seen that their mother could do it all, many consider men as extraneous. When asked what was the most important thing in *fathering*, many said they had no idea what a father did. Many women may have picked up feelings about

THE TWO-PARENT FAMILY IS NOT THE BEST

their mother's desertion and have transferred these feelings to their own opinions about men.

When asked what qualities they desire in a mate, most desired androgenous qualities such as sense of humor, honesty, friendship, and companionship. They had the lowest percentage of women who desired stereotypical feminine qualities. As a comparison, 62% of the women in the single *father* group desired stereotypical feminine qualities of caring, listening, understanding, and only 20% of the women in the single *mother* group desired these qualities.

All people are said to have two sides to their personality, feminine and masculine with the desired ratio being half of each gender trait. Socialization requires girls to over-develop their feminine side and boys to over-develop their masculine side. Many boys then feel compelled to be *Macho* and many girls feel compelled to aspire to becoming beauty queens. Society does not tolerate very well the girl who is too masculine, nor the boy who is a *sissy*. Yet placed in certain circumstances, as for example, even an extremely feminine type girl abandoned in rugged terrain may develop her survival skills and may even kill animals in order to live. The *typical all-boy* growing up in the home of ballet teachers may become a ballet dancer.

In all likelihood, the father who finds himself, or chooses to place himself in the position of raising children, has either been conditioned to permit his feminine side and is a nurturing type man to begin with, or the act of raising children has brought out the nurturing side of his personality. As one man

SUMMARY AND ANALYSIS

recently told a researcher, now that he is a partner in a shared-custody arrangement after his divorce, during the week that he has his two small children he is much kinder to them than when he was at home with them with his wife and she was the principal nurturer and he was the disciplinarian. In any event, most of the single fathers who raised their daughters permitted the feminine side of their own personality and this was indirectly taught to their daughters who then desire mates who have nurturing traits. It must be said here that not all fathers in this research were nurturing-type men. Many were described as cold, uncommunicative, and even cruel. But most were responsible to their daughters' emotional and material needs.

Of the single mothers who raised their daughters, most, of necessity developed what might be considered the masculine side of their own personality, that of financial survival in a competitive man's world, becoming the providers, and many suppressed their feminine side. Their masculine side, being most in evidence, was picked up by their daughters who, in turn, desire either androgenous or strong masculine traits in their mate. Most women raised by single mothers had strong mothers and probably gravitate toward stereotypical masculine traits in other women. Many of them said they abhor weak women. Being associated with strong women gives girls a sense of possibilities for women.

Therefore women raised by nurturing single fathers not only have strong masculine traits but also strong feminine traits. But women raised by single *mothers* have more masculine traits than feminine traits. This is borne out by their perception of themselves in the Adjective Check List where a higher percentage scored in the upper percentile range in Masculine Attributes Scale (51%) then in the Feminine Attributes Scale (39%). The girl who grows up with a caring father in the home, has the opposite sex on which to "*bounce off*" her adolescent sexual development. If it is a healthy father-daughter relationship he will assure her that she is doing all right in her role of growing up to be a woman. The girl in the single mother home does not have that opposite sex parent who will approve of her feminine side.

4. Single Parent Families Have Advantages

A father in the home gives the appearance of stability, even though he may be uncommunicative, often absent, or abusive. A mother in the home gives the appearance of wholesomeness, even though she may be alcoholic, demanding, or intrusive. Under the best circumstances, with a father who is present, communicative, supportive and caring, and a mother who is gentle, loving and understanding, and because she does not work outside her home has unlimited time for her children, and where there is enough financial security in the home, a child is blessed. And there are such families. But they are the exception rather than the rule. Actually a family with a father and a mother who does not work outside the home represents only 8% of the families today.

SUMMARY AND ANALYSIS

Tradition, which is important in the biological parents group, has been destroyed in the single parent group. When one parent dies or leaves, whatever habitual patterns of family life there were, come to an end. For a long time, maybe even for years, there is a void. What to do at Christmas? Can the family take a vacation? As time goes on, the trauma of the shock subsides and new patterns evolve, usually without planning. One might say, "*new traditions*" replace the old.

People learn that they can survive what might have been seen as impossible to bear. Widows and divorcees find jobs to support their children and widowers pick up the threads of their lives and arrange for child care. The children go back to school after the funeral, or after the shock of being deserted by one of their parents. Though they are hurting inside, they play on the swings and teeter-totters and force themselves to learn their multiplication tables. They realize earlier than other children that a lot of the work of keeping the household running, rests on their shoulders. No doubt reluctantly and sadly at first they absorb the jobs of vacuuming rugs, getting dinner started, caring for younger children to keep them off the streets. But what they have learned in all of this is how to adapt, how to shed the old, and how to get on with the new.

These are hard lessons, and it is not recommended that children live through this kind of trauma in order to learn adaptation. But children who have survived hardship, and have had a supportive remaining parent, claim they are the stronger for it. Having to make a major life change in their future

THE TWO-PARENT FAMILY IS NOT THE BEST

will probably not be devastating. Many in all groups, including the biological parents group, have said that the problems they have survived have made them stronger.

Girls who are brought up by single parents, whether mothers or fathers, develop strong, independent personalities, but society has a problem with strong, independent women. These women are apt to be assertive, to know that they can get along without men, that they can try new things, that they can test authority. Many have had tremendous responsibilities most of their lives and most are ready and eager to open new doors for themselves because, for them, tradition is not sacred.

As one woman in the single father group wrote, "*I feel that I have obtained a great benefit from my childhood. I think because I had to be responsible for taking care of myself and my sister, etc., that I got a 'jump' on maturity, in relation to others my age. This has meant that there are levels of growth which I feel I have access to, which a majority of people don't seem to have.*" Other women in the single father group wrote, "*I believe that one good parent -- mother or father -- is better than one or two lousy ones. But I am well aware of the burdens of raising children alone. I would not chose to do it that way. It was not my father's choice either.*" "*I think it would be an advantage to have both parents, only if they were happy together, of course.*" "*I feel like being raised by my dad was beneficial. I saw a man's point of view clearer than many women ever see.*"

Another in the single father group wrote, "*I do feel that I've been very fortunate in being brought*

SUMMARY AND ANALYSIS

up by my father. I grew up faster than my peers in several ways. For instance, by age 10, I was given a weekly allowance which I had to budget to buy all of my own clothes, school lunches and entertainment. My father wanted me to do well in school but didn't have the time to make sure I was doing my work. I had to discipline myself." "I think that in some ways growing up with only one parent had advantages because it taught us to grow up and to cope with life as it came." "On the whole - I think being a female brought up by a father has its advantages. One tends to learn more of the male attitudes, more of the 'can do's' than the female 'shouldn't do's'. One also gets to side step the mother-daughter competition I have observed in others." "I feel there were no disadvantages because my dad took over both roles." "Being raised by my father has made me more aggressive and assertive, but males are not able to deal with aggressive females."

"The advantages were these: Dad was busy at work and we weren't always rigidly supervised. Sometimes we were free to read what we wanted, therefore developing our own independent thoughts, experiment with things, sex, drugs, etc..Because we were branching into things, our father was often pulled along. His mind had to grow too, whether or not he agreed with all our ideas or supported all of our activities. For that, we're better off. I get a little guilty, if I consider this an advantage as a result of my mother's death. It's very possible that we would have had this growth with a mother around, too." "I think I'm a stronger woman and more resistant to being intimated by some things because I wasn't taught to be."

THE TWO-PARENT FAMILY IS NOT THE BEST

"I feel that having been raised by my father was both an advantage and a disadvantage. Of course it would have been better to have had both a mother and father, loving and supportive of each other and their children. This is Utopia. I feel the perfect family does not exist, and am only now beginning to be mature enough to make the best of what we had. I think I have an inner strength many women never will have. Because of growing up with no female role model, I was forced to learn to rely on my own intuition and intelligence. This makes me no better nor worse than other women. However it does make me inherently stronger."

"Having no female role model to look to, I am very much into equality and equal representation of women and their rights." "In the long run the experience was probably an advantage especially since I was subsequently widowed. Because of my father's leaving me to solve my own problems, I was not afraid as some widows are, that I couldn't take care of myself. I already knew that." "I did gain a resourcefulness in this process. I had no one to find things for me, or iron my skirt, or help me to get my way with my father. I learned how to take care of myself and get what I needed out of life."

"I have never thought that I was better off being raised by a single parent, but I know that I am no worse off because of it. I know that a lot of single parents try to be both mother and father. My father was like that for awhile. He was a lousy mother but he was an outstanding father. And that was enough." "I had the opportunity to see that men can lovingly raise children. I have the drive/motivation for a good career and the en-

couragement to be independent. Not a stereotypical upbringing at all."

Many women in both the single parent groups wrote that they didn't have to *'play dumb,'* or learn to practice *'feminine wiles,'* to *'get a man.'* They didn't have to depend on a man for financial security or to complete them as human beings. They also said that many men feel threatened by independent, autonomous women. But that, they said, was the man's problem, not theirs.

While the loss of a parent was not without trauma for the women in this study, for some there is compensation. For instance, for women in the single father family who never knew their mother, or women in any group who were badly treated by their mothers, it is said that in adulthood, in having and caring for their own children these women experience themselves as the "*mothered child*" which they never were. These women transfer to their children the love and understanding which they did not receive and in so doing restore their own lack of mothering to themselves.

There is also the advantage in single parent families that a girl does not have to compete with her mother for the affection of her father, or a boy does not have to compete with his father for the affection of his mother.

One woman appreciates not having a mother. *"What I remember and cherish most about my motherlessness was the lack of hovering by an adult -- the constant supervision most of my girlfriends had to endure. Although I was asked to account for my whereabouts and actions, where I went and what I did was left lar-*

THE TWO-PARENT FAMILY IS NOT THE BEST

gely to my own judgment. I was able to satisfy my curiosity, adventuresomeness, and love of exploring easily. Dad had raised us early to be able to look after and make decisions for ourselves so we wouldn't have to rely on others, even him, unnecessarily. I believe it was because he taught us <u>how</u> to think, rather than <u>what</u> to think that he was able to trust us with a great deal of freedom and responsibility.

Of course there are disadvantages, expressed mainly in this manner: "*Growing up with a father and no mother was very difficult. I never really felt as though my father understood such things as the need for new clothes, allowance, money, or phone calls to other friends.*" "*My general impression would be that in spite of some advantages it is more difficult and less desirable to grow up with only a father.*"

Another who mentions both the advantages and disadvantages wrote, "*I don't feel as if I've missed very much. I have had a lot of wonderful experiences. Yet I do believe I missed a wonderful experience when I grew up without a mother. I grew up as a happy person, yet I do believe that on the sub-conscious level something was always missing.*" In families where there are two parents, many children have been exposed to severe parental fighting from which children of single parents were spared, though many related to fighting before a divorce. One in the single father group wrote, "*I used to witness fights among my friends' parents and remember feeling lucky I didn't have to see my own parents fight.*"

Then, what might be considered a disadvantage of the single parent family, as one woman wrote, "*One of the hardest things for me as I remem-*

SUMMARY AND ANALYSIS

ber was the feeling of helplessness when my mother would be angry with me. The child of the single parent has no recourse, no one with any power to complain to - certainly no one to 'play off' against the other."

As one in the biological parents group wrote about her parents' fighting, "*screaming and shouting were conversational tones.*"

Another research study was conducted at Mills College, Oakland, California, directed by Nicole La Freniere, which involved women raised with a father present and women raised where there was no father. In using the Adjective Check List, the results indicated that women raised by single mothers scored higher than women raised with fathers present, on *Dominance, Endurance, Ideal Self, Nurturing Parent,* and *Adult Scale*. The results of the Mills College study indicated even stronger personality strengths for women raised by single mothers than did this research study, possibly because of the methodology. Nevertheless the results tend toward the same direction. The report on the Mills College study describes the results further. "*This indicates that the women with absent fathers describe themselves as ambitious, assertive, confident, gregarious, practical, and self-seeking. Their concept of self and ideal correspond more closely than that of the father-present women, indicating personal adjustment.*"

Currently the statistics on new births is that 13% of all babies born are born to unwed, teenage mothers. Also, the Census Bureau, January, 1988 reported that one-fifth of all children live in single parent homes, and that 25% of all the family com-

THE TWO-PARENT FAMILY IS NOT THE BEST

positions are single parent families. The report also found that single parents are far more likely to be less educated, earning less money, and unemployed. Whatever the disparity between two-parent families and single parent families, the difference is even greater when white and black or hispanic families are considered, with white single parents having advantages in all respects. Nevertheless, while these are definite and serious disadvantages of single parenthood which must be considered, there are also advantages for children in single parenthood. The comments here from the women who have grown up in single parent homes, and the results of the Research Questionnaire, combined with the results of the Adjective Check List used in this research and also the use of the Adjective Check List at Mills College, suggest advantages.

Most statistics on single families refer to single mothers. It is as if the single father family does not exist. Yet, even without statistics, there is an awareness that fathers raising their children by themselves is a growing phenomenon. Eventually the statistics may tell us about the level of education of a single father, his salary range and type of employment as the statistics now tell us about single mothers. For instance, in a study made by the National Association of Social Workers of single mothers in 12 states in 1987, 60% of the mothers said they believed their families were stronger than two-parent families, and 25% said they were just as strong.

Generally conceded to be the root of many social problems, the single parent family, which invariably means the single mother family, has been the scapegoat for many of this country's ills. It is usually the female who is either directly or indirectly blamed. The common erroneous complaint has been, "*If only women would stay home and take care of their kids there wouldn't be so many divorces, kids wouldn't be dropping out of school and getting into trouble. There would be better morals.*" As history has recorded, the virtue of a country rests on the virtue of its women. A woman raising children by herself, or even an employed mother in a two parent family, is not held up as an ideal mother.

To combat the negative and sometimes hostile attitude about single parent families, society should be made aware of the advantages for children of single parenthood. There is a smug and erroneous assumption that two parent families are the best for children, an assumption which should be corrected. In addition to helping to provide career and child care opportunities for single parents, it would be good for single parents today to know of the strength of the children grown to adulthood who were raised by single parents.

5. Most Children With Step Mothers are

Emotionally and Otherwise Abused

While there were some disturbingly sad anecdotes from women in all groups in this research, the most consistently cruel came from the women who had grown up with a step mother. Not that all step mothers were cold and uncaring. There were several who were dearly loved by their step daughters. But these were rare. Not only did the step mothers cause grievous unhappiness for the girls in these families, but their own biological fathers, married to their step mothers, failed their daughters.

These girls had nowhere else to go. One of their parents had died so it wasn't as though there had been a divorce and then remarriages and a second set of parents. Sometimes relatives of the deceased parent attempted to help, but often the step parent prevented the girl from seeing these relatives. It is almost as though the step parent was more or less jealous of the ghost of their spouse's first spouse.

On every question, when comparing answers from women who had step mothers with those of women who were in the step parent group but had their own biological mother, there is almost a two to one difference in the degree of either helpfulness or loss. For instance, on the question, "*Do you feel because of your family situation that you lost your childhood?*" 30% of the women who had biological mothers in this group answered, "*Yes,*" compared with 58% of the women with step mothers. To the question, "*Was your childhood happy?*" 63% with biological mothers in this step parent group answered, "*Yes,*" compared with 37% of the women with step mothers.

To the question, "*Was your father there for you?*" 36% with step fathers answered "*Yes,*" compared with but only 32% with biological fathers in this group. "*Was your mother there for you?*" 32% of

SUMMARY AND ANALYSIS

the women with step mothers answered "*Yes,*" compared with 60% of the women with biological mothers in this step parent group. Biological fathers were not very helpful for their daughters when the mother had died.

Thirty-two percent of the step mothers used alcohol excessively compared with 15% of the biological mothers in this step parent group. Fifteen percent of women in this step parent group with step fathers said their fathers used alcohol excessively compared with 20% of the girls' biological fathers. Twenty-eight percent of the step mothers beat their daughters compared with 12% of the biological mothers.

This group, as a whole, has the highest percentage (27%) of women who had been sexually abused. When the group is separated as to those with step mothers and those with step fathers, it is the group with step fathers that has the highest rate of sexual abuse. Thirty-eight percent of the women with step fathers had been sexually abused, mostly by their step fathers, though neighbors, step brothers, family friends, a janitor and a teacher contributed to this percentage. Sixteen percent of women with step mothers had been sexually abused, the abusers included brothers, step brothers, an uncle and a cousin.

This step parent group has the highest percentage of women who had fantasy mothers (56% of those with step mothers, and the highest percentage of those with fantasy fathers,(42%) of those with step fathers. Almost half of the women with step mothers did not get along with their step mothers at all. The group as a whole has the highest percentage who have *hostile* relationships with women, the highest which have *negative* relationships with women, the highest which have *difficult* relationships with women, and the highest percentage which has *hostile* relationships with men. Thirty-one percent of women in this group are overweight.

In spite of the difficulties for many girls in growing up in a step parent family, many achieved success after they left their families. Once again, it is recognized that college degrees and earned income are not the only measures of success, but they are one measure. Thirty-three percent of the women in the step parent group graduated from college, the highest percentage of all groups. Twenty-two percent received graduate degrees. Equalled only by the women in the single father group, 29% of the women in this step parent group are employed in professional positions, and exceeding the other three groups, 24% of this group are employed in the managerial positions. This group has the highest percentage who earned $30,000. to $49,000. in 1987.

It is the step parent group that had the highest percentage scoring over the 50th percentile range on Autonomy on the Adjective Check List. Autonomy is described by the Scale as "*To act independently of others or of social values and expectations.*" If one survives emotional hardship, one apparently develops a strong sense of independence. Though many were emotionally and some physically and sexually abused, most of the women in this group were capable of getting on with their lives. Being autonomous, they have achieved a separation from their earlier traumatizers. And as they have the highest percent which scored high in the personality trait, *"Change,"* on the Adjective Check List, described as *"seeks novelty of experience and avoids routine,"* most of the women in this group may very well keep life interesting for themselves and others.

WHAT IS A MOTHER?

Is a mother female? Is it a prerequisite that a mother give birth? When we speak of the mother-infant bond as the strongest bond known to humans, what of those infants whose mothers died or abandoned them at birth and had no mother with whom to bond? What if the first infant bonding is with a male? Wouldn't the strongest bond for that infant be the father-infant bond and wouldn't it be as strong? As Phyllis Chesler asks in her article, "*What is a Mother?*" in *Ms.* May, 1988, "*Is the father only an income-generating sperm donor? Or is he as potentially 'maternal' as any biological mother?*"

If, as is claimed, girls learn mothering from having been mothered, then what of the boys who have also been mothered? Did they not learn mothering as well? And if so, what did they do with that learning? If most women have a desire to be mothers, as is claimed, do all men instinctively also have a desire to mother?

We seem to take our conclusions about the roles of mothers and fathers both from nature and from early societies. In hunting-gathering societies, for instance, it was believed that women didn't join the hunt as often as men because they needed to stay close to the compound to nurse their infants. Actually women stayed close to the compound to gather nuts and fruits and other foods so that the men coming home from the hunt empty-handed would have something to eat because the hunt is an unreliable

SUMMARY AND ANALYSIS

source of food. The male/female work division was based on which gender had breasts.

Yet there are tribal societies even now where the men stay in the compound to tend the children all day while the women go into the fields to cultivate and harvest. In the village of Taute in the West Sepik of New Guinea, women go deep into the bush in the morning to chop and harvest the Sago Palm for food for the group and they do not return until nightfall. Their husbands have the major responsibility for childcare. When it begins to get dark, the children and men stand at the edge of the jungle and call to the women to come home before it gets dark, before the bush spirit gets them.

In the world of nature most species are cared for by the females, but even in nature there are exceptions. It cannot be said categorically that it is not natural for males to raise offspring. In some species the father takes over the role of mothering. The male Lotus bird incubates the eggs while the female goes in search of a new partner. He feeds and transports them until they can get along on their own.

So it isn't that men can't mother, but rather that the male mother is not fully, culturally accepted. He is either an aberration, or an object of great respect for taking on a task considered foreign to his nature, as in Dustin Hoffman's movie, "*Kramer Vs. Kramer.*" Yet mothering may not be so foreign to a boy's nature, but rather it may be that he is conditioned out of that nature.

Most little boy babies are cuddled and hugged, adored, and lovingly nursed at their mothers' breasts, just as little girl babies are. Little

THE TWO-PARENT FAMILY IS NOT THE BEST

boys would play with dolls just as their sisters do, except his parents must forbid that or risk disgrace. The little girl may continue playing at mothering if she wishes, but the boy's desire to mother must be diverted to masculine activities such as playing with toy automobiles. He must be masculinized early before *dangerous* habits are formed.

There is nothing inherent in a girl's desire to play with dolls (speaking metaphorically) and nothing inherent in a boy's desire to play with toy cars. These personal preferences have to be carefully taught and it all starts when the girl is dressed in a ruffled dress and the boy in stern, straight trousers. True, the girl may these days also be wearing long pants, but she is probably adorned with a bow here and there. Not so with the boy. Frills and decorations are *"sissy stuff,"* and no matter how attractive, must be denied to boys.

Both boys and girls have to be prepared for the roles society requires of them. For girls who had mothers in their formative years and are going to be mothers, it is a continuous track from birth to motherhood. For boys who must later mother their children, if their wives should die or desert them and leave them with children these men wish to raise, the track, which had been taking them only along a masculinized route, now abruptly turns him back to those years when he was mothered. He may still be a stern, macho father, or he may let his feminine side come into action. Women do not have a corner on empathy. It's a human trait but not very well developed in men because of the way they are raised.

SUMMARY AND ANALYSIS

In mothering his young children by himself, he may be able to dredge up those suppressed memories of his mother's emotional and physical love for him. Or maybe he is one of the boys who had a nurturing father who believed there were other values as important as "*making a man*" of his son. Maybe he is one who was permitted to be vulnerable without being made ashamed. In that case, his children will be lucky because they will have a parent with an androgenous personality which they can embody in their own personalities.

One of the many things learned in this research is that men can do a good job raising children by themselves. True, not all did, but then neither did all women do a good job of mothering. The fact that men can be good sole parents, however, will not be generally accepted because most men probably don't *want* to raise children. Even though men can do as good a job in this important task as women, it will still be said, "*But children really should be raised by their mothers.*" This is said even though in the Middle Ages middle and upper class women put their children out to be wet nursed for the first year or two and mothers did not see their babies again until they were toddlers.

Nancy Chodorow writes in her book, *The Reproduction of Mothering*, "*That women mother is basic to the sexual division of labor and generates a psychology and ideology of male dominance as well as an ideology about women's capacities and nature.*" Is there anything wrong with a sexual division of labor?s Nothing, Karen Horney, psychiatrist, writes, except that historically the division of labor cannot

THE TWO-PARENT FAMILY IS NOT THE BEST

be separated from sexual inequality. Who profits from the sexual division of labor? Not the women who fill low-paying caregiver jobs.

Because attitudes change slowly, and because it is to men's advantage, both at home and in the employment world, that women continue to be the principal providers of child care, we will, for many years, hear that mothers should really be the ones to raise their children.

As one woman raised by a step mother writes, "*I think that having a step mother gave me a broader idea about what 'mothering' is all about, and that many people can 'mother' you. After my mother died, I was 'mothered' by my father and an aunt who lived close by. Then my step mother brought her own 'brand' of 'mothering'. As I have grown older other people have met my nurturing needs in different ways and I was open to that.*"

There is a myth about working mothers which needs to be explored here. It is often said that women who work outside the home are contributing to the corruption of the country. An example of this, of how working mothers are blamed for the breakdown of the morals of the country was evident recently at the University of Utah. Linda Ellerbee, a speaker at the "*Women in the Workplace Conference,*" quoted Gordon Hinckley, a Mormon leader: "*It is my opinion that the very situation of an ever increasing number of mothers out of the home and in the workplace is a root cause of many problems of delinquency, drugs and gangs, both male and female.*" There are no studies to indicate that working mothers cause delinquency, or that non-working mothers prevent delinquency.

SUMMARY AND ANALYSIS

Even if there were some credence to Mr. Hinckley's comments, which there aren't, he does not concern himself with the fact that most mothers work because they have to, that they either have no husband, or their husbands earn less than $10,000 a year.

The vice president of the American Academy of Pediatrics, Dr. Antoinette Eaton, recently stated, as quoted in the May 22, 1990 *Los Angeles Times*, "*...most studies of children older than six months have shown no difference in development between children in day care and children cared for by their mothers.*" She was quoted, "*I can say without hesitancy that there is no proof that the mother working outside the home has a deleterious effect. The real issue is that the environment must be one that is most conducive to the child's development -- whether it's at home or at a day-care center.*"

A mother is more what one does than what one is. A mother is the one who provides the continuity of nurturing, health care and sustenance for the child. Although a father will have a more difficult time of it because he has been taught to be a non-mother, a mother can be a man.

THE TWO-PARENT FAMILY IS NOT THE BEST

WHAT IS A FATHER?

It is extremely difficult to change a society's belief. We have a dogma about motherhood. It says simply that mothers should stay home and raise the children. Because women wish to please men, they adapt to men's wishes. At one time the only way women could survive was to find a man to support them. They were obliged to defer to men and to keep them happy. Men's wishes became women's wishes. Consequently men's wishes about women raising children are incorporated in women's psyche and actually become women's need, or *part of women's nature*. But as mentioned in the section on *What is a Mother?* if needing to mother is part of a woman's nature, why isn't it also part of a man's nature?

There is an ongoing program in Harlem where black men are coming forward to help with black babies born addicted to crack cocaine. They come into the hospital wards and sit and hold the babies. As the author, Toni Morrison said, "*This is helping the babies, but just think what it's doing for the men.!*"

Because the woman carries the child in her womb and gives birth, does this exclude the father from the need to nurture the child he has fathered? Or is it that his maternal needs were subordinated as he was masculinized?

Though we have a firm dogma about motherhood, we do not provide the basics to support this. We do not provide the services or the help which would permit most women to stay home and take

SUMMARY AND ANALYSIS

care of their children, such as low cost housing, adequate pay for husband's menial jobs, or even minimum health care. Businesses hire mothers, often to do jobs that pay less than those which men do, yet our dogma insinuates that if a mother works she is really neglecting what the dogma says is her first responsibility. It is as though all women had husbands, or if they did, all husbands earned enough to support their families above the poverty level. To be "*a good mother,*" often means a mother should spend most of her hours with her children, though there is cause to believe that this may be harmful to both the children and the mother.

When a woman is described as "*a good mother,*" it will generally be understood what is meant. But when a man is described as "*a good father,*" the definition is somewhat blurred because the dogma about fathers is less precise. It says that fathers should "*be there*" for their children, though it doesn't really say what they should do, once they are "*there.*" It says fathers should not abandon their children, fathers should give advice when needed, fathers should provide money. But the dogma doesn't require any *specific* activity with their children, such as the dogma requires of mothers, like feeding children and making sure they are warm and secure.

Fatherhood does not demand such consistent performance as does motherhood. Society is not very much concerned about men being good fathers but society is very concerned about women being good mothers. As a matter of fact, much of the blame for the country's ills comes to rest on some suspicion

THE TWO-PARENT FAMILY IS NOT THE BEST

that too many women are not being good mothers. When the crime rate goes up, when unemployment goes up, when educational standards go down, when the school drop-out rate goes up, the tendency is to look to the women. Women are seen as the ones who should hold the family together. There seldom are complaints that fathers are absent, or if they are home that they are preoccupied with interests other than their children. We have no dogma about working fathers.

The responsibility for raising children and preserving the "*ideal*" almost *pure family* is seen as women's job. It is believed by many that if mothers don't do a good job, society suffers. It is as though the whole moral fiber of the country depends on women. This harkens back to the days of the Vestal Virgins in Ancient Rome when the Virgins were symbolic of Rome's purity, no matter what atrocities the Romans were committing. The Vestal Virgins were selected to keep the fires burning at the sacred hearth of the goddess Vesta. They were sworn to virginity for thirty years. If any were found guilty of sexual relations they were burned to death. This reliance on women's purity for men's morality is also reminiscent of the ancient laws which forbid women from drinking wine for fear they would relax too much and their sexual drive would take over. In other words, that they could be easily seduced and would no longer be *virtuous*.

Throughout history the moral standing of a country rests on its women. Men can go off to war, kill and plunder and rape, but the ideal is that they come home to virtuous women to be comforted and

SUMMARY AND ANALYSIS

purified. Womanhood, as exemplified in motherhood, is protected terrain, because men's psyche needs to rely on this balance. The woman at home to soothe and to cleanse is a necessary myth for the male who battles the dragon each day. Regardless of how dependent this country's Gross National Product is on female employment, working mothers are still blamed for the country's ills. They are not home to tend the children and the returning warriors. But what happens to the male psyche that tells the male employer that women should be home mothering, at the same time that he hires women in order for his corporation to make a profit? What happens to the nobility of his soul? And what are his beliefs about his role as a father?

How have men been prepared for fatherhood? In a recent study of over 700 junior high school students, girls were still narrowing their choices for jobs in the future to four: nurse, secretary, teacher, and mother. Boys listed options without limit, and no boy mentioned *"father."* Fatherhood is visualized by many as a passive activity. The better fathers take on the roles of interacting with their children, of giving advice, of being a good role model, and of providing financial support. For these better fathers there is much more to fatherhood than being, as Chesler says, an *"income generating sperm donor."*

Without a father, one might ask, who would give the children a male point of view? That's easy. All they have to do is turn on the T.V. The *world is a male point of view*. Children are said to watch more hours of T.V. than they spend in school. What do

THE TWO-PARENT FAMILY IS NOT THE BEST

they see on T.V? Men. Men running governments, making military decisions, men making touchdowns and home runs, men merging huge corporations, men with bullet-proof vests storming crack houses, and men being led away in handcuffs. It is impossible to avoid the male point of view.

What then is a father? "*A father,*" one person suggested, "*is not so important in the family when the children are very young, except maybe as the disciplinarian. But when the children are older, then it's important for the father to give advice and to take his children fishing.*"

He was then asked, "*What if his children are girls?*"

"*Oh, I hadn't thought about it that way. Well, I don't know. It would be good for him to be around when she goes on dates and he can give the boy the once-over.*"

"*Would he take his little girl fishing?*"

The man raised his shoulders and held them for a minute, pondering. "*Maybe.*"

The dogma about fatherhood says, further, that fathers should be there for sons and daughters when they enter puberty to smooth the son's road into manhood and to approve or disapprove the daughter's blossoming femininity and her dates. Generally speaking, a mother's role is an active role, to care for her children until adulthood, but a father's role is more passive until the children are in their teens.

It is true that mothers can be fathers and fathers can be mothers and there are advantages in single parent families. It is also true that in two

SUMMARY AND ANALYSIS

parent families the ideal would be, from their children's birth, for *both* parents to love, nurture, advise, provide for and then release them at adulthood. Fathers who permit their softer side to emerge, who participate in what is considered *mothering*, provide good role models for their daughters and their sons, and in addition they allow their sons to develop *their* softer side, their feminine side. They can steer their sons away from that sense of betrayal many boys feel when they must turn from the exclusive love of their mothers in the passage to become a man. The sons can learn to communicate, to not fear intimacy, to not hold women in contempt, and can learn to be nurturing fathers in their turn.

As it is now, most men assume that if they don't take care of their children, someone else will. Women, however, assume that if they don't take care of their children, they won't be cared for. Yet fathers have raised children successfully as indicated by the comments from women in this study and also as indicated by history books. Thomas Jefferson, James Madison and Cotton Mather were all raised by their fathers. Jefferson's earliest memories are about his father caring for him when he was an infant.

It's time to change the dogma about mothering so that it includes an expanded dogma about fathering. Since there is very little *required* of fathers by society now, except financial security, their sphere should be broadened to include them in the human process of helping an infant develop to adulthood. Currently *mothering* is a verb which includes almost exclusive care and raising of children. *Fathering* is a verb which means impregnating. Thoughtful,

THE TWO-PARENT FAMILY IS NOT THE BEST

responsible, loving men want more than that. The dogmas of the past do not fit the present.

SUMMARY AND ANALYSIS

WHAT IS A FAMILY?

The answer changes with the times. As was mentioned in the Introduction to this book, the earliest families from the beginning of human existence on earth until the Age of Cultivation about 15,000 to 10,000 B.C., consisted of mothers and their children. It was not known until the beginning of animal husbandry that males had any part in procreation. Knowledge of the physical reproduction process was a long time coming. In these early "*single mother*" families, the male important to a woman and her children was the woman's brother. The consequences of sexual activity were unknown. As mentioned previously, a woman believed she became honored by the Child Spirit when she passed a certain tree in the forest, or swam in the lagoon at a certain height of the moon. Women were considered supernatural and were revered because they could create human life.
    With the Age of Cultivation people realized that if cattle with horns were placed in an area with cattle with udders, the ones with udders some moons later would reproduce themselves. Men related this to men's sexual life and realized the children which the women had always claimed as theirs exclusively, were actually the men's. Children were an important asset because they could hoe the gardens and watch the cattle. Children became men's property.
    This was happening in a time in history when property was becoming important. Prior to the Age of Cultivation when people lived nomadic lives they

THE TWO-PARENT FAMILY IS NOT THE BEST

did not value possessions which would have to be carried as they moved from place to place in search of food. With the knowledge that grain planted in the ground and watered would, in time, sprout from the earth and provide food for the group, came, for many tribes, the end of a wandering lifestyle and the beginning of the desire for personal property.

After believing for so long that men had no part in reproduction, with the Age of Cultivation and animal husbandry there was then a realization that men were vital to the creation of other human beings. For many thousands of years it was believed that men were the *most* important. Even as late as the Golden Age of Greece around 400 B.C. Aristotle, the greatest scientist of his time, proclaimed that woman made no contribution to human creation other than being the vessel which carried the man's child. As explained in <u>Women's Roots,</u> *"This theory persisted until after the invention of the microscope, sixteen hundred years later. In 1786 Spallanzani discovered male germ cells, and in 1843, the fusion of male and female cells was understood. In 1879, barely 100 years ago, this fusion was demonstrated by Hermon Fol. Little wonder that prehistoric primitives had no knowledge of paternity when our own scientific civilization has only so recently learned the actual human procreative process."*

After paternity was understood, how, then, did the family change? Not very much for awhile. Women and children lived separately from men who lived in the Men's House. The husbands visited their wives but returned to the Men's House which held the clan's sacred items and in which secret tribal rituals were held from which women were excluded and in which boys entering puberty were initiated and made privy to the tribal secrets.

With the knowledge of paternity and the value of property there was a change in the activities of women. As men, contemplating their own death, desired to pass on their property to their sons, they needed to ensure that the sons were theirs. Women's sexual freedom was then curtailed. She must be available from then on only to her husband. Monogamy was not required of her husband. It was the birth of the double standard.

The family with the restriction of the wife's activities continues through history. The husband may or may not live with his wife or have much to do with her. In ancient Athens upper class women were required to remain in the women's quarters. They could go out of their homes chaperoned only for two reasons -- to shop or to go to funerals. Husbands had liasons with courtesans, and/or homosexual relations which were stylish at that time. As only the children born of citizen men could become citizens, a wife's continual confinement in her own home helped to guarantee that her children were her husband's.

Through the Middle Ages and the Renaissance almost all middle and upper class marriages were arranged by parents. While many of these marriages evolved into loving partnerships, and many were probably monogamous, the purpose of marriage was not to unite two people in love, but to join large landholdings or to end disputes between neighbors. The family was a husband, wife and children with husbands frequently away from home doing

THE TWO-PARENT FAMILY IS NOT THE BEST

battle for his Lord, often encasing his wife in a Chastity Belt before he left to ensure her fidelity. He must guarantee that his children were his. The law of property depended on the chastity of wives.

Modern family in the United States, until the massive influx of women into the labor market after World War II, consisted of a husband and wife who remained at home to care for their children. It is no wonder that a woman unable to have children must have been nearly devastated as the purpose of her life under those conditions was to bear children.

A man's manliness depended on being able to afford to keep a wife at home. Men would not permit wives to work on pain of losing status. The more household help he could employ the more he gained status. Many middle and upper class women were reduced to a condition of genteel idleness. They had maids, laundresses, governesses, gardeners, cooks. What was there for them to do except embroider and play a musical instrument? Many did more of course, but not because it was expected.

Though the family of husband, wife at home, and children now comprises only 8% of the total families in this country, it is still held up as the "*ideal*", the "*normal*," or for some confused reason, the "*nuclear*" family. What is "*normal*" for one time and place is not necessarily "*normal*" for another time and place. Professionals in the field of family relations are frustrated as they try to make the public understand that the family, as was known in history, barely exists today.

If "*nuclear*" is supposed to refer to the family as it was in the beginning of humans on earth, then the word is used erroneously because the "*nuclear*" family was a mother and her children. It is believed that those who first used phrases such as "*normal*," and "*nuclear*" and "*ideal*," intended the phrases to mean a family with a mother who stayed home, father, and children. The "*ideal*" or "*normal*" or "*nuclear*" family is a myth of romanticists and conservatives who on one hand want women to stay home, and on the other hand want them to be available for jobs when they are needed. It is politically and economically expedient to preserve the myth of the "*ideal*" family. There is no "*ideal*" family.

At present the U.S.Census Bureau reports that the demographics regarding families in the United States include: 29% married couples without children, 27% married couples with children, 8% other families with children, 6.6% other families without children, 4.4% other nonfamily households and 24% men and women living alone. These figures include gay and lesbian couples, some of whom are raising children, their own or adopted. There is no discussion of what family structures exist within the 8% of "*other families with children.*" This must include single parents, mostly female, and many grandparents who are now raising children because of the drug problems of the children's mothers. The 27% of "*married couples with children*" must include step parents. Also, though married couples with children represent 27% other statistics elaborate on this. Only 8% of all families have a mother who stays home.

An important statistic related to this study tells us that since 1980 single-mother families have

THE TWO-PARENT FAMILY IS NOT THE BEST

increased by 32%. But what is more startling and pertinent to this study is that since 1980 single-father families have increased 75%.

In the armed services, as of February, 1991, there were 67,000 single parents, two-thirds of them men.

Another report which comes from the American Demographics Association gives more specific information about some children. Their figures tell us that 27% of white children and 63% of black children do *not* live in households with both of their biological parents. Of those children, most live with their biological mother only, slightly less than half as many as live with their biological mother only, live with their biological mother and step father. Those living with a biological father only, or a biological father and step mother, represented less than 2% of those not living with both biological parents.

Another Census report, "*Marital Status and Living Arrangements*" dated May, 1988, stated that 2.3 million unmarried couples of the opposite sex are living together and 700,000 are raising children. There are 1.5 million couples of the same sex living together, including 92,000 with children. Of children under age 18, 24% live with just one parent. In households of the same sex, 803,000 were two men and of those 11,000 had children. Households with two females numbered 748,000 and included 81,000 children. Families come in many different forms.

In the state of California, a group of people living as a family can now obtain an ornate color certificate certifying that they are "*The family of -----.*"

SUMMARY AND ANALYSIS

Today there are many different family groups. For instance, there are people who are raising children but not adopting them because the biological parents are not able to care for their children. The certificates provide a certain sense of "*belonging*" to people who might otherwise feel unconnected to a family. They help the foster parents obtain health care for children, and give homosexual partners visiting rights in hospitals.These registered documents are issued under a section of the California Corporations Code and have been used by garden clubs, fraternities and homeowners associations.

Discussions about the importance of the "*normal*" family persist, both in the media and in government circles. When the so-called "*breakdown of the family,*" is referred to as the cause of the breakdown of morals in the country, the word, "*breakdown*" usually is translated, "*divorce*." It is as though if all men and women stayed married, even if the marriages were empty, somehow the country would be better off. Those who call for the return to the "*ideal*" family, would bring back families that would not fit this time in history. For one thing, as mentioned before, our country, no matter how its government may criticize working mothers, depends for its Gross National Product on the production of women. Secondly, women have changed. Most are beginning to believe that they should have an important role in issues which concern them and their children. They do not sit back and wait for their husbands to come home from work to tell them what goes on in the world. Women are involved in all the major social issues such as nuclear disarmament movements, en-

THE TWO-PARENT FAMILY IS NOT THE BEST

vironmental issues, childcare and health care legislation. Women, either as single women or married women with families, are coming into the world view and participating as fully as they are permitted to do.

The family will survive because it is forever changing. The so-called "*breakdown of the family,*" is simply the "*changing of the family.*" But changing the public understanding of what the family is today, is as difficult as changing the dogma of motherhood. Yet institutions which survive are those which change with the times. The family, which is defined here as any group of two or more people who live together with some basis for mutuality, will survive as long as human beings need each other. Where there are children, the family composition is irrelevant to the child's healthy development. What matters is the quality, the durability and the dependability of the personal relationships.

SUMMARY AND ANALYSIS

IMPLICATIONS FOR THE FUTURE

REWRITING THE MYTH OF THE TWO PARENT FAMILY

Changing myths seems impossible, especially when there are advantages to some people to keep them. The myth that the two parent family is the best, is just that -- a myth. Myths serve an important purpose and are the basis of religion and governments. But they are not based on fact. Our government is founded on the myth of equality. Actual equality does not exist but it is something to aspire to. The myth that the two parent family is best for children served a purpose. It was something to aspire to and no doubt kept fathers in families who might otherwise have left their wives and children, at a time in history when women did not work and were therefore dependent on a man for subsistence.

Many happy two-parent families have existed throughout history, and many unhappy two parent families have survived, locked in emotional misery because divorce was scandalous, (a method for preserving the myth) because women could not earn a living, and because of the power of the myth. Unhappy people stayed in marriages *"for the sake of the children,"* -- a great burden to put on children -- and themselves. .

Because women in the biological parents group in this research had as much strife in their childhood as the women in other groups, it is time to rewrite the myth of the two parent family being best for children.

Among much of what has been learned in this research is that maintaining the myth of the superiority of the two parent family not only lends itself to deceit but it is also harmful to those *not* in a two parent family. If a child is not in what is considered the *best* or the *normal* family arrangement, she/he feels *different* as most of the women in this research felt who were not in the biological parents group. Being in what is perceived as a second class situation can tarnish a child's self-esteem. Many women expressed a sense of shame which they felt in their childhood because of their single parentage.

While most of the women in this research who lived in single or step parent families overcame that sense of being outside the norm, it was something the children today should *not* have to overcome. There are and will be so many children growing up in single parent homes that their numbers should help relieve stress about not having both parents, and should keep them from feeling so different. But more importantly, they should know that the two parent family, which is held up to them as the ideal, in which they have no part, is, *as a category,* no better than *their* family category.

The increase in the number of single parent families and the lower financial ability of single parent families means that there will be more children living in poverty because most single parents are women. When the media refers to single parent families it is understood that the single parent is a woman. The growing number of single *father* families is practically ignored. It is known that single father families fare better economically than single mother families because men generally earn more money.

Now and in the future, conferences on family life must include some recognition that families *other* than two parent families deserve respect, support, encouragement and praise for doing a difficult job. Single parents and children of single parents need to know that *any* family, *including single and step parent families,* which has financial security, good personal relationships, which cares about its children and promotes their healthy interests, is a good family for children.

REWRITING THE DOGMA OF MOTHERHOOD

AND FATHERHOOD

From what has been learned in this research it is important to change the dogma that it is women's *nature* to raise the children and man's *nature* to be the family provider. This belief was developed by men and by women and it can be changed by women and men. Such a division of labor expands men's horizons and limits women's. Women subscribe to this dogma because they want to please men, and be-

THE TWO-PARENT FAMILY IS NOT THE BEST

cause most women probably do enjoy raising children. But it has been learned here that almost without exception mothers can do anything a father can and vice versa.

The dogma that women should raise the children heaps guilt on women who don't *want* to have children, or, if they do have children, on those who would like to be or are employed, or on those who would like to stay home and raise their children but who need the money for basic family needs. The division of labor, based on the assumed qualities of women to nurture, influences the jobs women acquire when they enter the labor market. Most jobs for women are service oriented, assisting other people. These jobs pay less than men's jobs which are production oriented. The gender roles in the labor market, based on the dogma, are part of the structure of sexual discrimination.

At any given time in history, different factions may develop different beliefs. The group which has the power will develop a dogma which will help it stay in power and will make the dogma acceptable to the weaker group by saying that "*it is nature,*" or "*it's in the Bible.*" or "*it's in the Koran,*" etc.

It is often said that women should stay home for the first five years, as though there is some magical number in five years. Yet studies show that caring people who are not biological mothers can do as good a job as mothers in raising children. The most recent research indicates that children need a group of people to care for them consistently. But many mothers will be made to feel guilty when they leave their infants in a good child care center even if there

SUMMARY AND ANALYSIS

is no evidence to indicate that this is harmful to the child. In fact, as the psychiatrist, Karen Horney, suggests in her collection of essays *'Feminine Psychology'*, *"exclusive single parenting is bad for mother and child alike...mothers in such a setting are liable to overinvest or overwhelm the relationship...children are better off in situations where love and relationship are not a scarce resource, controlled and manipulated by one person."*

The basis for the initial insistence on women as mothers is derived from the fact that women give birth to children. Any efforts to include men as equal partners in early and later child raising is often repudiated on the grounds that because she gave birth it is she who should mother. Built into this argument, but not mentioned, are the advantages to men who then do not have to change diapers and feed their infants, and to the business world which profits from the division of labor which carries over into female/male employment.

DAUGHTERS OF SINGLE PARENTS

What did the women in this research learn growing up with a single parent? Most said, in spite of childhood difficulties, they learned to be independent, resourceful, dependable, self-reliant and self-confident. These findings as related to girls growing up with single mothers were similar to those of the Mills College study. Characteristics that

THE TWO-PARENT FAMILY IS NOT THE BEST

develop in single parent homes would seem to provide an almost inexhaustible pool of strong citizens on whom this country could depend to enhance its well-being. But, in fact, strong, independent women are feared by most men in power. Strong, independent women are referred to as *aggressive*, a trait admired in men. But before too long men will need to recognize and accept the fact that most women do not generally have the same characteristics that their mothers had. With the tremendous growth in the number of single parents who will be raising responsible, independent girls because their single parents work, there will be in the near future girls grown to adulthood who can make their way in the world without depending on men.

Typical of this prophetic situation is the analogy of two tropical birds in New Guinea studied by a Smithsonian zoologist, as reported in the December 1989 issue of *Scientific American*. This zoologist studied two species, the Manucodes and the Raggiana. The male Manucodes works with his mate to build the nest and then stays with her until the nestlings are able to fly. He is a dutiful, faithful mate. He and she spend all their time searching for and bringing food back to the nest. On the other hand, the male Raggiana spends most of his time at the male hang-out, known as a *lek*, fluffing his plumage and hanging upside down squawking at the passing females. When a female Raggiano wants a male for mating purposes she goes to the *lek* and casually makes her selection. In an instant the nuptials are over, she flies off to the nest she has made by herself and never sees the male again.

SUMMARY AND ANALYSIS

How is this difference between the males of each species explained? It takes two Manucodes, male and female, to keep their offspring alive. They harvest fruit which is not very nutritious, though plentiful. The Raggiana, in comparison, are capable of picking insects out of bark because they have harder beaks than the Manucodes, and they can also crack nuts. As this kind of food is more nutritious than fruit, the offspring do not need to be constantly fed as the Manucodes do. It only takes one Raggiano to take care of the nestlings.

Among human species it only takes one parent to take care of human children. Two would be desirable because they could spell each other from the continuous responsibility, but two are not a necessity and in many cases, are actually harmful to children. This country will soon have a vast population raised by single parents. The highest percentages in this research, who enjoyed equality with their brothers were the women raised by single parents. Single parents will send their daughters into the adult world expecting to be treated equally. These daughters will expect to take their place in the country's decision-making.

CONCLUSION

When a parent of college-age children read this book in manuscript form she told the author, "*I wish I'd read this book before I had children. I'd have done a lot of things differently.*" Just what those things would have been were not discussed. But the women in this research spoke to her almost as *Everychild*. Sort of a cosmic child saying these are the things we desperately need.

This research verifies, how we love or harm our children remains with them forever. As in the law of physics, nothing passes out of existence. Everything remains, possibly in a different form or in a different place. The joys of childhood are transferred to other people in other places as the child matures. The pain absorbed by the four-year-old may explode in a temper-tantrum, or it may not erupt until the child is grown, or it may simmer always, affecting decisions, and relationships.

The voices in this book tell us that childrens' needs are simple and can be easily met. Ten minutes a day of uninterrupted time may be all it takes for a child of any age to feel secure in a parent's love. Or sitting down on the floor and watching a child's TV show with the children now and then, instead of watching a major league football game. This may be a sacrifice for some fathers, but the child will be proud of the sense of importance given to what might otherwise be denigrated as "*kids' stuff*," i.e. unimportant to big people. Taking children and their interests seriously is what children want most. That

SUMMARY AND ANALYSIS

requires little time and no money. Or the teenager may only want to know that his parent is standing by to pick him up from a party if the party gets rough. A security that tells him *"I'll be there if you need me."*

As parents, we are often frightened because we seldom feel we are doing the right thing and there is little by which we can gauge ourselves. The reassuring pages of Dr. Spock are seldom read today. The reassuring pages of this book should be telling parents to listen to their children, to give them the gift of time, as many women in this research are now doing with their own children.

Though these women grew up years ago, the dynamics of family living and the emotional needs of children are much the same as today. And though important, money is the least of those needs. Children who had few toys and not very good clothes, made do with simple things and appreciated the family love. There were those who had neither financial security nor love who learned to compensate and who found love in their adult lives and are working to give their children the love they themselves did not experience as children. There are other women in this research who will probably always bear the scars of an injured childhood.

Though we teach many skills in our schools, parenting is one skill almost never taught. This is a skill we are supposed to be born with, like the mother bear and her cubs, or the sparrow and her chicks. But human life is more complex than feeding offspring and teaching the young to forage for themselves. Unlike those species, we do not dismiss our offspring as soon as they can hold a spoon. Human beings are

THE TWO-PARENT FAMILY IS NOT THE BEST

responsible for nurturing the psychological as well as the physical well-being of their children. And having the responsibility, parents have the obligation to do their children no harm.

The women in this research, in all groups, said that nurturing was the most important quality of parenting, not only for mothering, but also for fathering. This research shows that men can do a good job of nurturing, that is, the ability to nourish, and to provide encouragement so the child will grow, not only physically but also emotionally and intellectually. That would mean, for instance, providing enough stimulation so the small child learns to talk, providing enough outside contacts and experiences so the child learns to be curious and wants to learn more, and providing enough appropriate physical contact so the child feels physically secure and emotionally comfortable with herself and with the people who care for her.

As mentioned before, Freud had asked, *"What do women want?"* We know from the voices on these pages that women want in their mates the stereotypically feminine qualities of listening, caring and nurturing. Freud never asked, *"What do the children want?"* He would have learned that children want parents, mothers and fathers, with the same characteristics. Now, we should ask, *"What do parents want?"* The researchers in this study suggest that parents want to not be so fearful of doing the wrong thing. Women in this research who now have young children, speak of raising them with love, but also with trepidation. That is not unique to women here. Most parents are fearful.

SUMMARY AND ANALYSIS

Psychologists have frightened us about parenting. As a consequence, the parent has fears and the child has fears but for different reasons. The parent senses criticism and the child, who is trying to make a life, is fearful. The parent's fear is communicated to the child who then has a double fear. It's important to both the parent and the child that the fears are at least diminished. The relationship between the parent and child will exist forever so it's best to make it as relaxed as possible. The parent can set the tone and ask his child, "*How can I make life easier for you? What can I provide for you that isn't a toy?*" This is not to say that parents should be totally self-sacrificing as that would be understandably harmful to children.

We should get more comfortable with ourselves and not be afraid now and then of asking our children, "*How am I doing? What are you missing from me? From your father?*" Let's go right to the children and ask them. It won't cost anything. It will take some effort, but parents will feel good about it. And if the child is not afraid of his parent, and if he has learned to explore his emotions, he will speak freely.

This book is a call from the voices of yesterday's children to all parents, men and women, and to all who raise children, to step aside and evaluate, from a child's view, how well they are parenting. This is a call to arms -- a call to loving arms.

APPENDIX A: Questionnaire - Women Raised by Fathers Only

The Questionnaire in this Appendix is modified to eliminate fill-in blank spaces. The questionnaire for each group is different only where it is made appropriate for the particular group circumstance.

Demographics

1. How did you learn about this research?

2. Who is the person (not by name) primarily responsible for your upbringing?

3. Your age, Race, Nationality

4. Your height and weight

5. Married, Single, Widowed, Divorced, Separated

6. How many times married?

7. How many children do you have and their ages?

8. How many grandchildren do you have?

9. What is your occupation?

10. Your yearly income in contrast to household income?

11. Approximate size of town where you grew up.

12. In what part of the country did you grow up?

13. Last grade completed in school.

14. Degrees and Subject.

15. Political party.

16. Your religion now.

17. Do you feel you were discriminated against?

THE TWO-PARENT FAMILY IS NOT THE BEST

18. If yes, please explain.

19. Do you feel you were singled out as being different?

20. If yes, please explain.

21. Did you have physical fights?

22. If so, please explain with whom, not by name.

23. Did you feel older than your years?

24. Your religion when growing up.

25. How often attend religious services now?

26. What organizations, if any, do you belong to?

GROWING UP

27. Did you lose your mother because of death, divorce, desertion, forced separation? Please explain.

28. How old were you when you lost your mother?

29. If you were old enough to remember, how did you feel when you lost your mother?

30. Was your father helpful at this time?

31. After you lost your mother, if you had a female role model, who was she (not by name, but her relationship to you)?

32. If you had a fantasy mother, what was she like?

33. If you lost your mother when you were in grammar school or before, what did you do most of the time after school?

34. If you lost your mother when you were in grammar school or before, what do you think people were saying about you? (friends, friends' parents, teachers, neighbors)

35. Did any of these things hurt your feelings?

36. If you lost your mother when you were in junior or senior high school, what did you usually do after school?

APPENDIX A

37. If you lost your mother when you were in junior or senior high school, what do you think people were saying about you?

38. Was there alcohol in your home?

39. Did your father drink moderately or often to excess?

40. What were your hobbies?

41. Were you sexually abused?

42. If so, by whom, not by name?

43. What were your regular activities after you lost your mother?

44. Did your father use ordinary spanking as disciplinary measure?

45. Did your father beat you?

46. If your father beat you, was it seldom or frequently?

47. What was your father's principal occupation when you were growing up?

48. When you were growing up was your father's income lower, middle or upper?

49. Did your father freely talk about his personal life?

50. If he did, was this a burden to you?

51. Was your father at home most of the time when he was not working?

52. About how many hours a week did he work?

53. What did you admire most about your father?

54. What did you dislike about your father?

55. Do you consider your father exceptional, average, other. Please explain.

56. Complete the sentence: My father was proud of me when I_____.

THE TWO-PARENT FAMILY IS NOT THE BEST

57. Who told you the facts of life?

58. Were you were encouraged in things other girls were not?

59. If so, what things?

60. Were you "on your own," more than other children?

61. If so, what effect did this have on you?

62. If your father did not remarry, why do you think he did not?

63. Do you believe your father permitted you to take more risks than your friends' parents permitted?

64. What did you miss most about not having a mother?

65. If you had had a mother, how do you think your life would have been different?

66. Do you feel you were "the little mother?"

67. If so, please explain.

68. Do you feel you were "the little wife?"

69. If so, please explain.

70. Number of brothers younger and older.

71. If you had a brother, did he do household chores?

72. Generally, were you treated equally?

73. If not, what were those areas?

74. Did all members of your family, including your father, share equally in household work?

75. Number of sisters younger and older.

76. Was your father "there for you" when you needed him?

77. After you lost your mother, were neighborhood children permitted to play in your home?

78. If not, why not?

APPENDIX A

79. If there was a woman present in your home when you were growing up, indicate her relationship to you and if she was very important, moderately important, or not important to you.

80. Do you feel your family was closer knit than others?

81. Please explain.

82. Did your father love your mother?

83. Did your father help in his parents' home when he was growing up?

84. Did your father love his mother?

85. When your father was growing up, did he have two parents in his home? Mother only? Father only?

86. After you lost your mother, did your father have girl friends?

87. If he did, did he bring them home?

88. When you were growing up did your father have less than five girl friends?

89. Did your father have more than five girl friends?

90. If he did have girl friends did you like this, not like this, or were you indifferent?

91. After you lost your mother, how many times did your father remarry?

92. If your father remarried, how did you get along with your stepmother? Very well, moderately well, not at all?

93. When you were in school did you participate in extra-curricular sports?

94. If you did, were you considered good, average, poor?

AS YOU ARE NOW

95. What is your relationship with your father now?

THE TWO-PARENT FAMILY IS NOT THE BEST

96. Did you feel because you lost your mother you had lost your childhood?

97. If so, please explain.

98. What are the three most important things about your personality due to having been raised by a father only?

99. What do you think is the most important thing about "mothering?"

100. What do you think is the most important thing about "fathering?"

101. Do you think a father can be a good substitute for a mother?

102. If you are a mother, how do you evaluate yourself?

103. What are the things a mother can do that a father can't, as a parent?

104. Do you believe there should be total equality of the sexes or modified?

105. If "modified" please explain.

106. In their abilities do you think that men and women are pretty much the same or basically different?

107. In their feelings do you think that men and women are pretty much the same or basically different?

108. If you are not married is it because the opportunity has not presented itself yet, but you hope it will, or you enjoy men but don't want the commitment, or you don't care to be involved with a man, or you don't care much for men, or it would be difficult to find a man "as good as Daddy."

109. If you don't already have children, would you like to?

110. If not is it because you don't like children, or you don't think you would make a good mother, or they would interfere with your plans, or other reasons explained here.

APPENDIX A

111. If you have children, how has your upbringing affected your mothering?

112. If you have children, how do you think they rate you as a mother?

113. If you are heterosexual, to what do you attribute this?

114. If you are homosexual, to what do you attribute this?

115. Have you ever known anyone else who was raised by a father only?

116. Do you feel that because you were raised by a father that you are different?

117. Please explain.

118. Has being brought up by a father made it easier or more difficult in your interaction in the work place?

119. Please explain either choice in #118.

120. How has being brought up by a father affected your relationships with men?

121. How has being brought up by a father affected your relationships with women?

122. If you have siblings, how do you rate your personal relationship with them now, close, average, or distant?

123. What do you look for in a mate or a lover?

APPENDIX B: The Adjective Check List

In addition to the questionnaire which was developed specifically by the research associates for this particular study, the standardized Gough Adjective Check List was also used. This, as was mentioned before, is a list of 300 adjectives which the respondents are asked to relate to, checking those which describe themselves. Sample items include adjectives such as *anxious, commonplace, egotistical, confused, practical, evasive, active.* In this study the Adjective Check List was used as an expansion on the results of this study. Would the results of the Check List corroborate and validate the results of the questionnaire designed for this research, or would the results of the Check List refute the results of the questionnaire? Would it provide the opportunity to make further comparisons between the four groups of women?

The Adjective Check List was first developed by Harrison Gough, Ph.D., and has been used since 1952. Quoting from the Adjective Check List Manual, 1983 Edition, ". . *the studies and research reports in which the ACT [Adjective Check List] has played a significant role now number almost 700, and in the 1978 edition of Buros's Mental Measurements Yearbook, the ACL had attained the 26th position in the list of the 100 most frequently used and cited tests in psychology."* As one reviewer wrote, *"...its primary use has been in the area of self-description...The primary strength of the ACT has been, and remains, that of a research instrument tied to theoretical developments in the area of personality...the primary application remains theoretical as opposed to clinical in nature...As such, researchers and theoreticians are likely to find the test more interesting and useful than would a practicing clinician. "*

The three researchers and theoreticians conducting this study selected the Gough Adjective Check List because of its authenticated reliability, and because it can be self-ad-

THE TWO-PARENT FAMILY IS NOT THE BEST

ministered, that is, sent by mail to respondents throughout the United States, to Canada, Spain, and England and returned by mail for entry into the computer for analysis.

The Check List assesses 37 aspects of a person's personality drawn from 300 adjectives. Various groups of adjectives fall into specific trait categories. For instance, adjectives which are scattered throughout the two pages such as *aggressive, ambitious, argumentative, assertive, outspoken,* etc. fall into the Dominance trait. There is little likelihood, when the respondent is checking the list, that she can know that these adjectives are related to a particular trait.

In addition to the first three categories on the Adjective Check List, *Total number of adjectives checked; Number of favorable adjectives checked;* and *Number of unfavorable adjectives checked,* which assess a person's outgoing approach, their favorable or unfavorable opinion of them*selves,* the check list is comprised of adjectives which assess 34 personality traits. A Description of the Scales is included as Appendix C. As some of the following may not be self-explanatory, it will be helpful to refer to the Appendix. The personality traits include: *Communality; Achievement; Dominance; Endurance; Order; Intraception; Nurturance; Affiliation; Heterosexuality; Exhibition; Autonomy; Aggression; Change; Succorance; Abasement; Deference; Counseling Readiness; Self-Control; Self-Confidence; Personal Adjustment; Ideal Self; Creative Personality; Military Leadership; Masculine Attributes; Feminine Attributes; Critical Parent; Nurturing Parent; Adult; Free Child; Adapted Child; High Origence, Low Intellectence; High Origence, High Intellectence; Low Origence, Low Intellectence: Low Origence, High Intellectence.*

When the Adjective Check Lists were completed by the respondents they were sent to the Consulting Psychologists Press in Palo Alto, California, and entered into their computer scanner. The results were returned to the researchers for this study, who in turn sent the respondents a copy of the scanned results with a Description of

APPENDIX B

the Scales to enable them to study the profile of their personality as they had defined it by their selection of the specific adjectives.

For this research study then, the profiles of each respondent were charted as to where, on a scale of one to one hundred, each woman in each group placed herself by the number of adjectives she checked related to a specific trait. That is, on the variable of Total number of adjectives checked, (which incidentally, with a high score indicates "High-scorers on number checked appear to be expressive individuals, eager to explore the world around them, but somewhat inconstant and even capricious in their reactions...") does the respondent in the particular group score below 50% or above 50%. And subsequently, how do the respondents by group compare on each trait?

It is sometimes an asset that a group has a high percentage of women scoring above 50% on a trait and sometimes it is not desirable. For instance, on the variable Number of favorable adjectives checked, a high score is desirable because the women who check many favorable adjectives are, according to the ACL Manual, seen "*as adaptable, outgoing, protective of those close to them, cheerful in the face of adversity, and productive as workers.*" However, a high score is not desirable in the variable Number of *unfavorable*, adjectives checked as the woman is describing herself unfavorably, often. The chart below lists the 37 variables or traits, but in order to fully understand their significance it is necessary to consult the Description of the Scales in Appendix C. The chart is included here to provide a comparison between groups.

The percentage of respondents scoring 51% - 100% in each group in each variable follows: (F = Single Father Group; M = Single Mother Group; B = Biological Parents Group; S = Step parent group.) An asterisk next to the traits indicates, for that trait the lowest score is most desirable.

THE TWO-PARENT FAMILY IS NOT THE BEST

Scored 51% - 100% on Trait by Group	F	M	B	S
No. adjectives checked	38%	63%	49%	59%
No. favorable adj.ckd.	59%	40%	69%	59%
*No. unfavorable adj.ckd.	27%	45%	22%	35%
Communality	52%	38%	39%	43%
Achievement	64%	57%	71%	66%
Dominance	68%	62%	74%	59%
Endurance	54%	51%	68%	55%
Order	54%	55%	69%	55%
Intraception	65%	55%	65%	63%
Nurturance	63%	42%	60%	59%
Affiliation	43%	34%	51%	48%
Heterosexuality	50%	55%	47%	63%
Exhibition	56%	48%	63%	57%
Autonomy	48%	55%	53%	58%
*Aggression	54%	60%	56%	54%
Change	33%	45%	48%	51%
*Succorance	21%	30%	22%	32%
*Abasement	24%	34%	34%	32%
Deference	41%	28%	38%	29%
Counseling Readiness	59%	64%	53%	57%
*Self-control	47%	33%	39%	30%
Self-confidence	68%	49%	74%	64%
Personal Adjustment	53%	38%	62%	55%
Ideal Self	77%	51%	73%	58%
Creative Personality	67%	64%	75%	64%
Military Leadership	64%	50%	73%	63%
Masculine Attributes	67%	51%	64%	50%
Feminine Attributes	53%	39%	41%	39%
*Critical Parent	58%	57%	58%	52%
Nurturing Parent	54%	37%	60%	53%
Adult Scale	65%	51%	78%	59%
Free Child	51%	57%	56%	65%
*Adapted Child	35%	39%	20%	36%
Hi Org.-Low Int.	41%	50%	31%	45%
*Hi Org.-Hi Int.	39%	58%	44%	37%
Low Org-Low Int	48%	36%	47%	38%

APPENDIX B

Low Org-Hi Int	74%	53%	72%	69%

Assigning *"positive," "negative,"* and *"neutral"* labels to the 37 personality traits by the three researchers and a random sample of others, those traits numbered 3, 15, 17, 18, 21, 29, 33, and 35 were labeled *"negative."* For instance, number 15, *"Aggression,"* as described in the Description of the Scales reads, *"The high scorer on aggression is a competitive and aggressive person who views others as rivals to be vanquished. The high-scorer's impulses are strong, often undercontrolled, and tend to be expressed with little regard for the courtesies of conventional society. The low-scorer is patient, seeks to avoid conflict, makes few if any demands on others, and in interpersonal life is forbearing and conciliatory."* This was classified by the researchers and a random sample of others as a *negative* trait.

The traits 13, 14, 20, 26, and 31 were classified as *"neutral,"* being neither a more desirable characteristics than an undesirable characteristic. All the other traits, as defined by the Description of the Scales, were classified as *positive* traits.

Number values were then assigned to traits, as for instance, "over 50% in a positive trait = +1," "over 50% in a negative trait = -1" and "neutral traits = 0), the larger the score the more desirable traits within the group. By this method it was determined that the single father group had a score of 23, the biological parents group had a score of 20 as well as the step parents group which also had a score of 20. The single mother group had a score of 14.

The percentage of women in the single mother group scoring 51% - 100% in many traits is considerably lower than the percentages in the other three groups. There are particularly low percentages for this group on *Number of favorable adjectives checked, Nurturance, Affiliation, Exhibition, Self-confidence, Personal Adjustment, Ideal Self,* and *Nurturing Parent.* The women in this group have the highest percentage on *Counseling Readiness* which is described as a positive trait.

THE TWO-PARENT FAMILY IS NOT THE BEST

The biological parents group had the highest percentage which checked the *Number of Favorable Adjectives* and the highest percentages for the following traits: *Achievement, Dominance, Endurance, Order, Intraception, Affiliation, Exhibition, Self-confidence, Personal Adjustment, Creative Personality, Military Leadership, Nurturing Parent,* and *Adult Scale.* And the lowest percentage scoring in one of the least desired traits, *Adapted Child.*

The single father group had the highest percentage which checked *Communality, Nurturance, Deference, Ideal Self, Masculine Attributes, Feminine Attributes, Low Origence-Low Intellectence,* and *Low Origence-High Intellectence.* This group also had the lowest percentage scoring in least desired traits such as *Aggression, Succorance, Abasement.*

The step parent group had the highest percentage which checked *Heterosexuality, Autonomy, Change, Free Child,* and the lowest percentage scoring in *Self over-control, Critical Parent,* and a tie with the same low percentage as the single father group in *Aggression.*

The single mother group had the highest percentage which checked *Number of Adjectives Checked, Counseling Readiness, High Origence-Low Intellectence.*

Biological Parent Families

In the initial questionnaire which all women responded to, referred to as the Research Questionnaire, the women listed what they believed to be their three most important personality traits. The women in the biological parents group viewed themselves as having predominantly stereptypical feminine traits, though on the first trait 46% listed stereotypical masculine traits. But for the second and third traits, the highest percentages were for stereotypical feminine traits such as *high esteem for family, cleanliness, decorating a home, love of children, cheerfulness, caring for others, loving and patient, tolerant, calm, being lovable.*

APPENDIX B

This correlates with the Adjective Check List, as the biological parents group has the highest percentages who scored 51% - 100% in traits which are considered to be stereotypically feminine. But they also have high percentages in traits which are stereotypically masculine. In *Number of Favorable Adjectives Checked* the description reads, "*adaptable, outgoing individuals, protective of those close to them, cheerful in the face of adversity, and productive as workers.* Women are seen as adaptable, protective, cheerful. This is essentially a stereotypically feminine characteristic as described.

This group also had the highest percent scoring 51% - 100% in *Achievement* described as "*hard-working, goal directed, determined to do well and usually does. The motivation to succeed seems to lie less in competitive drives than in an insistent need to live up to high and socially commendable criteria of performance.*" Stereotypically, women are seen as non-competitive and wanting approval. *Dominance "strong-willed, ambitious, determined, and forceful...free of self-doubt in the pursuit of goals, and little if at all inhibited by the disapproval or opposition of others".* This describes stereotypical masculine traits.

Endurance "*strong sense of duty, work conscientiously, and eschew frivolity and the nonessential. Conservation of the tried and true is deemed more important than the discovery of the new and different.*" Women growing up in the so-called "*nuclear*" family are apt to have a more conservative view of how things should be and how people should stick to what's been done before. Typically these girls are brought up in *conventional* homes and taught to not rock the boat. Whereas girls in the other three groups grew up in more unusual family situations.

A high percentage of women in the biological parents group scored 51% - 100% on *Order* which is described as "*seeks objectivity and rationality, is firm in controlling impulse, and unswerving in pursuit of goals. Setbacks and distractions are not easily endured, nor are change and variety welcomed".* This, too, fits the image of the conservative, whether male or female.

Many of the remaining traits on which a high percentage of the biological parents group scored 51% - 100% reflect well-adjusted personalities with strong conservative traits of falling in line with things as they are, which is stereotypically feminine. In the *Military Leadership* trait there are both feminine and masculine qualities. The high scorer holds fast to duty which is considered masculine, yet *exerts a steadying influence on others,* which is feminine *and is not at all temperamental or high-strung* which is not stereotypically feminine.

In the description of the *Nurturing Parent,* the role of conciliatory mediator is evident - a role perceived as stereotypically feminine. The *nurturing parent prefers continuity and the preservation of old values to rapid changes and shifts in convention; they seek to sustain relationships and to foster feelings of courtesy and respect between parent and child, the young and the old, the advantaged and the disadvantaged.-- in fact, between any two persons.*

The Creative Personality Scale, in which a high percentage of the biological parents group scored between 51% - 100%. is described as follows: "*The high-scorer on Cps is venturesome, aesthetically reactive, clever, and quick to respond. Intellectual characteristics such as breadth of interests, cognitive ability, and ideational fluency are also apparent.*" This describes both masculine and feminine traits. Being *venturesome* is considered stereotypically masculine, being *aesthetically reactive* is considered stereotypically feminine. Nevertheless this trait is of particular interest because on this trait seventy-five percent of the women in this group scored above 51%. However, a high percentage of all women scored above 51% on *Creative Personality.* This 75% for the biological parents group compares with 67% of the single father group, and 64% each for the single mother and step parent group. It could be said that most of the women who volunteered for this research study are *venturesome, quick to respond,* and have intellectual characteristics such as breadth of interests, cognitive ability, and ideational fluency.

Something more needs to be said here about the Creative Personality Scale. In Part 1, a correlation was made between girls who were permitted risks and those who were not, with how they later rated themselves on the Adjective Check List Creativity Personality Scale. From that correlation in Part 1 under "RISKS," it was learned that *"for each group of women, the percentage scoring in the upper 60th percentile range of the Creative Personality Scale was higher for women who were permitted risks than for women who were not."*

Specifically by group, of those who were permitted risks, in the single mother group 23% scored over 60%, those not permitted risks, 12% scored over 60% on the Creative Personality Scale. In the biological parents group, of those permitted risks, 53% scored over 60%, of those not permitted risks, 28% scored over 60%. In the step parent group, of those permitted risks, 50% scored over 60%, and those not permitted risks, 35% scored over 60%. In the single father group, this was fairly evenly divided between those who were permitted risks and scored over 60% on the Creative Personality Scale. That is, of those permitted risks, 29% scored over 60%, and of those not permitted risks, 28% scored over 60% on the Creative Personality Scale. Taken as a whole group, however, not just those women who had been permitted risks, a slightly higher percentage of women in the biological parents group scored in the 51% - 100% range of the Creative Personality Scale than did the other groups.

The *Adult Scale* in which a high percentage of women in the biological parents group scored 51% - 100% would be considered stereotypically masculine. *"The high-scorers on Adult Scale is production, work-centered, reliable, and ambitious, but these admirable virtues are to some extent attained at the cost of spontaneity, jollity, and the ability to enjoy respite and tranquility. The high-scorer is self-disciplined, commendably attentive to duties and obligations,* but uncomfortable in the expression of affection, love, or tenderness.

In both the Research Questionnaire and the Adjective Check List, the women in the biological parents group see themselves as having both masculine and feminine traits, the feminine traits being mostly in the area of obedience to convention, the masculine traits being mostly in the are of tending to duty.

Single Father Families

The women in the single father group, in both the Research Questionnaire and the Adjective Check List view themselves as independent with stereotypical masculine traits. On the Research Questionnaire, when asked to list three personality traits as the result of their upbringing, 72% of the single father group listed masculine traits for their first trait, 61% for their second trait, and 55% for their third trait. On the Adjective Check List, in addition to *Nurturance* which is discussed below, this group, has the highest percentages of women scoring 51-100% on *Communality (appears to be reliable, considerate, free of pretense, and comfortable in interpersonal relationships); Deference (conscientious, unassuming, and patient. Deferring to others without loss of self-respect, they prefer anonymity and freedom from conflict, to the winning of interpersonal victories); Ideal Self (characterized by interpersonal effectiveness and goal-attaining abilities...elements of narcissistic ego inflation...tend to be rated as well-adjusted by observers...but as less likeable); Masculine Attributes (...for both sexes. High scorers will be seen as ambitious and assertive, impatient when blocked or frustrated, quick to take the initiative and get things moving and stubbornly insistent on attaining their goals); Feminine Attributes (Prompts positive reactions from others and in turn treats them in a cooperative, considerate, and sympathetic manner. Values intimacy and mutuality in relationships with others) Low Origence, Low Intellectence (Unpretentious, uncomplicated, forbear-*

ing individual, protective of close friends, forthright, rule-respecting, and content with his or her role and station in life); Low Origence, High Intellectence (Analytical, logical, astute, intellectually capable and self-disciplined, and fully prepared to undertake the planning and hard work necessary for the attainment of rationally established goals).

This group has the <u>lowest</u> percentages (low scores being desirable in these traits) in *Aggression, Succorance,* and *Abasement,* as defined in the Description of Scales as: Aggression: *The low scorer is patient, seeks to avoid conflict, makes few if any demands on others, and in interpersonal life is forbearing and conciliatory.* Succorance: *The low-scorer is independent, relatively unbothered by self-doubt and equivocation, and effective in setting and attaining goals.* Abasement: *The low-scorers are assertively self-confident and respond quickly; they insist on obtaining what they judge to be their just rewards.*

It is interesting that women in the single father group, who might be expected to be devoid of nurturing because they did not have a mother, have the highest percentage on the Adjective Check List who scored 51% - 100% in *nurturance,* Also 53% of this group scored in the 51% - 100% range on the trait for *nurturing parent.* This correlates with the Research Questionnaire on which the single father group had the highest percentage (79%) who evaluated themselves as *very good* mothers, and 87% who said their *children* rated them as *very good* mothers.

Single Mother Families

When asked to list their three most important personality traits on the original Research Questionnaire, the highest percentage of women in the single mother group, for their first, second, and third traits listed stereotypically masculine traits. The traits on which this group was listed as having the highest percentage of women scoring 51% - 100% were *Number of Adjectives Checked, Counseling*

THE TWO-PARENT FAMILY IS NOT THE BEST

Readiness, and High Origence- Low Intellectence. The description for *Number of Adjectives Checked* is "*High scorers on No. Ckd appear to be expressive individuals, eager to explore the world around them but somewhat inconstant and even capricious in their reactions. The high-scorer seems to be an attractive person, vivacious and quickly enthusiastic, but at the same time somewhat self-seeking and lacking in responsibility.* This would not be considered stereotypically masculine.

As for *Counseling Readiness,* the description reads, "*The high-scoring female in Crs appears to be an intelligent, inner-directed, capable, but acerbic individual, dissatisfied with her status, dubious about the dependability and support of her associates, and not at all ready to submit to the demands of the conventional female role. She does not arouse nurturant feelings in others and may in fact provoke responses of disapproval or rejection. Counseling would attempt to reduce conflicts in her views of self and to foster the development of less abrasive, opposition-inducing interpersonal techniques.*

Not arousing nurturant feelings in others would indicate that this is not a stereotypical feminine trait. Sixty-four percent of the women in this group scored in the 51% - 100% range for this trait. This was followed by 59% of the women in the single father group, 57% in the step parent group, and 53% in the biological parents group. Though it seems that the group which could profit most from counseling is the single mother group, over 50% of women in all groups checked adjectives which indicated that they could possibly profit from counseling.

The single mother group also had the highest percentage of women who scored in the 51% - 100% range on *High Origence, Low Intellectence.* The description for this reads, "*Possess strong instincts, a taste for merrymaking, and easy distractibility. ... Easygoing and accepting of both self and others.*" Less than 50% of all groups scored 51% - 100% on this trait. This would appear to be a stereotypically feminine trait.

Of all traits in which the highest percentage of a particular trait was in the single mother group, not one appears to be a stereotypically masculine trait. That is not to say that this group did not score in the stereotypically masculine traits; just that they were not the highest percentage in those traits.

Of the single mother group, the one group raised primarily by women who are stereotypically considered nurturers, only 39% scored in the 51% - 100% range in *Feminine Attributes*. Only 37% scored in that range in *Nurturing Parent*, and only 42% scored in that range for *Nurturance*. These are the lowest percentages for all groups in each of these stereotypically feminine traits. Women in the single father had the highest percentages in *Feminine Attributes*, *Nurturance*, and the second highest percentage in *Nurturing Parent*.

Step Parent Families

On the original Research Questionnaire, when asked to list their three most important personality traits, the women in this group listed masculine traits for their first and second traits and feminine traits for their third trait.

The highest percentage of women who scored 51% - 100% on *Autonomy* was in the step parent group. This is definitely a stereotypically masculine trait. The description reads, *"Those who score high on Aut are independent and autonomous, but also assertive and self-willed. They tend to be indifferent to the feelings of others, and are viewed as egotistical and headstrong.*"

The highest percentage of women who scored 51% - 100% on *Heterosexuality* was in the step parent group. The description of this trait is, *"The high-scorer on Het plunges into life with gusto, responds warmly to interpersonal encounters, likes the company of the opposite sex, has vigorous erotic drives, and appears to be blessed by good health and abundant vitality."*

The highest percentage of women who scored in the 51% - 100% range on *Change,* was in the step parent group. This trait is described as, "*Takes pleasure in change and variety, persons high on Cha are typically perceptive, spontaneous, and aesthetically-minded. They comprehend problems and situations rapidly and incisively, and they have confidence in themselves and welcome the challenges found in disorder and complexity.*" This appears to be stereotypically feminine as it refers to *aesthetics* and indirectly to adaptability which is ascribed to women. This is not to say that men are not aesthetic. But only stereotypically are women considered more aesthetic than men.

Sixty-five percent of the women in this group scored in the 51% - 100% range on the *Free Child* trait. The *Free Child* is described as "*ebullient and enterprising, not at all inclined to exercise self-restraint or to postpone gratifications.*" However else this trait may be categorized, it could not fit a stereotypically masculine trait.

This group had the lowest percentage of women who scored in the 51% - 100% range on *Self-Control.* In this case the lowest percentage is the most desirable. The description reads, "*The high-scorer on S-Cn is an admirable individual from the standpoint of sobriety, diligence, and attention to duty, but these virtues seem to be attained at the cost of spontaneity and the enhancement of self.In short, the high-scorer is not so much controlled as over-controlled.*" As only 30% scored high, then it can be said that 70% of the women in the step parent group are not over-controlled. Rigidity is seen as a masculine trait, therefore having a low percentage who scored in this high range indicates that the women in this group are not rigid and therefore tend to be more stereotypically feminine.

The women in the step parent group listed their personality traits in the original Research Questionnaire as predominantly masculine, and on the Adjective Check List their percentages are higher for masculine traits (50%) than for feminine traits (30%). They also have a high percentage on several traits which are stereotypically

APPENDIX B

masculine, as for instance *Exhibition, Self-confidence, Military Leadership, Achievement, and Dominance,* but they did not have the *highest* percentages in these traits.

Conclusion

Whether or not the responses from the original Research Questionnaire correlate positively with the responses from the Adjective Check List is difficult to determine. In some cases they do and in some cases they do not. It cannot be said that any one particular group of people has a particular trait. That is the stuff of discrimination -- of transferring from a specific to a generality. For instance, it might have been said that girls raised by their fathers would not have adequate feminine traits, that children raised by both biological parents would have a better start in life and therefore become more successful. But neither of these statements is true.

When there are discrepancies between the results of the Research Questionnaire and the Adjective Check List it would probably be best to rely on the trait selected by the respondent in the Adjective Check List. In the original Research Questionnaire the respondent might describe herself as, for instance, *independent*. She may very well believe that she is independent. Yet when she checks the adjectives on the Adjective Check List she may not check those which describe someone who is independent. Those adjectives, as listed in the Manual for the Adjective Check List which have adjectival correlations for *Autonomy,* which is in itself defined as, *"To act independently of others or of social values and expectations,"* are *"adventurous, argumentative, arrogant, assertive, clever, complicated, conceited, curious, cynical, daring, egotistical, headstrong, imaginative, impatient, impulsive, independent, individualistic, interests wide, opinionated, original, outspoken, pleasure-seeking, rebellious, restless, sexy, sharp-witted, sophisticated, spontaneous, temperamental, touchy, unconventional, and uninhibited."* The person checking the 300 adjectives does not know which ones fall into the category of *Autonomy*, or *independent*. It is a check on her ability to define herself. Incidentally, as the chart shows, a higher percentage (58%) of women in the step parent group scored in the higher ranges on autonomy than other groups as stated before. The most that can be said is that a larger percentage of one group than another scored in the 51% - 100% range on a specific trait.

APPENDIX C - Description of the Scales Used in Adjective Check List

1. Total number of adjectives checked: No. Ckd

High-scorers on No. Ckd appear to be expressive individuals eager to explore the world around the but somewhat inconstant and even capricious in their reactions. The high-scorer seems to be an attractive person, vivactious and quickly enthusiastic, but at the same time somewhat self-seeking and lacking in responsiblity. Low-scorers on No. Ckd are less urgent, narrower in interests, more reserved and conventional, and less likely to behave impulsively or erratically. The ego ideal of the low-scorer sets standards of moderaton, sobriety, and good judgment. That of the high-scorer values versatility, spontaneity, and the enhancement of self in action.

2. Number of favorable adjectives checked: Fav

High-scorers are seen as adaptable, outgoing individuals, protective of those close to them, cheerful in the face of adversity, and productive as workers. The desirability of their self-descriptions, in other words, is not a fraud or deception; on the contrary, high-scorers on Fav appear to be quite justified in ascribing these favorable items to themselves.

3. Number of unfavorable adjectives checked: Unfav

The high-scorer on Unfav may be characterized as a disbeliever, pessimistic about the future, changeable, headstrong, and quick to take offense or umbrage. The good fortune or success of others is seen as unearned and unfair. Self-doubt and self-rejection lead to feelings of bitterness and hostility toward others. The low-scorer on

Unfav is more dependable, more tactful, less judgmental, and less easily offended.

4. Communality: Com

The high-scorer on Com appears to be a reliable person, considerate of others, free of pretense, and comfortable in interpersonal relationships. The low-scorer is ambivalent in relating to others, may express opposition in deviant ways, tends to be contentious and defensive, and finds it difficult to conform to the every-day expectations of interpersonal life.

5. Achievement: Ach

The high-scorer on Ach is a hard-workig, goal-directed individual, who is determined to do well and usually does. The motivation to succeed seems to lie less in competitive drives than in an insistent need to live up to high and socially commenable criteria of performance. Others acknowledge the energy and enterprise displayed by the high-scorer, but also see elements of coercion, impatience, and self-aggrandizement. The low-scorer is less effective, less venturesome, and less persistent, but at the same time an easier and more congenial companion whose diffidence has a certain charm.

6. Dominance: Dom

The high-scorer on Dominance is a strong-willed, ambitious, determined, and forceful individual, free of self-doubt in the pursuit of goals, and little if at all inhibited by the disapproval or oppostion of others. The high-scorer is affiliative and adroit in directing the group's actions toward the attainment of socially worthy objectives. The low-scorer lacks confidence, prefers to be on the perphery of group enterprise, and shuns situations calling for competition or the assertion of self.

7. Endurance: End

High-scorers on End have a strong sense of duty, work conscientiously, and eschew frivolity and the nonessential. Conservation of the tried and true is deemed more important than the discovery of the new and different. Low-scorers are changeable, easily distracted or redirected, leisurely, and informal individuals who take pleasure in new experiences and the endless variety of everyday life.

8. Order: Ord

The high-scorer on Ord seeks objectivity and rationality, is firm in controlling impulse, and unswerving in the pursuit of goals. Setbacks and distractions are not easily endured, nor are change and variety welcomed. The low-scorer is less inhibited and more expressive, but at the same time less able to persevere in a steady pace of work toward a distant goal. The high-scorer prefers tasks demanding self-discipline and diligent effort; the low-scorer, wanting quicker gratification, takes pleasure in the here and now.

9. Intraception: Int

High-scorers are seen as logical and foresighted, and as valuing intellectual and cognitive matters. Low-scorers appear to have a narrower range of interests, to be somewhat superstitious, and to be less capable in coping with stress or trauma. High-scorers tend to be complex and internally differentiated, whereas low-scorers tend to be simple and prosaic.

10. Nurturance: Nur

The high-scorer on Nur appears to like people; to have a cooperative, unaffected, and tactful social manner; and to be sympathetic and supportive in temperament. The low-scorer avoids close ties, is wary of others, and is dubious of others' intentions and defensive of his or her own.

11. Affiliation: Aff

The high-scorer on Affiliation is comfortable in social situations, likes to be with people, and adapts easily to the changing demands of group process. Little if at all given to soul-searching, the high-scorer glosses over inner complexities and prefers to take people and events at face value. The low-scorer agonizes over the meaning of relationships, complicates them, and fears involvement. An underlying current of anxiety and preoccupation makes wholehearted participation in social interation difficult if not impossible.

12. Heterosexuality: Het

The high-scorer on Het plunges into life with gusto, responds warmly to interpersonal encounters, likes the company of the opposite sex, has vigorous erotic drives, and appears to be blessed by good health and abundant vitality. Thinking too much, as it were, the low-scorer keeps people at a distance, fears the challenges and opportunities of interpersonal life, and falls back on a too narrow and restricted role repertoire.

13. Exhibition: Exh

The high-scorer on Exh is a forceful, obtrusive, and even bombastic individual, insistent on winning attention, impatient with opposition and delay, and quite willing to coerce or manipulate someone whose acquiescence is desired. The low-scorer is cautious, holds back, avoids conflict, and gives in so as to escape interpersonal stress or controversy. Lacking confidence in themselves, low-scorers shrink from any encounter in which they will be visible or "on stage."

14. Autonomy: Aut

Those who score high on Aut are independent and autonomous, but also assertive and self-willed. They tend to be indifferent to the feelings of others, and are viewed as egotistical and headstrong. Low-scorers are more conventional, seek security in the tried and true, avoid risks, and welcome direction from trusted superiors.

15. Aggression: Agg

The high-scorer on Agg is a competitive and aggressive person who views others as rivals to be vanquished. The high-scorer's impulses are strong, often undercontrolled, and tend to be expressed with little regard for the courtesies of conventional society. The low-scorer is patient, seeks to avoid conflict, makes few if any demands on others, and in interpersonal life is forbearing and conciliatory.

16. Change: Cha

Taking pleasure in change and variety, persons high on Cha are typically perceptive, spontaneous, and aesthetically-minded. They comprehend problems and situations rapidly and incisively, and they have confidence in themselves and welcome the challenges found in disorder and complexity. The low-scorer seeks stability and continuity in the environment, avoids ill-defined and risky situations, and tends to lack verve and imagination.

17. Succorance: Suc

The high-scorer on Suc feels inadequate in coping with stress and crises, avoids confrontation, and tends to retreat into fantasy. Others are seen as stronger and more effective, and their support is solicited. The low-scorer is independent, relatively unbothered by self-doubt and equivocation, and effective in setting and attaining goals.

THE TWO-PARENT FAMILY IS NOT THE BEST

18. Abasement: Aba

The high-scorers on Aba ask for little, submit to the wishes and demands of others, and avoid conflict at all costs. The interpersonal world is viewed with worry and foreboding, and others are seen as stronger, more effective, and more deserving. The low-scorers are assertively self-confident and respond quickly; they insist on obtaining what they judge to be their just rewards.

19. Deference: Def

The individuals scoring high on Def are typically conscientious, unassuming, and patient. Deferring to others without loss of self-respect, they prefer anonymity and freedom from conflict to the winner of interpersonal victories. The low-scorers on Def delight in competition, taking risks, and defeating rivals; their behavior tends to be headstrong and impulsive, frequently leading to conflict with others.

20. Counseling Readiness Scale: Crs

The high-scoring female on Crs appears to be an intelligent, inner-directed, capable, but acerbic individual, dissatisfied with her status, dubious about the dependability and support of her associates, and not at all ready to submit to the demands of the conventional female role. She does not arouse nurturant feelings in others and may in fact provoke respones of disapproval or rejection. Counseling would attempt to reduce conflicts in her views of self and to foster the development of less abrasive, opposition-inducing interpersonal techniques. The low-scoring female on Crs appears to have settled comfortably into the role of a gentle, unambitious, other-directed helpmate. Not at odds with herself or with others, she feels little need for counseling nor would counseling serve much purpose.

21. Self-Control: S-Cn

The high-scorer on S-Cn is an admirable individual from the standpoint of sobriety, diligence, and attention to duty, but these virtues seem to be attained at the cost of spontaneity and the enhancement of self. In short, the high-scorer is not so much controlled as over-controlled. The low-scorer has moved to the other end of the continuum, where impulses defy management and where interpersonal encounters involve a constant series of broken rules, contretemps, and altercations with others who refuse to set aside their own narcissistic claims.

22. Self-Confidence: S-Cfd

The high-scorers on S-Cfd are initiators, confident of their ability to achieve goals. They are not above cutting a few corners to create a good impression, and observers do see them as assertive, enterprising, and self-confident. The low-scorers have difficulty in mobilizing their resources and taking action; others view them as shy, inhibited, and withdrawn.

23. Personal Adjustment: P-Adj

The high-scorer on P-Adj has a positive attitude toward life, enjoys the company of others, and feels capable of initiating activities and carrying them through to conclusion. High-scorers may not possess psycho-dynamic self-understanding, but they do appear to possess the ability to "love and work," proposed by Freud as the critical criteria of personal adjustment. Low-scorers are anxious, high-strung, and moody, avoid close relationships with others, and worry about their ability to deal with the stresses and strains of their lives. Others see them as defensive, preoccupied, and easily distracted.

24. Ideal Seal Scale: Iss

High-scorers appear to be characterized by inter-personal effectiveness and goal-attaining abilities, as were high-scorers on P-Adj. In addition, there seem to be elements of narcissistic ego inflation. High-scorers on Iss should tend to be rated as well-adjusted by observers, on a par with high-scorers on P-Adj, but as less likable. Low-scorers as Iss appear to have poor morale, to feel defeated by life, and to find it difficult to set and attain goals. In these respects they resemble those who score low on P-Adj. But once more a new element enters the picture, as the low-scorers on Iss have several redeeming qualities from an interpersonal standpoint such as kindness, modesty, and consideration for the rights and wishes of others.

25. Creative Personality Scale: Cps

The high-scorer on Cps is venturesome, aesthetically reactive, clever, and quick to respond. Intellectual characteristics such as breadth of interests, cognitive abiity, and ideational fluency are also apparent. The low-scorer is more subdued, less expressive, more conservative, and less inclined to take action in complex, ill-defined situations.

26. Military Leadership Scale: Mls

The high-scorer on Mls is oriented toward duties and obligations, holds fast to an agreed-upon line of action, and works hard to see that consensual goals are attained. He or she exerts a steadying influence on others, values good organization and careful planning, and is not at all temperamental or high-strung. The low-scorer is much less convinced of the worth of unremitting effort and self-discipline, enjoys change and variety, and likes to probe limits to see if the rules can be bent or broken.

27. Masculine attributes scale: Mas

The interpersonal and descriptive implications of the Masculine Attributes scale are quite clear for both sexes. High-scorers will be seen as ambitious an assertive, impatient when blocked or frustrated, quick to take the initiative and get things moving, and stubbornly insistent on attaining their goals. Low-scorers will be seen as kind, gentle, and considerate, fatalistic about personal misfortune or adversity, vulnerable to attack and aggression, and willing to substitute day-dreams and fantasies for more direct or tangible experience. In their cathexes, high-scorers stress action, visible rewards, and vigorous assertion of self, whereas low-scorers value inner feelings and an intuitive evocation of identity.

28. Feminine attributes scale: Fem

The high-scorer on Fem prompts positive reactions from others and in turn treats them in a cooperative, considerate, and sympathetic manner. The low-scorer keeps others at a distance, is skeptical of their intentions, and rejects their overtures. Observers see the high-scorer as appreciative, cheerful, and warm, whereas the low-scorer is viewed as fault-finding, hard-headed, and opinionated. The high-scorer values intimacy and mutuality in relationships with others; the low-scorer prefers autonomy and detachment.

29. Critical Parent scale: CP

High-scorers on CP are easily angered, skeptical, and counteractive. In pursuing their own interests they are indifferent to those of others, irritated by interference or obstacles, and self-serving. Their narcissism renders them nearly impervious to the reactions they provoke, and in

THE TWO-PARENT FAMILY IS NOT THE BEST

fact they care little for what others may think or feel. Low-scorers are more cognizant and accepting of interdependency, less egoistic, and more tolerant of the fears and weaknesses of others. Low-scorers want to bring people together, to reduce conflicts, and to share in the rewards of social living. High-scorers claim more for themselves and see others as opponents to be overcome.

30. Nurturing Parent scale: NP

High-scorers on NP prefer continuity and the preservation of old values to rapid changes and shifts in convention; they seek to sustain relationships and to foster feelings of courtesy and respect between parent and child, the young and the old, the advantaged and the disadvantaged -- in fact, between any two persons. To low-scorers, routine is stifling; they seek change and variety, tend to be dissatisfied with their current status, and respond poorly to stress or social pressure. Others view the low-scorers as temperamental, hard to predict, and even self-defeating; high-scorers are seen as helpful, loyal, genuinely responsible, and as good persons from who to obtain counsel.

31. Adult scale: A

The high-scorer on Adult is productive, work-centered, reliable, and ambitious, but these admirable virtues are to some extent attained at the cost of spontaneity, jollity, and the ability to enjoy respite and tranquillity. The high-scorer is self-disciplined, commendably attentive to duties and obligations, but uncomfortable in the expression of affection, love, or tenderness. The low-scorer is more relaxed and responsive, but also less effective in coping with the demands of work and the responsibilities of adulthood.

32. Free Child scale: FC

The high-scorer on FC is ebullient and enterprising, not at all inclined to exercise self-restraint or to postpone gratifications. Others are swept along whether they like it or not, in a rush toward enjoyment. The low-scorer is moderate, slow to respond, and cautious in interpersonal encounters. Others see the high-scorer as entertaining, but also as aggressive. The low-scorer is viewed as self-denying and lacking in zest.

33. Adapted Child scale: AC

The high-scorers on AC experience great difficulty in setting aside subordinate childhood roles. They lack independence, feel unsure about coping with the demands of adult life, fear and avoid direct confrontation, and are easily disorganized by stress and trauma. Satisfaction is sought in daydreams and fantasies, not in the threatening context of contemporary reality. The low-scorers are autonomous and effective, but inconsiderate. To acieve independence, personal feelings are suppressed and the feelings of others ignored. The low-scorers strive for power, success, and tangible accomplishments in a world free of subjective concerns.

ORIGENCE-INTELLECTENCE SCALES

In 1975 George Welsh published a monograph in which creativity and intelligence were proposed as structural dimensions of personality. Intelligence may be defined as the ability to think abstractly, to detect logical relationships, and to apply general principles to the solution of specific problems. Creativity may be defined as the ability to think imaginatively, to bring new ideas and tangible products into being, to modify one's environment in accordance with aesthetic criteria, to picture the world of the past and the world of the future, and to discern the underlying elements of order in disorder, harmony in disharmony, and even sense in nonsense. Attempts to measure this constellation of attributes have typically followed a cognitive path by appealing to tasks that require ingenuity in problem-solving and the ability to overcome implicit assumptions and to shift quickly in the associational basis of linguistic classifications. Welsh's view was that the dispositional facet of creatitvity should be given more explicit attention and in fact raised to parity. He concluded that independent measures of creativity and intelligence should be employed.

34. High Origence, Low Intellectence: A-1

High-scorers on A-1 possess strong instincts, a taste for merrymaking, and easy distractibility. Low-scorers are prudent, vigilant, and programmed; they plan ahead and avoid intemperance and the undue expression of impulse. High-scorers are more easygoing and accepting of both self and others, whereas low-scorers take a firm stand on ethical issues and look askance at those who violate society's conventions.

35. High Origence, High Intellectence: A-2

The high-scorer on A-s is self-sufficient, strong-willed, original in thought and perceptions, aesthetically sensitive, indifferent to convention, and much annoyed by those who are uninsightful, intellectually maladroit, or lacking in perspicacity. In spite of many talents, the high-scorer on A-2 is scarcely more comfortable with his or her own inner needs and reactions than with those of other people. Intimacy based on the candid sharing of emotionally significant feelings is sensed as dangerous and hence avoided. The low-scorer is a more mundane, practical, ordinary individual, less temperamental, more predictable, and less apt to lash out at others for their ineptitude and intellectual blunders.

APPENDIX C

36. Low Origence, Low Intellectence: A-3

The high-scorer on A-3 is an unpretentious, uncomplicated, forbearing individual, protective of close friends, forthright, rule-respecting and content with his or her role and station in life. The low-scorer is intelligent and inventive, but at the same time anxious, ill at ease, worrying, and preoccupied; keeping people at a distance, the low-scorer is skeptical about their intention and tends to feel alienated.

37. Low Origence, High Intellectence: A-4

The high-scorer on A-4 is analytic, logical, astute, intellectually capable and self-disciplined, and fully prepared to undertake the planning and hard work necessary for the attainment of rationally established goals. The low-scorer is less controlled, more changeable, and more easily influenced by illogical concerns. Whereas the high-scorer finds it hard to unbend and give in to whim and impulse, the low-scorer delights in informality and letting go.

BIBLIOGRAPHY

Banks, Russel, *Affliction,* New York: Harper & Row Publishers, 1989.
Bigner, Jerry J., *Parent-Child Relations: An Introduction to Parenting,* 2nd Ed., New York: MacMillan Publishing Co., 1985.
Chodorow, Nancy, *The Reproduction of Mothering,* California: University of California Press, 1978.
Durant, Will, *The Story of Civilization,* New York: Simon & Schuster, 1954-1967, Vol I, p. 49.
Gough, H.C., and Heilbroun, A.B., *The Adjective Check List,* California: Consulting Psychologists Press, 1980.
Horney, M.D., Karen, *Feminine Psychology,* New York: W. W. Norton & Company, Inc., 1967.
Leonard Linda Schierse, *The Wounded Woman,* Colorado: Shambhala Publications, Inc., 1982.
Miller, Alice, *Thou Shalt Not Be Aware,* New York: New American Library, 1986.
Miller, Alice, *For Your Own Good, Hidden Cruelty in Child-rearing and the Roots of Violence,* New York: Farrar, Straus, Giroux, tr. 1984.
Orthner, D.C., Brown, T., Ferguson, T., *Single Parent Fatherhood: An Emerging Family Life Style,* Family Coordinator, 1976, 25(4), 429-437.

Plath, Sylvia, *The Collected Poems,* ed. Ted Hughes, New York: Harper & Row Publishers, 1981.
Rubin, Lillian, *Intimate Strangers,* New York: Harper & Row, Publishers, 1983.
Victor, G., and Wilding, P., *Motherless Families,* London: Routledge and Kegan Pault Ltd., 1972.
Walkerman, Elyce, *Father Loss,*
Wallerstein, Judith, *Second Chances: Men, Women, and Children a Decade After Divorce,* New York: Ticknor & Fields, 1989.

ACV 8755

BERTRAND LIBRARY BUCKNELL UNIVERSITY
89001 0015 36194

WITHDRAWN
From Bertrand Library

the Ellen Clarke Bertrand Library

DATE DUE

NOV 2 9 1992			
APR 1 9 1993			
DEC 2 9 '93			
OCT 3 1 1994			
FEB 2 1 1997			
DEC 2 1 1998			
SEP 2 8 2001			
MAY 1 3 2004			
NOV 2 0 2006			
DEC 1 8 2006			
GAYLORD			PRINTED IN U.S.A.